Essays on Economics and Economists

R. H. Coase

The University of Chicago Press
Chicago and London

The University of Chicago Press, Chicago 60637
The University of Chicago Press, Ltd., London

© 1994 by The University of Chicago
All rights reserved. Published 1994
Paperback edition 1995
Printed in the United States of America
02 01 00 99 98 97   2 3 4 5

ISBN: 0-226-11103-2 (paper)

Library of Congress Cataloging-in-Publication Data

Coase, R. H. (Ronald Henry)
    Essays on economics and economists / R. H. Coase.
        p.   cm.
    Includes 15 previously published papers and an original
preface.
    Includes bibliographical references and index.
    1. Economics.   2. Economic policy.   3. Economics—
History.   4. Economists—Biography.   5. Marshall, Alfred,
1842–1924.
    HB34.C54   1994
    330—dc20   93-26174
                                                       CIP

Contents

Contents

ECONOMISTS

Preface

My desire to publish this collection of essays is no doubt largely motivated by vanity. But, as Adam Smith pointed out, characteristics of human beings which appear to us as in some degree disagreeable may nonetheless bring social benefits. I hope this will be true in this case. The first essay in part one, "Economics," reprints my Alfred Nobel Memorial Prize lecture given in Stockholm in December 1991. I was asked by the Royal Swedish Academy of Sciences to discuss, for an audience which consisted of interested members of the public as well as trained scientists, the work for which the award had been made. This enabled me to deal with the present state of the subject of industrial organisation and to consider what needs to be done to improve it. The next three essays examine some general questions concerning how economists go about their business: how they tackle the problems of the economic system, choose their theories, decide what questions come within the purview of their subject or give advice on public policy. The opinions expressed in these essays are, I believe, different from those held by many, perhaps most, economists. I am hoping that having these essays read will increase my market share.

The last three essays in this part are of a somewhat different character. That on "The Market for Goods and the Market for Ideas" was strongly denounced by the American press after it was presented at a meeting of the American Economic Association but the interesting question it poses has been largely ignored by economists. The year 1976 saw the bicentenary of the publication of the *Wealth of Nations,* and as part of the celebrations of this anniversary I gave two lectures, one at the University of California at Los Angeles on the *Wealth of Nations* and another at the University of Chicago on "Adam Smith's View of Man." They demonstrate the greatness of Adam Smith, from whose works we still learn. But this raises a troublesome question: What have we been doing in the last two hundred years?

The second part, "Economists," starts with four papers on Alfred Marshall. In my youth I thought about what I should do in my declining years and decided that an interesting project with which to fill them would be to write a biography of Alfred Marshall. I set about collecting material in preparation for this period, and the work resulted in these papers. However, when my declining years arrived, I found that I was still heavily engaged in economic research and had no idle time to fill. I had therefore to abandon this project. Fortunately a biography of Alfred Marshall is being prepared by Professor Peter Groenewegen of the University of Sydney, and we will soon learn the truth about this great economist and flawed human being.

There follow remembrances of three economists that I knew very well: Arnold Plant, my teacher and mentor, Duncan Black, a colleague in my first position at the Dundee School of Economics and a close friend until his death, and George J. Stigler, friend and colleague of my later years at the University of Chicago. The section ends with a personal account of economics at the London School of Economics in the 1930s, a period in which much exciting and important work was carried out at that great institution.

Economics

ONE

The Institutional Structure of Production

In my long life I have known some great economists but I have never counted myself among their number nor walked in their company. I have made no innovations in high theory. My contribution to economics has been to urge the inclusion in our analysis of features of the economic system so obvious that, like the postman in G. K. Chesterton's Father Brown tale, "The Invisible Man," they have tended to be overlooked. Nonetheless, once included in the analysis, they will, I believe, bring about a complete change in the structure of economic theory, at least in what is called price theory or microeconomics. What I have done is to show the importance for the working of the economic system of what may be termed the institutional structure of production. In this lecture I shall explain why, in my view, these features of the economic system were ignored and why their recognition will lead to a change in the way we analyse the working of the economic system and in the way we think about economic policy, changes which are already beginning to occur. I will also speak about the empirical work that needs to be done if this transformation in our approach is to increase our understanding.

In speaking about this transformation, I do not wish to suggest that it is the result of my work alone. Oliver Williamson, Harold Demsetz, Steven Cheung, among others, have made outstanding contributions to the subject, and without their work and that of many others, I doubt whether the significance of my writings would have been recognised. While it has been a great advantage of the creation of the Prize in Economic Sciences in Memory of Alfred Nobel that, by drawing attention to the significance of particular fields of economics, it en-

The 1991 Alfred Nobel Memorial Prize Lecture in Economic Sciences, delivered 9 December 1991, in Stockholm, Sweden. © The Nobel Foundation 1991.

courages further research in them, the highlighting of the work of a few scholars, or, in my case, one scholar, tends to obscure the importance of the contributions of other able scholars whose researches have been crucial to the development of the field.

I will be speaking of that part of economics which has come to be called industrial organisation but, to understand its present state, it is necessary to say something about the development of economics in general. During the two centuries since the publication of the *Wealth of Nations,* the main activity of economists, it seems to me, has been to fill the gaps in Adam Smith's system, to correct his errors and to make his analysis vastly more exact. A principal theme of the *Wealth of Nations* was that government regulation or centralised planning were not necessary to make an economic system function in an orderly way. The economy could be co-ordinated by a system of prices (the "invisible hand") and, furthermore, with beneficial results. A major task of economists since the publication of the *Wealth of Nations,* as Harold Demsetz has explained,[1] has been to formalise this proposition of Adam Smith. The given factors are technology and the tastes of consumers. Individuals, who follow their own interest, are governed in their choices by a system of prices.

Economists have uncovered the conditions necessary if Adam Smith's results are to be achieved and where, in the real world, such conditions do not appear to be found, they have proposed changes which are designed to bring them about. It is what one finds in the textbooks. Harold Demsetz has said rightly that what this theory analyses is a system of extreme decentralisation. It has been a great intellectual achievement and it throws light on many aspects of the economic system. But it has not been by any means all gain. The concentration on the determination of prices has led to a narrowing of focus which has had as a result the neglect of other aspects of the economic system. Sometimes, indeed, it seems as though economists conceive of their subject as being concerned only with the pricing system and anything outside this is considered as no part of their business. Thus, my old chief and a wonderful human being, Lionel Robbins, wrote in *The Nature and Significance of Economic Science,* about the "glaring deficiencies" of the old treatment of the theory of production with its discussion of peasant proprietorships and industrial forms: "It

1. Harold Demsetz, *Ownership, Control and the Firm* (1988), vol. 1, 145.

suggests that from the point of view of the economist 'organisation' is a matter of internal industrial (or agricultural) arrangement—if not internal to the firm, at any rate internal to 'the' industry. At the same time it tends to leave out completely the governing factor of all productive organisation—the relationship of prices and cost."[2]

What this comes down to is that, in Robbins's view, an economist does not interest himself in the internal arrangements within organisations but only in what happens on the market, the purchase of factors of production and the sale of the goods that these factors produce. What happens between the purchase of the factors of production and the sale of the goods that are produced by these factors is largely ignored. I do not know how far economists today share Robbins's attitude but it is undeniable that microeconomics is largely a study of the determination of prices and output, indeed this part of economics is often called price theory.

This neglect of other aspects of the system has been made easier by another feature of modern economic theory—the growing abstraction of the analysis, which does not seem to call for a detailed knowledge of the actual economic system or, at any rate, has managed to proceed without it. Bengt Holmstrom and Jean Tirole, writing on "The Theory of the Firm" in the recently published *Handbook of Industrial Organization,* conclude at the end of their 63-page article that "the evidence/theory ratio . . . is currently very low in this field."[3] Sam Peltzman has written a scathing review of the *Handbook* in which he points out how much of the discussion in it is theory without any empirical basis.[4]

What is studied is a system which lives in the minds of economists but not on earth. I have called the result "blackboard economics." The firm and the market appear by name but they lack any substance. The firm in mainstream economic theory has often been described as a "black box." And so it is. This is very extraordinary given that most resources in a modern economic system are employed within firms, with how these resources are used dependent on administrative deci-

2. Lionel C. Robbins, *The Nature and Significance of Economic Science* (1932), 70.

3. Richard Schmalensee and Robert D. Willig, eds., *Handbook of Industrial Organization* (1989), 126.

4. Sam Peltzman, "The Handbook of Industrial Organization: A Review Article," *Journal of Political Economy* (February 1991):201–17.

sions and not directly on the operation of a market. Consequently the efficiency of the economic system depends to a very considerable extent on how these organisations conduct their affairs, particularly, of course, the modern corporation. Even more surprising, given economists' interest in the pricing system, is the neglect of the market or more specifically the institutional arrangements which govern the process of exchange. As these institutional arrangements determine to a large extent what is produced, what we have is a very incomplete theory.

All this is beginning to change and in this process I am glad to have played my part. The value of including such institutional factors in the corpus of mainstream economics is made clear by recent events in Eastern Europe. These ex-communist countries are advised to move to a market economy, and their leaders wish to do so, but without the appropriate institutions no market economy of any significance is possible. If we knew more about our own economy, we would be in a better position to advise them.

What I endeavored to do in the two articles cited by the Royal Swedish Academy of Sciences was to attempt to fill these gaps or more exactly to indicate the direction in which we should move if they are ultimately to be filled. Let me start with "The Nature of the Firm" (1937). I went as a student to the London School of Economics in 1929 to study for a bachelor of commerce degree, specialising in the Industry group, supposedly designed for people who wished to become works managers, a choice of occupation for which I was singularly ill-suited. However, in 1931, I had a great stroke of luck. Arnold Plant was appointed professor of commerce in 1930. He was a wonderful teacher. I began to attend his seminar in 1931, some five months before I took the final examinations. It was a revelation. He quoted Sir Arthur Salter: "The normal economic system works itself." And he explained how a competitive economic system co-ordinated by prices would lead to the production of goods and services which consumers valued most highly. Before being exposed to Plant's teaching, my notions on how the economy worked were extremely woolly. After Plant's seminar I had a coherent view of the economic system. He introduced me to Adam Smith's "invisible hand."

As I had taken the first year of University work while still at high school, I managed to complete the requirements for a degree in two years. However, university regulations required three years of residence before a degree could be granted. I had therefore a year to spare. I then had another stroke of luck. I was awarded a Cassel Travelling Scholarship by the University of London. I decided to spend the year in the United States, this being treated as a year's residence at the London School of Economics, the regulations being somewhat loosely interpreted.

I decided to study vertical and lateral integration of industry in the United States. Plant had described in his lectures the different ways in which various industries were organised but we seemed to lack any theory which would explain these differences. I set out to find it. There was also another puzzle which, in my mind, needed to be solved and which seemed to be related to my main project. The view of the pricing system as a co-ordinating mechanism was clearly right but there were aspects of the argument which troubled me. Plant was opposed to all schemes, then very fashionable during the Great Depression, for the co-ordination of industrial production by some form of planning. Competition, according to Plant, acting through a system of prices, would do all the co-ordination necessary. And yet we had a factor of production, management, whose function was to co-ordinate. Why was it needed if the pricing system provided all the co-ordination necessary?

The same problem presented itself to me at that time in another guise. The Russian Revolution had taken place only fourteen years earlier. We knew then very little about how planning would actually be carried out in a communist system. Lenin had said that the economic system in Russia would be run as one big factory. However, many economists in the West maintained that this was an impossibility. And yet there were factories in the West and some of them were extremely large. How could the views expressed by economists on the role of the pricing system and the impossibility of successful central economic planning be reconciled with the existence of management and of these apparently planned societies, that is, firms, operating within our own economy?[5]

I found the answer by the summer of 1932. It was to realise that there were costs of using the pricing mechanism. What the prices are have to be discovered. There are negotiations to be undertaken, con-

5. A fuller account of these events will be found in Oliver E. Williamson and Sidney G. Winter, eds., *The Nature of the Firm, Origins, Evolution and Development* (1991), 34–47.

tracts to be drawn up, inspections to be made, arrangements to be made to settle disputes, and so on. These costs have come to be known as transaction costs. Their existence implies that methods of co-ordination alternative to the market, which are themselves costly and in various ways imperfect, may nonetheless be preferable to relying on the pricing mechanism, the only method of co-ordination normally analysed by economists. It was the avoidance of the costs of carrying out transactions through the market that could explain the existence of the firm, in which the allocation of factors came about as a result of administrative decisions (and I thought it did explain it).

In "The Nature of the Firm" I argued that in a competitive system there would be an optimum of planning since a firm, that little planned society, could only continue to exist if it performed its co-ordination function at a lower cost than would be incurred if co-ordination were achieved by means of market transactions and also at a lower cost than this same function could be performed by another firm. To have an efficient economic system it is necessary not only to have markets but also areas of planning within organisations of the appropriate size. What this mix should be we find as a result of competition. This is what I said in my article of 1937. However, as we know from a letter I wrote in 1932, which has been preserved, all the essentials of this argument had been presented in a lecture I gave in Dundee at the beginning of October 1932.[6] I was then twenty-one years of age and the sun never ceased to shine. I could never have imagined that these ideas would some sixty years later become a major justification for the award of a Nobel prize. And it is a strange experience to be praised in my eighties for work I did in my twenties.

There is no doubt that the recognition by economists of the importance of the role of the firm in the functioning of the economy will prompt them to investigate its activities more closely. The work of Oliver Williamson and others has led to a greater understanding of the factors which govern what a firm does and how it does it. And we can also hope to learn much more in future from the studies of the activities of firms which have recently been initiated by the Center for Economic Studies of the Bureau of the Census of the United States. But it would be wrong to think that the most significant consequence for economics of the publication of "The Nature of the Firm" has been to direct atten-

6. Ibid., 34–35.

tion to the importance of the firm in our modern economy, a result which, in my view, would have come about in any case. What I think will be considered in future to have been the important contribution of this article is the explicit introduction of transaction costs into economic analysis.

I argued in "The Nature of the Firm" that the existence of transaction costs leads to the emergence of the firm. But the effects are pervasive in the economy. Businessmen in deciding on their ways of doing business and on what to produce have to take into account transaction costs. If the costs of making an exchange are greater than the gains which that exchange would bring, that exchange would not take place and the greater production that would flow from specialisation would not be realised. In this way transaction costs affect not only contractual arrangements but also what goods and services are produced. Not to include transaction costs in the theory leaves many aspects of the working of the economic system unexplained, including the emergence of the firm, but much else besides. In fact, a large part of what we think of as economic activity is designed to accomplish what high transaction costs would otherwise prevent or to reduce transaction costs so that individuals can negotiate freely and we can take advantage of that diffused knowledge of which Friedrich Hayek has told us.

I know of only one part of economics in which transaction costs have been used to explain a major feature of the economic system, and that relates to the evolution and use of money. Adam Smith pointed out the hindrances to commerce that would arise in an economic system in which there was a division of labour but in which all exchange had to take the form of barter. No one would be able to buy anything unless he possessed something that the producer wanted. This difficulty, Smith explained, could be overcome by the use of money. Thus, a person wishing to buy something in a barter system has to find someone who has this product for sale but who also wants some of the goods possessed by the potential buyer. Similarly, a person wishing to sell something has to find someone who both wants what he has to offer and also possesses something that the potential seller wants. Exchange in a barter system requires what W. Stanley Jevons called "this double coincidence."

Clearly the search for partners in exchange with suitable qualifications is likely to be very costly and will prevent many potentially beneficial exchanges from taking place. The benefit brought about by the use of money consists of a reduction in transaction costs. The use of money also reduces transaction costs by facilitating the drawing up of contracts as well as by reducing the quantity of goods that need to be held for purposes of exchange. However, the nature of the benefits secured by the use of money seems to have faded into the background so far as economists are concerned and it does not seem to have been noticed that there are other features of the economic system which exist because of the need to mitigate transaction costs.

I now turn to that other article cited by the Swedish Academy, "The Problem of Social Cost," published some thirty years ago. I will not say much here about its influence on legal scholarship, which has been immense, but will mainly consider its influence on economics, which has not been immense, although I believe that in time it will be. It is my view that the approach used in that article will ultimately transform the structure of microeconomics—and I will explain why. I should add that in writing this article I had no such general aim in mind. I thought that I was exposing the weaknesses of A. C. Pigou's analysis of the divergence between private and social products, an analysis generally accepted by economists, and that was all. It was only later, and in part as a result of conversations with Steven Cheung in the 1960s, that I came to see the general significance for economic theory of what I had written in that article and also to see more clearly what questions needed to be further investigated.

Pigou's conclusion and that of most economists using standard economic theory was (and perhaps still is) that some kind of government action (usually the imposition of taxes) was required to restrain those whose actions had harmful effects on others (often termed negative externalities). What I showed in that article, as I thought, was that in a regime of zero transaction costs—an assumption of standard economic theory—negotiations between the parties would lead to those arrangements being made which would maximise wealth, and this irrespective of the initial assignment of rights. This is the infamous Coase Theorem, named and formulated by George Stigler, although it is based on work of mine. Stigler argues that the Coase Theorem follows from the standard assumptions of economic theory. Its logic cannot be questioned, only its domain.[7] I do not disagree with Stigler.

7. George J. Stigler, "Two Notes on the Coase Theorem," *Yale Law Journal* (December 1989):631–33.

However, I tend to regard the Coase Theorem as a stepping stone on the way to an analysis of an economy with positive transaction costs. The significance to me of the Coase Theorem is that it undermines the Pigovian system. Since standard economic theory assumes transaction costs to be zero, the Coase Theorem demonstrates that the Pigovian solutions are unnecessary in these circumstances. Of course, it does not imply, when transaction costs are positive, that government actions (such as government operation, regulation or taxation, including subsidies) could not produce a better result than relying on negotiations between individuals in the market. Whether this would be so could be discovered not by studying imaginary governments but what real governments actually do. My conclusion: Let us study the world of positive transaction costs.

If we move from a regime of zero transaction costs to one of positive transaction costs, what becomes immediately clear is the crucial importance of the legal system in this new world. I explained in "The Problem of Social Cost" that what are traded on the market are not, as is often supposed by economists, physical entities but the rights to perform certain actions, and the rights which individuals possess are established by the legal system. While we can imagine in the hypothetical world of zero transaction costs that the parties to an exchange would negotiate to change any provision of the law which prevents them from taking whatever steps are required to increase the value of production, in the real world of positive transaction costs such a procedure would be extremely costly and would make unprofitable, even where it was allowed, a great deal of such contracting around the law. Because of this, the rights which individuals possess, with their duties and privileges, will be, to a large extent, what the law determines. As a result, the legal system will have a profound effect on the working of the economic system and may in certain respects be said to control it.

It is obviously desirable that rights should be assigned to those who can use them most productively and with incentives that lead them to do so. It is also desirable that, to discover (and maintain) such a distribution of rights, the costs of their transference should be low, through clarity in the law and by making the legal requirements for such transfers less onerous. Since this can come about only if there is an appropriate system of property rights (and that the rights are enforced), it is easy to understand why so many academic lawyers (at least in the United States) have found so attractive the task of uncovering the character of such a property rights system and why the subject of "law and economics" has flourished in American law schools. Indeed, work is going forward at such a pace that I do not consider it overoptimistic to believe that the main outlines of the subject will be drawn within five or ten years.

Until quite recently most economists seem to have been unaware of this relationship between the economic and legal systems except in the most general way. Stock and produce exchanges are often used by economists as examples of perfect or near-perfect competition. But these exchanges regulate in great detail the activities of traders (and this quite apart from any public regulation there may be). What can be traded, when it can be traded, the terms of settlement and so on are all laid down by the authorities of the exchange. There is, in effect, a private law. Without such rules and regulations, the speedy conclusion of trades would not be possible. Of course, when trading takes place outside exchanges (and this is almost all trading) and where the dealers are scattered in space and have very divergent interests, as in retailing and wholesaling, such a private law would be difficult to establish and their activities will be regulated by the laws of the state.

It makes little sense for economists to discuss the process of exchange without specifying the institutional setting within which the trading takes place since this affects the incentives to produce and the costs of transacting. I think this is now beginning to be recognised and has been made crystal clear by what is going on in Eastern Europe today. The time has surely gone in which economists could analyse in great detail two individuals exchanging nuts for berries on the edge of the forest and then feel that their analysis of the process of exchange was complete, illuminating though this analysis may be in certain respects. The process of contracting needs to be studied in a real world setting. We would then learn of the problems that are encountered and how they are overcome, and we would certainly become aware of the richness of the institutional alternatives among which we have to choose.

Oliver Williamson has ascribed the non-use or limited use of my thesis in "The Nature of the Firm" to the fact that it has not been made "operational," by which he means that the concept of transaction costs has not been incorporated into a general theory. I think this is correct. There have been two reasons for this. First, incorporating transaction costs into standard economic theory, which has been based on the assumption that such costs are zero, would be very difficult, and economists who, like most scientists, as Thomas Kuhn has told us, are extremely conservative in their methods, have not been inclined to attempt it. Second, Williamson has also pointed out that although I was correct in making the choice between organisation within the firm or through the market the centrepiece of my analysis, I did not indicate what the factors were that determined the outcome of this choice and thus made it difficult for others to build on what is often described as a "fundamental insight." This also is true. But the interrelationships which govern the mix of market and hierarchy, to use Williamson's terms, are extremely complex, and in our present state of ignorance it will not be easy to discover what these factors are.

What we need is more empirical work. In a paper written for a conference of the National Bureau of Economic Research I explained why I thought this was so. This is what I said: "An inspired theoretician might do as well without such empirical work, but my own feeling is that the inspiration is most likely to come through the stimulus provided by the patterns, puzzles and anomalies revealed by the systematic gathering of data, particularly when the prime need is to break our existing habits of thought."[8] This statement was made in 1970. I still think that in essentials it is true today. Although much interesting and important research was done in the seventies and eighties and we certainly know much more than we did in 1970, there is little doubt that a great deal more empirical work is needed. However, I have come to the conclusion that the main obstacle faced by researchers in industrial organisation is the lack of available data on contracts and the activities of firms. I have therefore decided to do something about it.

Believing that there is a great deal of data on contracts and the activities of firms in the United States available in government departments and agencies in Washington, D.C., and that this information is largely unknown to economists, I organised a conference at the University of Chicago Law School in the summer of 1990. Government officials presented papers describing what data was available and how to get access to it and also reported on some of the research being carried out in their departments. The audience consisted of academic

8. R. H. Coase, *The Firm, the Market, and the Law* (1988), 71.

economists. It was, as a colleague remarked, a case of supply meeting demand. The proceedings of this conference were published in a special issue of the *Journal of Law and Economics*.[9]

Another development with which I am associated is the establishment of the Center for Research on Contracts and the Structure of Enterprise at the Business School of the University of Pittsburgh. This center will make large-scale collections of business contracts and will prepare databases which will be made available to all researchers, whatever their institution. Nor should we forget the work now getting started at the Center for Economic Studies of the Bureau of the Census.

This greater availability of data and the encouragement given to all researchers working on the institutional structure of production by the award to me of the Nobel prize should result in a reduction in that elegant but sterile theorizing so commonly found in the economics literature on industrial organisation and should lead to studies which increase our understanding of how the real economic system works.

My remarks have sometimes been interpreted as implying that I am hostile to the mathematisation of economic theory. This is untrue. Indeed, once we begin to uncover the real factors affecting the performance of the economic system, the complicated interrelations among them will clearly necessitate a mathematical treatment, as in the natural sciences, and economists like myself, who write in prose, will take their bow. May this period soon come.

I am very much aware that many economists whom I respect and admire will not agree with the opinions I have expressed, and some may even be offended by them. But a scholar must be content with the knowledge that what is false in what he says will soon be exposed and as for what is true, he can count on ultimately seeing it accepted, if only he lives long enough.

9. *Journal of Law and Economics* 34(2), pt. 2 (October 1991).

TWO

How Should Economists Choose?

I had a close relationship with Warren Nutter at the University of Virginia. I came to admire him for the thoroughness with which he carried out his researches, for the conscientiousness with which he performed his academic duties, and for the courage he displayed in doing what he believed to be right. Warren Nutter was an excellent economist, which is rare, but he was something rarer still, a truly moral man. Frank Knight, who was so much admired by Warren Nutter, tells us that the "basic principle of science—truth or objectivity—is essentially a moral principle, in opposition to any form of self-interest. The presuppositions of objectivity are integrity, competence and humility."[1] Integrity, competence, and humility—these three qualities sum up Warren Nutter's character. He knew that in economic affairs people are mainly motivated by self-interest, but he did not believe that this was their sole motivation and certainly he thought it should not be. In his own actions, Warren Nutter cared as much for others as he did for himself. As a colleague and friend, I knew him to be utterly reliable. It is our good fortune that he devoted himself to the service of economics. We are all in his debt.

To have been asked to deliver one of the Warren Nutter memorial lectures is a great privilege. But it is not easy to prepare a lecture of a standard that will truly honour Warren Nutter's memory. There is also the problem of choosing a topic appropriate to the occasion. On this

The third G. Warren Nutter Lecture in Political Economy, delivered November 18, 1981, at the American Enterprise Institute for Public Policy Research, Washington, D.C. Published by the American Enterprise Institute in pamphlet form in 1982, it was reprinted in *Ideas, Their Origins and Their Consequences*, edited by Frank S. Kaulback, Jr. (1988). Reprinted here by permission of the American Enterprise Institute.

1. Frank H. Knight, *Freedom and Reform* (New York: Harper & Brothers, 1947), 244.

score, however, I believe I have succeeded and that Warren Nutter would have found the questions I will be discussing of great interest and would have treated my point of view with sympathy.

Many economists, perhaps most, think of economics as the science of human choice, and it seems only proper that we should examine how economists themselves choose the theories they espouse. The best-known treatment of this question is that of Milton Friedman, who, in "The Methodology of Positive Economics," his most popular paper (in itself a somewhat suspicious circumstance), tells us "how to decide whether a suggested hypothesis or theory should be tentatively accepted as part of" the positive science of economics. As you all know, the answer he gives is that the worth of a theory "is to be judged by the precision, scope, and conformity with experience of the predictions it yields. . . . The ultimate goal of a positive science is the development of a 'theory' or 'hypothesis' that yields valid and meaningful . . . predictions about phenomena not yet observed."[2]

I should say at once that I do not consider Milton Friedman's answer satisfactory. At this point, I fear that many in this audience will be inclined to regard this statement as lese majesty. But I hasten to reassure them by saying that it is my belief that my way of looking at this question is more consonant with Friedman's general position as expressed in *Capitalism and Freedom* or *Freedom to Choose* than with that found in "The Methodology of Positive Economics." I should add that I am in no sense well informed in the philosophy of science. Words like epistemology do not come tripping from my tongue. What I have to say consists of reflections based on what I have observed about the actual practice of economists.

The view that the worth of a theory is to be judged solely by the extent and accuracy of its predictions seems to me wrong. Of course, any theory has implications. It tells us that if something happens, something else will follow, and it is true that most of us would not value the theory if we did not think these implications corresponded to happenings in the real economic system. But a theory is not like an airline or bus timetable. We are not interested simply in the accuracy of its predictions. A theory also serves as a base for thinking. It helps us to understand what is going on by enabling us to organise our

2. Milton Friedman, "The Methodology of Positive Economics," in *Essays in Positive Economics* (Chicago: University of Chicago Press, 1953), 3–4, 7.

thoughts. Faced with a choice between a theory which predicts well but gives us little insight into how the system works and one which gives us this insight but predicts badly, I would choose the latter, and I am inclined to think that most economists would do the same. No doubt it would be their belief that ultimately this theory would enable us to make predictions about what would happen in the real world; but since these predictions would emerge at a later date (and probably would also be about different things), to assert that the choice between theories depends on their predictive powers becomes completely ambiguous.

Friedman enlarges his argument by maintaining that theories are not to be judged by whether their assumptions are realistic. Let me quote what he says:

> Consider the density of leaves around a tree. I suggest the hypothesis that the leaves are positioned as if each leaf deliberately sought to maximize the amount of sunlight it receives, given the position of its neighbors, as if it knew the physical laws determining the amount of sunlight that would be received in various positions and could move rapidly or instantaneously from any one position to any other desired and unoccupied position. . . . Despite the apparent falsity of the "assumptions" of the hypothesis, it has great plausibility because of the conformity of its implications with observation.[3]

Let us suppose that it is true that the assumption that a leaf subscribes to *Scientific American* and the *Journal of Molecular Biology* and that it understands what is contained therein enables us to predict what the distribution of leaves around a tree will be. Such a theory nonetheless provides a very poor basis for thinking about leaves (or trees). Our problem is to explain how leaves come to be distributed on a tree given that a leaf does not have a brain. Similarly, to take an example in economics, we could have predicted over the last few years what the American government's policies on oil and natural gas would be if we had assumed that the aim of the American government was to increase the power and income of the OPEC countries and to reduce the standard of living in the United States. But I am sure that we would prefer a theory that explains why the American government, which

3. Ibid., 19–20.

presumably did not want to bring about these results, was led to adopt policies which harmed American interests. Testable predictions are not all that matters. And realism in our assumptions is needed if our theories are ever to help us understand why the system works in the way it does. Realism in assumptions forces us to analyse the world that exists, not some imaginary world that does not.

It is, of course, true that our assumptions should not be completely realistic. There are factors we leave out because we do not know how to handle them. There are others we exclude because we do not feel the benefits of a more complete theory would be worth the costs involved in including them. Their inclusion might, for example, greatly complicate the analysis without giving us greater understanding about what is going on. Again, assumptions about other factors do not need to be realistic because they are completely irrelevant. If we wish to show that enforcement of a minimum wage will lead to unemployment among less productive workers, it is unnecessary to be accurate about the exact way in which capital gains are taxed. There are good reasons why the assumptions of our theories should not be completely realistic, but this does not mean that we should lose touch with reality.

I now turn to what is, from my point of view, the strangest aspect of "The Methodology of Positive Economics." It is that what we are given is not a positive theory at all. It is, I believe, best interpreted as a normative theory. What we are given is not a theory of how economists, in fact, choose between competing theories but, unless I am completely mistaken, how they ought to choose. When Friedman says that the "ultimate goal of a positive science is the development of a 'theory' or 'hypothesis' that yields valid and meaningful . . . predictions about phenomena not yet observed," I cannot help mentioning that a science has no goals, only individuals have goals. What has to be shown if Friedman's criteria are to be accepted as a positive theory is that individual economists actually choose among competing theories according to these criteria. I will show the difficulty of interpreting Friedman's argument in this way by considering three episodes, all of which occurred in my youth and, unlike more recent events, I remember vividly. These are episodes in the 1930s in which economists changed their views, that is, changed the theories they espoused. I will mainly be discussing what happened in economics in England, but these were times when, to a very considerable extent, this was what happened in economics.

The first episode I will discuss is local, but the economists involved were among the best in the world. In February 1931, Friedrich Hayek gave a series of public lectures entitled "Prices and Production" at the London School of Economics, and in September 1931 these lectures were published as a book. They were undoubtedly the most successful set of public lectures given at LSE during my time there, even surpassing the brilliant lectures Jacob Viner gave on international trade theory. The audience, notwithstanding the difficulties of understanding Hayek, was enthralled. What was said seemed to us of great importance and made us see things of which we had previously been unaware. After hearing these lectures, we knew why there was a depression.

Most students of economics at LSE and many members of the staff became Hayekians or, at any rate, incorporated elements of Hayek's approach in their own thinking. With the arrogance of youth, I myself expounded the Hayekian analysis to the faculty and students at Columbia University in the fall of 1931. What now strikes me as odd is the ease with which Hayek conquered LSE. I think this was in part the result of a lack of precision in the existing analysis or, at any rate, in our grasp of it, so that Hayek's analysis seemed to give a well-organised and fruitful way of thinking about the working of the economic system as a whole. As far as I can see, the Hayekian analysis did not make predictions except in the sense that it explained why there was a depression. What can be said is that the analysis seemed to be consistent with everything we observed. To show that this was so, Lionel Robbins published in 1934 *The Great Depression*, the only one of his works, as he tells us, that he wishes he had not written.[4]

The next episode I will consider was by no means local, although I viewed it from the London School of Economics. It was a worldwide phenomenon. This was the Keynesian revolution. I will not labour its importance—that is conceded by the great majority of economists. I need only quote the statement of John Hicks: "The Keynesian revolution is the obvious example of a big revolution [in economics]; there

4. Lord Robbins, *Autobiography of an Economist* (London: Macmillan, 1971), 154, 160.

are not more than two or three others which might conceivably be compared to it."[5]

While in the case of Hayek I thought (incorrectly) that I understood what was going on, I was never under such an illusion in the case of Keynes. By that time, I was wholly absorbed in what is now called microeconomics. What I mainly remember from this period is that everything I said on the subject was wrong because savings equaled investment. Fortunately I am not concerned so much with the substance of Keynes's *General Theory* as with the circumstances of its acceptance by the economics profession. For there can be no question that Keynes triumphed. Nor did it take very long. The *General Theory* was published in February 1936. Although some of the early reviews were hostile or lukewarm, it was soon apparent that the economics profession was, for the most part, going to adopt the Keynesian approach. Abba Lerner, for example, published his influential account of the Keynesian system in the *International Labour Review* in October 1936. As Paul Samuelson has said:

> The *General Theory* caught most economists under the age of thirty-five with the unexpected virulence of a disease first attacking and decimating an isolated tribe of South Sea islanders. Economists beyond fifty turned out to be quite immune to the ailment. With time, most economists in between began to run the fever, often without knowing or admitting their condition.[6]

I cannot vouch for the accuracy of Samuelson's account of the difference in the response of economists in the United States to Keynes's *General Theory* according to their age, but it has very little relevance to events in England; there were, in fact, very few economists there who were older than fifty in 1936. Among those who were at Cambridge or were associated with Keynes when the *General Theory* appeared, apart from Keynes himself, who was fifty-two, only A. C. Pigou was over fifty, and he proved not to be immune to the Keynesian

5. Sir John Hicks, "'Revolutions' in Economics," in Spiro Latsis, ed., *Method and Appraisal in Economics* (Cambridge: Cambridge University Press, 1976), 208.
6. Paul A. Samuelson, "The General Theory," in Robert Lekachman, ed., *Keynes' General Theory: Reports of Three Decades* (New York: St. Martin's Press, 1964), 315–16.

"disease," as Samuelson describes it. D. H. Robertson was then forty-five, R. F. Harrod thirty-six, Joan Robinson thirty-two, Richard Kahn thirty, J. E. Meade twenty-eight. The economists at LSE were even younger. Robbins was thirty-seven, Hayek thirty-six, Hicks thirty-one, Lerner thirty-two, and Nicky Kaldor twenty-seven at the time the *General Theory* was published.

Whether the acceptance of Keynes's system of analysis was or was not affected by the age distribution of economists in Britain, its success was such that by the outbreak of war in 1939, it could be said to be the orthodox approach among British economists. In fact, Robbins, as director of the Economics Section of the War Cabinet Office, enthusiastically supported the proposals in the White Paper on Employment Policy issued in 1944. And Sir William Beveridge, who had attacked the *General Theory* in 1937 as theory untested by facts, was to publish his *Full Employment in a Free Society,* also in 1944, assisted by a number of Keynesians, including Kaldor.

This swift adoption of the Keynesian system came about, I believe, because its analysis in terms of the determinants of effective demand seemed to get to the essence of what was going on in the economic system and was easier to understand (at least in its broad outlines) than alternative theories. That the Keynesian system offered a cure for unemployment without requiring any sacrifices, provided a clearly defined role for government, and a policy easy to carry out (as it then appeared) added to its attractiveness. It can hardly be maintained that the Keynesian analysis was adopted because it yielded accurate "predictions about phenomena not yet observed." It is true that Keynes claimed to demonstrate that the economic system could function in such a way as to bring about persistent mass unemployment. But mass unemployment could not be described in the 1930s as a phenomenon "not yet observed." And it is not without relevance that the alternative theory that was displaced, or at any rate displaced at LSE, was that of Hayek, a theory which also explained why the economic system could operate in such a way as to lead to mass unemployment. Keynes's analysis was adopted in the main because it seemed to make more sense to most economists. Or, as I put it earlier, it provided a better base for thinking about the problems of the working of the economic system as a whole. And to those economists who were less concerned about the niceties of the analysis, Keynes's policy recommendations undoubtedly provided a sufficient reason for many of them to adopt his theory and to reject that of Hayek.

The third episode I will consider is concerned with the change in the way in which economists analysed the working of a competitive system following the publication in 1933 of Edward Chamberlin's *Theory of Monopolistic Competition* and Joan Robinson's *Economics of Imperfect Competition*. These books were, as George Stigler has said, "enthusiastically received."[7] Robert L. Bishop exaggerated somewhat, but not perhaps a great deal, when he said, writing in 1964, that it was "the consensus of economists" that these two books "touched off, in 1933, a theoretical revolution whose relative importance in the microeconomic area was comparable to that of the Keynesian analysis in macroeconomics."[8] These books were certainly an instant success, and their contents were quickly absorbed and used by economists interested in price theory. As an example, although these books appeared in 1933, I had completed by mid-1934 a paper in which I used the geometrical analysis of Mrs. Robinson to illuminate and extend Chamberlin's treatment of duopoly and had corresponded with both Chamberlin and Mrs. Robinson. This paper, "The Problem of Duopoly Reconsidered," was published in the *Review of Economic Studies* in 1935. At about the same time Kaldor wrote his article on "Market Imperfection and Excess Capacity," which was also published in 1935, in *Economica*. I have no doubt that there was similar activity in the United States among economists writing on price theory.

The speedy adoption of these new approaches was in large part due to the very unsatisfactory state of the existing price theory. That this was so had been demonstrated beyond doubt by the controversies in the *Economic Journal* in the 1920s and perhaps above all by Piero Sraffa's 1926 article. We were therefore looking for ways to solve the dilemmas these discussions revealed. These new books by Chamberlin and Mrs. Robinson, which started the analysis with the decisions of the individual firm and used new tools such as the marginal revenue schedule, seemed to offer the way out. They certainly gave us a lot to

7. George J. Stigler, "Monopolistic Competition in Retrospect," in *Five Lectures on Economic Problems* (London: London School of Economics, and Longmans, Green and Co., 1949), 12.

8. Robert L. Bishop, "The Theory of Imperfect Competition after Twenty Years: The Impact on General Theory," *American Economic Review* 54 (May 1964):33.

put on the blackboard and to explain to our students. They enlarged our analytical apparatus. They seemed to give us a better understanding of how a competitive system works, but whether this was really so is another matter.

My own view of the contribution of these books is not essentially different from that expressed by Stigler in his lecture "Monopolistic Competition in Retrospect" published in 1949. But what is particularly interesting and useful, given the questions I am discussing, is that in this lecture Stigler also appraised Chamberlin's theory of monopolistic competition using Friedman's methodological principles. He argued that Chamberlin's theory should be adopted "if it contains different or more accurate predictions (as tested by observation) than the theory of competition." His personal belief was that "the predictions of [the] standard model of monopolistic competition differ only in unimportant respects from those of the theory of competition." He added, however, that "this is a question of fact, and it must be resolved by empirical tests of the implications of the two theories (a task the supporters of the theory of monopolistic competition have not yet undertaken)."[9]

The fact that supporters of the theory of monopolistic competition had not made empirical tests comparing the predictions of the alternative theories of competition (and, I may add, do not appear to have made such tests in the years since Stigler wrote) lends support to the view that Friedman's methodology is not a positive but a normative theory. Certainly this is the way that Stigler used it. Stigler was not saying that supporters of the theory of monopolistic competition made such tests but did them badly and so came to the wrong conclusion. He was saying that they did not make them at all. Since they should have done so, this merits our disapproval.

If choosing theories in accordance with Friedman's criteria is to be treated as a positive theory, economists would need to adopt a procedure somewhat similar to the following. When a new theory is advanced, economists would compare the accuracy of its predictions, preferably about "phenomena not yet observed," with that of the predictions of the existing theory and would choose that theory which gave the best predictions. Nothing remotely resembling this procedure happened during the three episodes that I have discussed, two of which

9. Stigler, "Monopolistic Competition," 24.

are recognised as having involved very important changes indeed in economic theory. For one thing, in each case the new theory was adopted within a time period too short for such a procedure to be followed. I believe that these three cases will be found to be quite representative of the process by which one theory has displaced another in economics, in large part because I do not believe that the process could, in general, be otherwise. An insistence that the choice of theories be made in accordance with Friedman's criteria would paralyze scientific activity.

Except in the most exceptional circumstances, the data required to test the predictions of a new theory (statistics and other information) will not be available or, if available, will not be in the form required for the tests (and, even when put into this form, will need a good deal of manipulation of one sort or another before they can be made to yield the requisite predictions). And who would be willing to undertake these arduous investigations? Someone who believed in a new theory might be willing to make these tests to convince unbelievers that the theory yielded correct predictions. And someone who did not believe in a new theory might make these tests to convince believers that the theory did not yield correct predictions. But for the tests to be worthwhile, someone has to believe in the theory, at least to the extent of believing that it might well be true. There is little profit in undertaking an investigation that is expected to show that a theory in which no one believes yields incorrect predictions, and I doubt whether any editor of a professional journal could be found who would be willing to publish a paper giving the results of such an investigation. If all economists followed Friedman's principles in choosing theories, no economist could be found who believed in a theory until it had been tested, which would have the paradoxical result that no tests would be carried out. This is what I meant when I said that acceptance of Friedman's methodology would result in the paralysis of scientific activity. Work could certainly continue, but no new theories would emerge.

But the world is not like that. Economists, or at any rate enough of them, do not wait to discover whether a theory's predictions are accurate before making up their minds. Given that this is so, what part does testing a theory's predictions play in economics? First of all, it very often plays either no part or a very minor part. A great deal of economic theory, so-called pure theory (and this is most of economic theory), consists of logical constructions based on assumptions about human nature so basic that they are difficult to question, assumptions such as that, faced with a choice between $100 and $10, very few people will choose $10. The kind of prediction that results is that if the price of a commodity is reduced, more will be demanded, or if the price is increased, more will be supplied. But, of course, that this is so must have been known before economics existed as an academic study. Other parts of theory, and this applies particularly to monopoly theory, tell us that if something happens, the price will go up, go down, or remain the same, depending on demand and cost conditions. It goes without saying that its predictions are always accurate. It might be argued that what this theory does is to tell us, given the demand and cost conditions, whether the price will go up, go down, or remain the same, but it is not easy to discover in practice what demand and cost conditions really are, and they are commonly inferred from the result rather than the other way round.

Some of you may be inclined to think that, while what I have been saying no doubt applies very well to the economic theory of my youth, things are very different in present-day economics with its massive use of quantitative methods. No doubt things are different. But in what way? What I have to say is largely based on the quantitative articles published in the *Journal of Law and Economics* when I was editor, but I have no doubt that what they reveal is representative of other quantitative studies in economics. First of all, many of these papers cannot be said to test a theory at all. They are measurements of an effect, the nature of which was already well established but of which the magnitude was unknown. For example, economists would expect that governmental control of entry into banking would reduce the number of banks, but without a quantitative study we would be unable to estimate the extent of the reduction.[10] Of course, later on, theories may be developed to explain why some magnitudes are greater than others, and then such studies could be used to test such theories. But, generally speaking, this does not appear to be where we are at present.

Other papers take the form of a test of the theory espoused by the author: there is a model, then regressions, followed by conclusions. In almost all cases it will be found that the statistical results confirm the theory. Sometimes it does happen that some of the expected relationships are not statistically significant, but they will usually be found to

10. See Sam Peltzman, "Entry in Commercial Banking," *Journal of Law and Economics* 8 (October 1965):11–50.

be in the right direction. And when results are obtained that do not square with the theory, which occasionally happens, these results are not usually treated as invalidating the theory but are left as something calling for further study. I would not claim that such studies have never led the investigators to modify their theories, but such cases appear to be rather uncommon.

Some articles, of course, involve the testing of alternative theories, and this means that some theories are bound to come out worse. But I doubt whether such studies have often led to a change in the views of the authors. My impression is that these quantitative studies are almost invariably guided by a theory and that they may most aptly be described as explorations with the aid of a theory. In almost all cases, the theory exists before the statistical investigation is made and is not derived from the investigation.

I do not believe that, for the most part, economists could act in any other way. I am bolstered in this view by the fact that quantitative methods do not appear to be used in the natural sciences in a way essentially different from the way they are used in economics. At this point, I should acknowledge my indebtedness to Thomas Kuhn.

I first heard Milton Friedman expound his views on the methodology of positive economics one evening in London in the company of Ralph Turvey, at a time before Friedman's essay had been published. My immediate response was unfavourable. I voiced various objections to Friedman's views. But Adam Smith's impartial spectator, asked to report on this debate, would have said that I lost every round. Whatever argument I put forward, Friedman had a more telling counterargument. And yet I was not convinced. It was not until 1958—59, when Kuhn and I were both fellows at the Center for Advanced Study in the Behavioral Sciences at Stanford, that I learned about Kuhn's views and came to see exactly what it was about Friedman's methodological position that I did not like. But what most influenced me was not so much the argument that was later to appear in Kuhn's famous book *The Structure of Scientific Revolutions* (although I am in general agreement with its main thrust) as what he said in an earlier paper, "The Function of Measurement in Modern Physical Science", published in 1961.[11] Among other things, this paper makes clear that

11. Thomas S. Kuhn, "The Function of Measurement in Modern Physical Science," reprinted in *The Essential Tension* (Chicago: University of Chicago Press, 1977), 178.

quantitative methods are used in economics in essentially the same way as in the natural sciences.

I said that quantitative studies in economics are explorations with the aid of a theory. Consider what Kuhn wrote:

> *The road from scientific law to scientific measurement can rarely be traveled in the reverse direction.* To discover quantitative regularity one must normally know what regularity one is seeking and one's instruments must be designed accordingly; even then nature may not yield consistent or generalizable results without a struggle.[12]

I remarked earlier on the tendency of economists to get the result their theory tells them to expect. In a talk I gave at the University of Virginia in the early 1960s, at which Warren Nutter was, I think, present, I said that if you torture the data enough, nature will always confess, a saying which, in a somewhat altered form, has taken its place in the statistical literature. Kuhn puts the point more elegantly and makes the process sound like a seduction: "Nature undoubtedly responds to the theoretical predispositions with which she is approached by the measuring scientist."[13]

I also observed that a failure to get an exact fit between the theory and the quantitative results is not generally treated as calling for the abandonment of the theory but rather the discrepancies are put on one side as something calling for further study. Kuhn says this: "Isolated discrepancies . . . occur so regularly that no scientist could bring his research problems to an end if he paused for many of them. In any case, experience has repeatedly shown that in overwhelming proportion, these discrepancies disappear upon closer scrutiny."[14] Because of this, Kuhn argues that "the efficient procedure" is to ignore them, a conclusion economists will find easy to accept. Furthermore, Kuhn says:

> Anomalous observations . . . cannot tempt [a scientist] to abandon his theory until another one is suggested to replace it. . . . In scientific practice the real confirmation questions always involve the comparison of two theories with each other and with the world, not the comparison of a single the-

12. Ibid., 219 (emphasis in original).   13. Ibid., 200.   14. Ibid., 202.

ory with the world. In these three-way comparisons, measurement has a particular advantage.[15]

This last statement of Kuhn's has a special significance for economists. Quantitative studies, or qualitative studies for that matter, may give someone who believes in a theory a better idea of what that theory implies. But such studies (normally quantitative in the natural sciences and increasingly so in economics) also play, as Kuhn indicates, another and very important role. The choice economists face is a choice between competing theories. These studies, whether quantitative or qualitative, perform a function similar to that of advertising and other promotional activities in the normal products market. They do not aim simply at enlarging the understanding of those who believe in the theory but also at attracting those who do not believe in it and at preventing the defection of existing believers. These studies demonstrate the power of the theory, and the definiteness of quantitative studies enables them to make their point in a particularly persuasive form. What we are dealing with is a competitive process in which purveyors of the various theories attempt to sell their wares.

Failure to realise that we are dealing with a competitive situation seems to have led astray even so accomplished an economist as Don Patinkin. Consider this remark of his:

> What generates in me a great deal of skepticism about the state of our discipline is the high positive correlation between the policy views of a researcher (or, what is worse, of his thesis director) and his empirical findings. I will begin to believe in economics as a science when out of Yale there comes an empirical Ph.D. thesis demonstrating the supremacy of monetary policy in some historical period and out of Chicago, one demonstrating the supremacy of fiscal policy.[16]

I assume that Patinkin did not mean that the empirical findings are fabricated. If this were so, it would be a cause for disquiet. While there is, I suppose, some fraud in economics, it must be quite rare and is certainly not common at either Yale or Chicago. Patinkin expressed

15. Ibid., 211.
16. Don Patinkin, "Keynesian Monetary Theory and the Cambridge School," *Banca Nazionale del Lavoro Quarterly Review* (June 1972):142.

concern about the high positive correlation between the policy views of a researcher and his empirical findings. But this is how it should be. I would be very worried by a negative correlation: if, for example, an economist at Yale advocated reliance on fiscal policy while his Ph.D. thesis demonstrated the superiority of monetary policy. The policy views of an economist should accord with the results of his empirical investigations. What I think really worried Patinkin is that, according to his observations, the empirical findings at Yale and Chicago are not the same. Such differences could come about because researchers in the two universities use different methods for estimating the magnitudes of important variables in spheres in which measurement is very difficult. But I do not think that this is what Patinkin had in mind.

Assuming that Patinkin is right and that the empirical findings of economists at Yale and Chicago are not the same, this undoubtedly reflects a difference in their view about how the economic system operates, a difference, that is, in the theories espoused at the two universities. As Kuhn explains, this will inevitably lead to differences in the empirical findings. A belief that the empirical findings by research workers in all economics departments should be the same might lead an arrogant and ignorant university administration to attempt to destroy an economics department that had a distinctive character and to attempt to remake it so as to be like Yale (few would want all economics departments to be like Chicago). But that would be the way to mediocrity for that university as well as impeding the search for truth by restraining the competitive process.

Some may think that I have treated somewhat too literally what Patinkin said and have therefore failed to deal with the serious issue that inspired it. This may well be right. Earlier I said that many, I thought most, economists would choose to employ one theory rather than another because it afforded them a better base for thinking. Economists who choose theories using this criterion will not necessarily choose the same theory. They may be interested in different problems or approach the same problem in rather different ways or use different techniques of analysis, and these factors may lead them to prefer one theory rather than another. This does not bother me. In such cases there is little that should be done other than to leave economists free to choose.

But there are some motives for selecting one theory rather than another that are more worrying than others, and I think it was this concern that lay behind Patinkin's somewhat facetious remark. In public discussion, in the press, and in politics, theories and findings are adopted not to facilitate the search for truth but because they lead to certain policy conclusions. Theories and findings become weapons in a propaganda battle. In economics, whose subject matter has such a close connection with public policy, it would be surprising if some academic economists did not adopt the criteria of public discussion in selecting theories, that is, choose a theory because it lends support to a particular policy (perhaps the policy advocated by a particular political party). At the same time, they may belittle the work of other economists because it seems to have the wrong policy conclusions. Many of us will, I feel sure, be able to think of an instance of a scholar doing solid work who suffered because his policy conclusions were considered unacceptable at that time.

Yet, such instances notwithstanding, what is striking is how unimportant the influence of such behaviour is over the long period. As an example, consider what has happened to academic opinion on government regulation. Some fifteen or twenty years ago, economists, under the influence of Pigou and others, thought of the government as waiting beneficently to put things right whenever the invisible hand pointed in the wrong direction. The conclusions they drew for policy involved extensive government regulation. Studies made in the intervening years have shown that such regulation often has no effect or has effects opposite to those expected and was commonly introduced to serve the interests of politically influential groups. What has happened is that most economists have changed their views on policy to fit the new findings.

One might have expected, given the stakes involved, that the various groups active in the political arena could have procured economists to voice opinions which served their interests. There can be no question that the affiliation of economists with business or labour organisations or with political parties or even their engaging in consulting does threaten academic integrity. No doubt some economists have been corrupted. Yet my experience is that corruption of this sort, at any rate among economists of quality, is very uncommon or even nonexistent. As Stigler says: "I have seen silly people—public officials as well as private, by the way—try to buy opinions but I have not seen or even suspected any cases in which any important economist sold his professional convictions." Stigler is clearly troubled by the thought that this implies that economists are not maximising their money incomes, and so he adds:

> When we strive to solve a scientific problem, is ambition for our own professional status completely overshadowed by our love of knowledge? . . . When we write an article to demonstrate the fallacies of someone else's work, is our hatred for error never mixed with a tiny bit of glee at the display of our own cleverness?[17]

So if we have to admit that we are not maximising our money incomes, we can at least console ourselves by claiming that we are maximising our self-esteem.

It is also true that we value the respect of our colleagues. As Samuelson has said: "In the long run, the economic scholar works for the only coin worth having—our own applause."[18] The professional position of an economist depends on work that could not even be understood by the ordinary person. Samuelson does not owe his reputation to those of his writings that are read by the public but to papers that would be completely incomprehensible to them.

Just as is true for those working in the natural sciences, the activities of economists are regulated by, or at least much influenced by, professional organisations (universities or societies) in such matters as the design of courses, the requirements for degrees, the allocation of research funds, the standards for publication, and qualifications for employment. Respect and position are obtained by doing work which meets the standards of the economics profession. This regulation through professional organisations means that we are to a very considerable extent insulated from outside pressures. But we avoid that danger only by creating another. This danger is that the implementation of such standards, through its influence on courses, research funds, publication, and employment, none of which are necessarily completely

17. George J. Stigler, *The Intellectual and the Market Place* (New York: Free Press of Glencoe, 1963), 92.
18. Paul A. Samuelson, "Economists and the History of Ideas," *American Economic Review* 52 (March 1962):18.

unaffected by political considerations, may be so rigid as to impede the development of new approaches. If this happens, the likely response will be an attempt to form new professional groupings or to carry forward the work under other auspices. If professional organisation is sufficiently loose, as it tends to be in the United States, and the new approach has real promise, such efforts will probably succeed. It is not without significance that the new group of studies that has come to be known as "law and economics" has to a very considerable extent been carried forward in law schools rather than in economics departments, where the economists' somewhat narrow conception of the scope of their subject led them to be, at least initially, largely uninterested in the field.

For economists to be free to choose the theories that will be most helpful in guiding them in their work, and to invent new theories when the existing ones seem unsatisfactory, research has to be carried on within a relatively free educational structure, with universities, research institutes, and the foundations and other bodies that finance research all following independent policies and even within universities allowing a considerable degree of autonomy for schools and departments.

I started this talk by asking, How should economists choose? I have ended by discussing the organisation and finance of academic activities. I do not think that I have lost my way. Instead of confining ourselves to a discussion of the question of how economists ought to choose between theories, developing criteria, and relying on exhortation or perhaps regulation to induce them to use these criteria in making their choices, we should investigate the effect of alternative institutional arrangements for academic studies on the theories that are put into circulation and on the choices that are made. From these investigations we may hope to discover what arrangements governing the competition between theories are most likely to lead economists to make better choices. Paradoxically, the approach to the methodological problem in economics that is likely to be the most useful is to transform it into an economic problem.

In carrying out this task, we may draw inspiration from the example of Warren Nutter. As I said at the beginning of this talk, he possessed what Knight considered the essential attributes of a good scholar: integrity, competence, and humility. But Warren Nutter added courage. Fearless in the defense of the causes in which he believed, he calls to mind that heroic figure in Bunyan's *Pilgrim's Progress,* Valiant-for-Truth. And it may surely be said of Warren Nutter, as it was of Valiant-for-Truth, that when "he passed over . . . all the trumpets sounded for him on the other side."

THREE

Economics and Contiguous Disciplines

I wish to start with two general observations. First, what I have to say is largely based on my knowledge of developments within the United States and Britain. But I have sufficient confidence in the international character of science to believe that what can be observed in these countries is paralleled by similar developments elsewhere. My second observation is that a paper which deals with what is happening within a series of disciplines and which ranges so widely within economics itself, must inevitably mean, at any rate in my case, that it deals with many subjects about which the writer's knowledge is extremely vague. What I have to say will often have the character of assertion rather than of a conclusion based on a careful study of the literature in the many fields covered by my subject. I believe that such a careful study would confirm what I assert. But it is equally true that it may refute my views. Papers presented at international conferences are not usually high-risk ventures, but this one is. However, I do not think what is called for at this stage is a paper guarded by qualifications and

Presented at a conference of the International Economic Association held at Kiel, Germany, in 1975. Originally published as part of the conference proceedings in Mark Perlman, ed., *The Organization and Retrieval of Economic Knowledge* (London: Macmillan, 1977), and reprinted here by permission of the Macmillan Press on behalf of the Association.

This conference was supposedly organised for the benefit of librarians. I was asked to write this paper by Mark Perlman and Milton Friedman over lunch at the Quadrangle Club at the University of Chicago. Faced with the persuasive powers of this formidable pair, I was clearly out-gunned and there was little I could do but yield. The title of my paper was selected by the organisers of the conference. I was unsure about the meaning of "contiguous disciplines" but I interpreted the phrase as referring to the other social sciences which was, I believe, what the organisers had intended.

ECONOMICS AND CONTIGUOUS DISCIPLINES

difficult to attack because it says so little except what is generally accepted.

What is the subject with which I am dealing? What I am concerned with is what determines the boundaries between disciplines, in particular with what determines the boundaries between economics and the other social sciences, sociology, political science, psychology and the like (without excluding the possibility that there may be areas of overlap). What the boundaries are at any particular time can, of course, be discovered by examining the range of activities engaged in by members of any given professional association, by the subjects treated in the journals devoted to particular disciplines, by the courses given in university departments, by the topics covered in textbooks and by the books collected in libraries concerned with the various areas of knowledge. A forecast of the boundaries of a discipline is, thus, a forecast of what topics will be covered by professional associations, journals, libraries and the like. I have long considered the definition of economics which Kenneth E. Boulding attributed to Jacob Viner and has since often been repeated, "Economics is what economists do,"[1] as essentially sound but only if it were accompanied, which it never is, by a description of the activities in which economists actually engage.

If the question is asked, how do these boundaries between disciplines come to be what they are, the broad answer I give is that it is determined by competition. The process is essentially the same as that which determines the activities undertaken by firms or, to take another example, the extent of empires. Edward Gibbon describes how Augustus came to accept the boundaries of the Roman Empire. Gibbon says that it was easy for Augustus to discover that "Rome, in her present exalted situation, had much less to hope than to fear from the chance of arms; and that, in the prosecution of remote wars, the undertaking became every day more difficult, the event more doubtful, and the possession more precarious, and less beneficial."[2] The same kind of calculation ultimately led, and this is Gibbon's grand theme, to an abandonment of much of what had been contained within the Roman Empire and, finally, to its division within quite another set of bound-

1. Kenneth E. Boulding, *Economic Analysis* (New York: Harper, 1955), 3.
2. Edward Gibbon, *The Decline and Fall of the Roman Empire*, chap. 1.

aries. It is much the same with disciplines. The practitioners in a given discipline extend or narrow the range of the questions that they attempt to answer according to whether they find it profitable to do so, and this is determined, in part, by the success or failure of the practitioners in other disciplines in answering the same questions. Since different people are satisfied with different answers, victory is not necessarily clear-cut, and different answers and different ways of tackling the same question may exist side by side, each satisfying its own market. One group of practitioners need not drive another group from the field, but may merely, to use an economist's terminology, increase their own market share. Of course, when the number of those who are satisfied with the answers given by any group of practitioners becomes so small and/or the questions for which this is true are few or trivial, the field may be abandoned altogether except by those whose competence is so low elsewhere that they cannot compete in a wider, more active and more profitable market.

If we look at the work that economists are doing at the present time, there can be little doubt that economics is expanding its boundaries or, at any rate, that economists are moving more and more into other disciplines. They have become conspicuously active in political science, where they have developed an economic theory of politics and have done a great deal of empirical work analysing voting behaviour.[3] Economists have also moved into sociology and we now have an economic theory of marriage.[4] Nor should we be surprised that there is also an economic theory of suicide.[5] Other subjects on which econo-

3. Among the works on the economic theory of politics are Duncan Black, *The Theory of Committees and Elections* (Cambridge: Cambridge University Press, 1958); Anthony Downs, *An Economic Theory of Democracy* (New York: Harper, 1957); James Buchanan and Gordon Tullock, *The Calculus of Consent* (Ann Arbor, Mich.: University of Michigan Press, 1962); Mancur Olson, *The Logic of Collective Action* (Cambridge, Mass.: Harvard University Press, 1965); W. A. Niskanen, *Bureaucracy and Representative Government* (Chicago: Aldine, Atherton, 1971). For a study of voting behaviour, see George J. Stigler, "General Economic Conditions and National Elections," *American Economic Review* (May 1973).

4. Gary S. Becker, "A Theory of Marriage: Part I," *Journal of Political Economy* (July-August 1973); *idem.*, "A Theory of Marriage: Part II," *ibid.*, (March–April 1974).

5. Daniel S. Hamermesh and Neal M. Soos, "An Economic Theory of Suicide," *Journal of Political Economy* (January–February 1974).

mists have worked are linguistics,[6] education,[7] and national defence.[8] I am sure that it is only my lack of familiarity with what is going on in the other social sciences which restricts my list. One striking example, with which I am familiar, is the use of economics in the study of law.[9] The general movement is clear. Economists are extending the range of their studies to include all of the social sciences, which I take to be what we mean when we speak of economics' contiguous disciplines. What is the reason this is happening? One completely satisfying explanation (in more than one sense) would be that economists have by now solved all of the major problems posed by the economic system, and, therefore, rather than become unemployed or be forced to deal with the trivial problems which remain to be solved, have decided to employ their obviously considerable talents in achieving a similar success in the other social sciences. However, it is not possible to examine any area of economics with which I have familiarity without finding major puzzles for which we have no agreed solutions or, indeed, questions to which we have no answers at all. The reason for this movement of economists into neighbouring fields is certainly not that we have solved the problems of the economic system; it would perhaps be more plausible to argue that economists are looking for fields in which they can have some success.

Another explanation for this interest in neighbouring fields might be that modern economists have had a more broadly based education than those who preceded them and that, in consequence, their interests are wider, with the result that they are naturally dissatisfied with being restricted to so narrow a range of problems as that presented by the economic system. Such an explanation seems to me largely without merit. If we think of Adam Smith or John Stuart Mill or Alfred Marshall, the range of questions with which they dealt is greater than is

6. J. Marschak, "Economics of Language," *Behavioral Science* (April 1965).

7. John Vaizey, *The Economics of Education* (New York: Free Press of Glencoe, 1962); Theodore W. Schultz, *The Economic Value of Education* (New York: Columbia University Press, 1963); idem., *Investment in Human Capital* (New York: Free Press of Glencoe, 1970).

8. Charles J. Hitch and Roland N. McKean, *The Economics of Defence in the Nuclear Age* (Cambridge, Mass.: Harvard University Press, 1960).

9. See Richard A. Posner, *Economic Analysis of Law* (Boston: Little, Brown and Co., 1972).

37

commonly found in a modern work on economics. This impression is reinforced if we consider the articles which appear in most of the economics journals, which, to an increasingly great extent, tend to deal with highly formal technical questions of economic analysis, usually treated mathematically. The general impression one derives, particularly from the journals, is of a subject narrowing, rather than extending, its range. This seems inconsistent with the concurrent movement of economists into the other social sciences, but I believe that there is a connection between these two apparently contradictory developments.

If we are to attempt to forecast what the scope of economists' work is likely to be in the future—which is surely what is needed if we are to be helpful to the librarians and others for whose benefit this conference was planned—we have to understand why economists have been moving into the other social sciences and what the situation is likely to be in the future. To do this, we have to consider what it is that binds together a group of scholars so that they form a separate profession and enables us to say that someone is an economist, someone else a sociologist, another a political scientist and so on. It seems to me that what binds such a group together is one or more of the following: common techniques of analysis, a common theory or approach to the subject, or a common subject matter.

I need not conceal from you at this stage my belief that in the long run it is the subject matter, the kind of question which the practitioners are trying to answer, which tends to be the dominant factor producing the cohesive force that makes a group of scholars a recognisable profession with its own university departments, journals and libraries. I say this, in part, because the techniques of analysis and the theory or approach used are themselves, to a considerable extent, determined by what it is that the group of scholars is studying, although scholars in a particular discipline may use different techniques or approaches in answering the same questions. However, in the short run, the ability of a particular group to handle certain techniques of analysis or an approach may give them such advantages that they are able to move successfully into another field or even to dominate it. In making these distinctions, I do not wish to deny that techniques, approaches and subject matter will all exert some influence at any given time. Nor would I argue that it is inevitable that techniques and approach should exert their influence only in the short run. They could be dominant in the long run as well. But I believe that there are reasons for thinking that this will not usually be the case.

If my description of the binding forces of a scholarly discipline is correct and if my assessment of their long- and short-run influences is also valid, then we will have to decide whether the current movement by economists into the other social sciences is the triumph of a technique or of an approach, or whether such an extension of their work illuminates, and is interrelated with, the solution of the central questions which economists attempt to answer, that is, is necessitated by the nature of the subject matter which they study. To the extent that this movement is based on technique or approach, we can expect a gradual displacement of economists from their newly won ground. To the extent that it is necessitated by their subject matter, we may expect the range of studies undertaken by economists to be permanently broadened.

My first example of a technique, linear programming, is one which I am particularly unqualified to discuss but, fortunately, extensive discussion is not called for.[10] It is, if I understand correctly, a mathematical method for discovering the proportions in which inputs should be combined in order to achieve a certain result at minimum cost. Such a technique has, potentially, applications in many fields. It is, however, difficult to believe that such a highly mathematical technique could not be as easily acquired or as well handled by suitably endowed scholars in other disciplines. Indeed, some of these scholars might find such a technique easier to acquire or handle than would most economists. To the extent that economists have moved into other fields using linear programming, I would expect the forces of competition to be such that these economists would be largely displaced, although individual economists might still do useful work using linear programming. In any case, it seems improbable that knowledge of a technique such as linear programming would become such an essential part of any discipline as to outweigh command of the theory or knowledge of the subject matter. One would not expect economists to dominate such fields as nutrition or oil refinery engineering even if

10. On this subject, see J. R. Hicks, "Linear Theory," *The Economic Journal* (December 1960).

Economics

(which seems improbable) economists as a class were particularly adept in linear programming.

The employment of quantitative methods, now so commonly part of the equipment of the modern economist, has also enabled a number of economists to move into neighbouring disciplines. To the extent that economists find it easier to acquire these techniques and/or can handle them with greater dexterity than can their colleagues in the other social sciences (in part because they use them so frequently), it is possible that this may offset their unfamiliarity with the subject matter of these other disciplines and the analytical framework within which these other social scientists work. But it seems a rather fragile basis for predicting a long-run movement by economists into the other social sciences.

My next example, cost-benefit analysis, is more difficult to discuss.[11] My guess would be that the great bulk of the incursions made by economists into contiguous and not-so-contiguous disciplines in recent years has been in connection with the undertaking of cost-benefit studies. Cost-benefit analysis seems to me best described as a technique. But since it is essentially applied price theory, having as its aim the giving of a monetary value to what is gained and what is lost by following a particular course of action, it is certainly an activity in which economists have some obvious advantages. However, since these studies are usually carried out with a view to facilitating decision-making, particularly by public bodies, with the problem to be investigated selected by such bodies, rather than with a view to understanding the system of which these public bodies are a part, and since economists working in unfamiliar fields will tend to rely on the work of others for their data, economists engaged in these studies will tend to play a useful but subordinate role, except to the extent that the particular decisions being investigated are closely related to their main concerns.

More important and more persuasive is the view, which I associate with the name of Gary Becker, that economic theory or the economic approach can form the means by which economists can work

11. On cost-benefit analysis, see A. R. Prest and R. Turvey, "Cost-Benefit Analysis: A Survey," *The Economic Journal* (December 1965); E. J. Mishan, *Cost-Benefit Analysis* (London: Allen and Unwin; New York: Praeger, 1971); G. H. Peters, *Cost-Benefit Analysis and Public Expenditures* (London: Institute of Economic Affairs, 1966).

40

in, if not take over, the other social sciences.[12] But before examining this point of view, I will consider what I believe to be the normal binding force of a scholarly profession, its subject matter. What do economists study? What do they do? They study the economic system. Alfred Marshall, in the first edition of the *Principles of Economics*, defined economics thus: "Political Economy, or Economics, is a study of man's actions in the ordinary business of life; it inquires how he gets his income and how he uses it."[13] A modern economist, George J. Stigler, has phrased it differently: "Economics is the study of the operation of economic organizations, and economic organizations are social (and rarely individual) arrangements to deal with the production and distribution of economic goods and services."[14] Both of these definitions of economics emphasise that economists study certain kinds of activity. And this accords well with the actual topics dealt with in a book on economics. What economists study is the working of the social institutions which bind together the economic system: firms, markets for goods and services, labour markets, capital markets, the banking system, international trade and so on. It is the common interest in these social institutions which distinguishes the economics profession.

A very different kind of definition is that of Lionel Robbins: "Economics is the science which studies human behaviour as a relationship between ends and scarce means which have alternate uses."[15] Such a definition makes economics a study of human choice. It is clearly too wide if regarded as a description of what economists do. Economists do not study all human choices, or, at any rate, they have not done so as yet. However, the view that economics is a study of all human choice, although it does not tell us the nature of the economic theory or approach which is to be employed in all of the social sciences, certainly calls for the development of such a theory.

12. See Gary S. Becker, "The Economic Approach to Human Behaviour," in *Essays in the Economic Approach to Human Behavior* (Chicago and London: The University of Chicago Press, 1976), 3–14.

13. Alfred Marshall, *Principles of Economics*, C. W. Guillebaud, ed., 9th variorum ed. (London and New York: Macmillan, for The Royal Economic Society, 1961), 2:131.

14. George J. Stigler, *The Theory of Price* (New York: Macmillan, 1952), 1.

15. Lionel C. Robbins, *The Nature and Significance of Economic Science* (London: Macmillan and Co., 1932), 15.

I said earlier that there are, at present, two tendencies in operation in economics which seem to be inconsistent but which, in fact, are not. The first consists of an enlargement of the scope of economists' interests so far as subject matter is concerned. The second is a narrowing of professional interest to more formal, technical, commonly mathematical, analysis. This more formal analysis tends to have a greater generality. It may say less, or leave much unsaid, about the economic system but, because of its generality, the analysis becomes applicable to all social systems. It is this generality of their analytical systems which, I believe, has facilitated the movement of economists into the other social sciences, where they will presumably repeat the successes (and the failures) which they have had within economics itself.

The nature of this general approach has been described by Richard A. Posner in his *Economic Analysis of Law:* "Economics is the science of human choice in a world in which resources are limited in relation to human wants. It explores and tests the implications of the assumption that man is a rational maximizer of his ends in life, his satisfactions—what we shall call his " 'self-interest'."[16]

By defining economics as the "science of human choice," economics becomes the study of all purposeful human behaviour and its scope is, therefore, coterminous with all of the social sciences. It is one thing to make such a claim, it is quite another to translate it into reality. At a time when the King of England claimed to be also King of France, he was not always welcome in Paris. The claim that economics is the science of human choice will not be enough to cause sociologists, political scientists and lawyers to abandon their field or, painfully, to become economists. The dominance of the other social sciences by economists, if it happens, will not come about simply by redefining economics but because of something which economists possess and which enables them to handle sociological, political, legal and similar problems better than the practitioners in these other social sciences. I take it to be the view of Becker and Posner that the decisive advantage which economists possess in handling social problems is their theory of, or approach to, human behaviour, the treatment of man as a rational utility-maximizer.

Since the people who operate in the economic system are the same

16. Posner, *Economic Analysis of Law,* 1.

people who are found in the legal or political system, it is to be expected that their behaviour will be, in a broad sense, similar. But it by no means follows that an approach developed to explain behaviour in the economic system will be equally successful in the other social sciences. In these different fields, the purposes which men seek to achieve will not be the same and, in particular, the institutional framework within which the choices are made is quite different. It seems to me probable that an ability to discern and understand these purposes and the character of the institutional framework (how, for example, the political and legal systems actually operate) will require specialized knowledge not likely to be acquired by those who work in some other discipline. Furthermore, a theory appropriate for the analysis of one of these other social systems will presumably need to embody features which deal with the important specific interrelationships of that system.

I am strengthened in this view by a consideration of the part played by utility theory in economic analysis. Up to the present it has been largely sterile. To say that people maximize utility tells us nothing about the purposes for which they engage in economic activity and leaves us without any insight into why people do what they do. As Stigler has told us, the chief implication of utility theory is that "if consumers do not buy less of a commodity when their incomes rise, they will surely buy less when the price of the commodity rises."[17] But that consumers demand more at a lower price is known to anyone, whether an economist or not, who is at all familiar with the operation of a market. Utility theory seems more likely to handicap than to aid economists in their work in contiguous disciplines. Recently, the work of Kelvin Lancaster on "characteristics analysis"[18] and of Becker on "commodities,"[19] which relate the satisfactions derived from goods and services to certain, specified, more fundamental needs, shows promise of being more fruitful. But it seems improbable that the list of

17. George J. Stigler, "The Development of Utility Theory," in *Essays in the History of Economics* (Chicago: University of Chicago Press, 1965), 155.

18. Kelvin Lancaster, "A New Approach to Consumer Theory," *Journal of Political Economy* (April 1966); *idem., Consumer Demand* (New York: Columbia University Press, 1971).

19. Gary S. Becker and Robert T. Michael, "On the New Theory of Consumer Behaviour," *The Swedish Journal of Economics* 75 (1973).

the important "commodities," to use Becker's term, will be the same in the various social sciences or that the "commodities" will be uncovered, except by specialists in those disciplines.

Economics, it must be admitted, does appear to be more developed than the other social sciences. But the great advantage which economics has possessed is that economists are able to use the "measuring rod of money." This has given a precision to the analysis, and since what are measured by money are important determinants of human behaviour in the economic system, the analysis has considerable explanatory power. Furthermore, the data (on prices and incomes) is generally available, so that hypotheses can be examined and checked. Marshall said that

> the steadiest motive to ordinary business work is the desire for the pay which is the material reward of work. The pay may be on its way to be spent selfishly or unselfishly, for noble or base ends; . . . but the motive is supplied by a definite amount of money: and it is this definite and exact money measurement of the steadiest motives in business life, which has enabled economics to outrun every other branch of the study of man.[20]

If it is true that the more developed state of economics, as compared to the other social sciences, has been due to the happy chance (for economics) that the important factors determining economic behaviour can be measured in money, it suggests that the problems faced by practitioners in these other fields are not likely to be dissipated simply by an infusion of economists, since in moving into these fields they will commonly have to leave their strength behind them. The analysis developed in economics is not likely to be successfully applied in other subjects without major modifications.

If I am right about the relative unimportance of technique as a basis for the choice of professional groupings, if subject matter is really the dominant factor, with the theory or approach in large part determined by the subject matter, what is the outlook for the work of economists in the other social sciences? I would not expect them to continue indefinitely their triumphal advance and it may be that they will be forced to withdraw from some of the fields which they are now

20. Marshall, *Principles of Economics*, 9th variorum ed., 1:14.

so busily cultivating. But such a forecast depends on the practitioners in the other disciplines making a competitive response. The success of economists in moving into the other social sciences is a sign that they possess certain advantages in handling the problems of those disciplines. One is, I believe, that they study the economic system as a unified interdependent system, and, therefore, are more likely to uncover the basic interrelationships within a social system than is someone less accustomed to looking at the working of a system as a whole. Another is that a study of economics makes it difficult to ignore factors which are clearly important and which play a part in all social systems. One such factor would be that, to a large extent, people choose their occupations on the basis of money incomes. Another would be that a higher price lowers the demand. Such factors may appear in various guises, but an economist is likely to see through them. Punishment, for example, can be regarded as the price of crime. An economist will not debate whether increased punishment will reduce crime; he will merely try to answer the question, by how much? The economist's analysis may fail to touch some of the problems found in the other social systems but often the analysis can be brought to bear. And the economist will take full advantage of those opportunities which occur when the "measuring rod of money" can be used.

But if the main advantage which an economist brings to the other social sciences is simply a way of looking at the world, it is hard to believe, once the value of such economic wisdom is recognised, that it will not be acquired by some practitioners in these other fields. This is already happening in law and political science. Once some of these practitioners have acquired the simple but valuable truths which economics has to offer— and this is the natural competitive response— economists who try to work in the other social sciences will have lost their main advantage and will face competitors who know more about the subject matter than they do. In such a situation, only the exceptionally endowed economist is likely to be able to make a significant contribution to our knowledge of the other social sciences.

Economists may, however, study other social systems, such as the legal and political ones, not with the aim of contributing to law or political science but because it is necessary if they are to understand the working of the economic system itself. It has come to be realised by many economists in recent times that parts of these other social systems are so intermeshed with the economic system as to be as much a

Economics

part of that system as they are of a sociological, political or legal system. Thus, it is hardly possible to discuss the functioning of a market without considering the nature of the property rights system, which determines what can be bought and sold and which, by influencing the cost of carrying out various kinds of market transaction, determines what is, in fact, bought and sold, and by whom.[21] Similarly, the family or household and the educational system are of concern to the sociologist but their operations affect the supply of labour to different occupations and the patterns of consumption and production and are, therefore, also of concern to the economist. In the same way, the administration of the regulatory agencies and antitrust policy, while part of the legal system and, as such, studied by lawyers, also provides the framework within which firms and individuals decide on their actions in the economic sphere.

The need to take into account the influence of other social systems, above all the legal system, in analysing the working of the economic system is now widely accepted by economists. It has resulted in numerous studies of the effect of the legal system on the performance of the economic system.[22] Such work, because of its focus on the economic system, is likely, in general, to be best done by economists. Unlike the movement by economists into the other social sciences, which has as its aim the improvement of these other social sciences, a movement which, for reasons I have already given, seems to me likely to be temporary, the study by economists of the effects of the other social systems on the economic system will, I believe, become a permanent part of the work of economists. It cannot be done effectively by social scientists unfamiliar with the economic system. Such work may be carried out in collabouration with other social scientists but it is unlikely to be well done without economists. For this reason, I think we may expect the scope of economics to be permanently enlarged to include studies in other social sciences. But the purpose will be to enable us to understand better the working of the economic system.

21. On property rights, see Erik Furubotn and Svetozar Pejovich, "Property Rights and Economic Theory: A Survey of Recent Literature," *Journal of Economic Literature* (December 1972).
22. It is necessary here only to refer to the kind of articles which appear in the *Journal of Law and Economics*.

FOUR

Economists and Public Policy

The large enterprise that I will be examining is the study of economics, and the performance that I will be appraising is not that of corporations but of my colleagues in the economics profession. The particular aspect of their work that I will be examining will be the part that economists play in the determination of public policy.

I know, of course, that there are some economists who argue that economics is a positive science and that all we can do is to explain the consequences that follow from various economic policies. We cannot say whether one policy is preferable to another, because to do so would require us to introduce value judgments, in the making of which we have no special competence. Thus we can say that certain agricultural policies (say collectivization) will lead to widespread starvation, but we cannot say whether collectivization is or is not desirable. Such self-restraint is I think unnecessary. We share (at least in the West) a very similar set of values, and there is little reason to suppose that the value judgments of economists are particularly eccentric. There will, of course, be instances in which, knowing the consequences of a change in policy, there will be differences in opinion as to whether the change is desirable. But such cases are, I believe, exceptions, and can be treated as such. I agree with Milton Friedman's judgment that

> currently in the Western World, and especially in the United States, differences about economic policy among dis-

Presented at the University of California at Los Angeles in a lecture series with the general title "Large Corporations in a Changing Society" in 1974. Originally published in J. Fred Weston, ed., *Large Corporations in a Changing Society* (New York: New York University Press, 1975), and reprinted here with the publisher's permission. My topic was chosen by the organisers. It had little to do with large corporations, at least as I interpreted the topic.

interested citizens derive predominantly from different predictions about the economic consequences of taking action—differences that in principle can be eliminated by the progress of positive economics—rather than from fundamental differences in basic values, differences about which men can ultimately only fight.[1]

Of course, if this is so, it has the result that an analysis of the consequences of alternative social arrangements becomes a prescription for policy (since we all share the same values). Thus it hardly matters, once it is established that a certain policy will lead to widespread starvation, whether we add that the policy would be undesirable—although to refrain from doing so on principle seems like an affectation. In general, one would expect that a statement of the consequences of alternative policies would bring its policy recommendations with it.

Whether they should or not, few economists do in fact refrain from making pronouncements on public policy, although the state of the economy (both here and elsewhere) suggests either that the advice given is bad or, if good, that it is ignored. Of course, there is the other possibility, more disturbing from some points of view but reassuring from others, that the advice is disregarded, whether it is good or bad. I happen to think that we are appallingly ignorant about many aspects of the working of the economic system, at least so far as that part of economics is concerned in which I am particularly interested—the economics of the firm and industry. I think we know very little about the forces which determine the organisation of industry or the arrangements which firms make in their transactions with one another. We have, of course, been told that when we consider the economics of the system as a whole, what is termed macroeconomic policy, that things are very different, at least since the appearance of Keynes's *General Theory,* and that we now know how to secure full employment coupled with a stable price level. I leave to others more knowledgeable in this field whether our present troubles are due to ignorance, impotence in affecting policy, or some other cause. But I do seem to have detected in recent years a degree of humility among workers in this field not hitherto observed.

1. Milton Friedman, "The Methodology of Positive Economics," in *Essays in Positive Economics* (Chicago: University of Chicago Press, 1953), 5.

Yet having said this, I would not wish to argue that economists do not have something valuable to contribute to the discussion of public policy issues. The problem is that economists seem willing to give advice on questions about which we know very little and on which our judgments are likely to be fallible, while what we have to say which is important and true is quite simple—so simple indeed that little or no economics is required to understand it. What is discouraging is that it is these simple truths which are so commonly ignored in the discussion of economic policy.

It requires no great knowledge of economics to know that at a lower price, consumers will buy a greater quantity. Or to know that as the price falls, producers will be willing to supply less. Even the combining of these two notions to show that, if the price is put low enough, producers will not be willing to supply as much as consumers wish to buy (so that what is called a "shortage" will result) is easy enough to understand. Indeed, the essentials of such a situation would be understood by many who have not studied economics at all. Yet consider an example. In the early 1960s, the Federal Power Commission began to regulate the field price of natural gas. The price was frozen at the 1959–60 level. It became apparent that this was lower than the price would have been without regulation. What followed was what one would expect. Consumption was encouraged; the discovery and exploitation of natural gas was discouraged. The effect of the regulation was at first masked by the short-term fall in the cost of coal and by a reduction in the quality of what was supplied (the consumer had less assurance of the availability of the gas in future). But as time went on, the nature of the regulation-induced shortage of natural gas (to use Paul MacAvoy's phrase) became obvious to the meanest intelligence, and the Federal Power Commission began to take steps to raise the price.

A number of studies have been made (by MacAvoy and others), and there is general agreement about what happened. One of these studies was carried out by Edmund Kitch at the University of Chicago Law School and was published in the *Journal of Law and Economics* in 1968.[2] Later Kitch decided that it would be a good idea if he updated his study. He then presented his findings in Washington, D.C., in 1971

2. Edmund W. Kitch, "Regulation of the Field Market for Natural Gas by the Federal Power Commission," *Journal of Law and Economics* (October 1968):243.

in a talk entitled "The Shortage of Natural Gas."[3] Much of the audience consisted of Washington journalists, members of the staff of congressional committees concerned with energy problems, and others with similar jobs. They displayed little interest in the findings but a great deal in discovering who had financed the study. Many seem to have been convinced that the law and economics program at the University of Chicago had been "bought" by the gas industry. In fact, this study had not been financed by any organisation of any kind connected with the gas or oil industries. But a large part of the audience seemed to live in a simple world in which anyone who thought prices should rise was pro-industry and anyone who wanted prices to be reduced was pro-consumer. I could have explained that the essentials of Kitch's argument had been put forward earlier by Adam Smith—but most of the audience would have assumed that he was someone else in the pay of the American Gas Association.

Adam Smith does not, of course, mention the natural gas industry, which did not exist in his time, but he deals with what is the same problem in his discussion of the corn trade. By corn Smith means, of course, wheat. I quote Smith:

> The interest of the inland [corn] dealer, and that of the great body of the people, how opposite soever they may at first sight appear, are, even in the years of the greatest scarcity, exactly the same. It is his interest to raise the price of his corn as high as the real scarcity of the season requires, and it can never be his interest to raise it higher. By raising the price he discourages the consumption, and puts everybody more or less, but particularly the inferior ranks of people, upon thrift and good management. . . . If by not raising the price high enough he discourages the consumption so little, that the supply of the season is likely to fall short of the consumption of the season, he not only loses a part of the profit which he might otherwise have made, but he exposes the people to suffer before the end of the season, instead of the hardships of a dearth, the dreadful horrors of a famine.[4]

3. Edmund W. Kitch, "The Shortage of Natural Gas," Occasional Paper of the University of Chicago Law School, no. 2 (Chicago, 1971).
4. Adam Smith, *An Inquiry into the Nature and Causes of the Wealth of Nations*, vol. 1 of *The Glasgow Edition of the Works and Correspondence of Adam Smith*, R. H. Campbell and A. S. Skinner, eds. (Oxford, 1976), 524.

But, as Smith points out, since the dealer will maximise his profits by adjusting the price at which he sells so that consumption over the season is equal to the supply, he is not likely to put the price too low. Smith adds:

> Whoever examines, with attention, the history of the dearths and famines which have afflicted any part of Europe, during either the course of the present or that of the two preceding centuries, of several of which we have pretty exact accounts, will find, I believe, that a dearth never has arisen from any combination among the inland dealers in corn, nor from any other cause but a real scarcity, occasioned sometimes, perhaps, and in some particular place, by the waste of war, but in by far the greatest number of cases, by the fault of the seasons; and that a famine has never arisen from any other cause but the violence of government attempting, by improper means, to remedy the inconvenience of a dearth. . . . When the government, in order to remedy the inconveniences of a dearth, orders all the dealers to sell their corn at what it supposes a reasonable price, it either hinders them from bringing it to market, which may sometimes produce a famine even in the beginning of the season; or if they bring it thither, it enables the people, and thereby encourages them to consume it so fast, as must necessarily produce a famine before the end of the season. The unlimited, unrestrained freedom of the corn trade, as it is the only effectual preventative of the miseries of a famine, so it is the best palliative of the inconveniences of a dearth; for the inconveniences of a real scarcity cannot be remedied; they can only be palliated.[5]

Of course, the beneficial role of the merchant in palliating the inconvenience of the scarcity is not understood. "In years of scarcity the inferior ranks of people impute their distress to the avarice of the corn merchant, who becomes the object of their hatred and indignation."[6] And Smith points out that this hostility to the merchant shows itself in the laws against "engrossing and forestalling," that is, the buying and holding of an inventory to sell at a higher price. Of course, Smith is able to show that the merchant will find his holding of stock profitable

5. *Ibid.*, 526–27.
6. *Ibid.*, 527.

only when it is desirable that he should do so. And Smith comments: "The popular fear of engrossing and forestalling may be compared to the popular terrors and suspicions of witchcraft."[7] Smith here attempts to discredit the idea that businessmen, by holding stocks, make prices higher than they would otherwise be, by likening it to a belief in witchcraft. Such an analogy would be less effective today—we also believe in witchcraft.

In the two hundred years which have passed since Adam Smith wrote, many economists have argued along much the same lines about the futility of a policy of holding prices below the competitive level. One of these was Edwin Cannan, of the London School of Economics, who wrote in 1915. He was, of course, writing about the price controls established in Britain at the beginning of World War I. He describes the public response to a rise in price:

> Buyers who have to pay higher prices suddenly become either "the poor" forced to reduce their consumption of necessary articles or else employers of a particularly needy and deserving class which will be thrown out of work by the rise. All the injured persons are at once represented as being iniquitously robbed by an unscrupulous gang of speculators, middlemen, blood-sucking capitalists, or rack-renting landlords against whom all the resources of the State ought to be brought forthwith. The ideal somewhat vaguely held seems to be an immediate return to the prices of a few months or a year ago.[8]

Of course, Cannan argues against price controls in the usual way. But he points to a paradoxical aspect of the situation: "When the price of a thing goes up, [people] abuse, not the buyers nor the persons who might produce it and do not do so, but the persons who are producing and selling it, and thereby keeping down its price."[9] So, if there is a "shortage" of wheat or beef or oil, we abuse those who are producing all the wheat, beef, or oil that we have and without whose efforts the "shortage" would have been still greater. The reason why people show

7. *Ibid.,* 534.
8. Edwin Cannan, "Why Some Prices Should Rise," written in 1915 in *An Economist's Protest* (1927), 16–17.
9. *Ibid.,* 18.

this hostility is that, as Cannan points out, if there is an unusual rise in prices, people

> are perfectly convinced that the rise with which they have to contend for the moment is unnatural, artificial, and wholly unjustifiable, being merely the wicked work of people who want to enrich themselves, and who are given the power to do so not by the economic conditions . . . but apparently by some absolutely direct and inexplicable interference of the Devil. This has been so since the dawn of history . . . but no amount of historical retrospect seems to be of much use. The same absurdity crops up generation after generation.[10]

I began this paper by saying that economists in their discussion of public policy often deal with questions which are difficult to analyse, about which we know very little, and on which, therefore, our recommendations, if followed, would very likely make things worse. On the other hand, the advice we do have to offer which would be valuable, if followed, consists of a few simple truths. However, history indicates that these are simple truths which people find it easy to reject—or ignore. When I first began thinking about what I would say, I did not anticipate the present oil problem (and I was not alone). But the character of the public discussion of this problem suggests that we are no better than those who went before us. We are a generation whose time has come. We observe the same attitudes that Cannan described, "the rise [of price] with which we have to contend at the moment" being "unnatural, artificial, and wholly unjustifiable . . . the wicked work of people who want to enrich themselves." This raises the question of what the role of an economist should be in a world which rejects the only solidly based advice that he has to give.

Frank Knight, in his presidential address to the American Economic Association in 1950, poses this question—and gives an appropriately depressing answer.

> I have been increasingly moved to wonder whether my job is a job or a racket, whether economists, and particularly economic theorists, may not be in a position that Cicero, con-

10. *Ibid.*, 23.

cerning Cato, ascribed to the augurs of Rome—that they should cover their faces or burst into laughter when they met on the street. . . . The free-traders, as has been said, win the debates but the protectionists win the elections; and it makes little difference in our policy which party wins, the avowed protectionists or the professed free-traders. Inflation is of course to be brought on as a more pleasant alternative to taxation and then suppressed by law and police action. . . . The serious fact is that the bulk of the really important things that economics has to teach are things that people would see for themselves if they were willing to see. And it is hard to believe in the utility of trying to teach what men refuse to learn or even seriously listen to. . . . Can there be any use in explaining, if it is needful to explain, that fixing a price below the free-market level will create a shortage and one above it a surplus? But the public's oh's and ah's and yips and yaps at the shortage of residential housing and surpluses of eggs and potatoes as if these things presented problems—any more than getting one's footgear soiled by deliberately walking in the mud.[11]

Knight says that, in consequence of this, his interest has tended to shift away from economic theory "to the question of why people so generally, and the learned elite in particular, as they express themselves in various ways choose nonsense instead of sense,"[12] which is one possible response to the situation, although not, I think, the only one open to us. Knight also says something else which is, I think, helpful to those of us who are looking for an alternative response: "Explanations of policy might conceivably get farther if we . . . ask *why* men believe and practice nonsense but in general act so much less irrationally than they argue—and what follows from that."[13]

If we took seriously the argument used by those who advocate price controls and similar measures, we would expect much more extreme, and less sensible, proposals than are actually put forward. Thus, some senators believe that lower prices for gasoline would benefit consumers, so they introduce a measure in Congress which would

11. Frank H. Knight, "The Role of Principles in Economics and Politics," *American Economic Review* (March 1951):2–4.

12. *Ibid.*, 2.

13. *Ibid.*, 4.

make the gasoline prices of last December [1973] mandatory, not the still lower prices that prevailed in the 1930s. The Federal Power Commission undertook in 1961 to regulate the field price of natural gas—so the level of prices which it determined should be charged in future was that prevailing in 1959–60. As Cannan said, writing long ago and about a different country: "The ideal somewhat vaguely held seems to be a return to the prices of a few months or a year ago." Similarly, politicians may make speeches which favor the elimination of all pollution; their proposals are much more moderate. Furthermore, I seem to observe that as the harm inflicted by the policy increases, the strength of the support for that policy decreases—which leads, if not to the elimination of the policy, at any rate to a moderation of it. The Federal Power Commission finally did act to raise the field price of natural gas, although it no doubt acted more slowly and made a smaller change than most economists would have liked. With a rise in the price of oil, concern about the fate of the caribou in Alaska became less pressing, and the Alaska Pipe Line is now likely to be built.

Although controls, such as price and wage controls, are introduced to prevent the basic economic forces from working, a study of the history of controls would show, I believe, that, over a longer period, there have been very few controls which have not been modified to take such forces into account, or even abandoned, so that market forces have free sway. My conclusion is that, although a policy may be misguided, we should not assume that its range, severity, and duration are not kept in check by recognition of the extent of the harm it produces. I do not myself understand why the political system operates in the way it does. Whether the interests opposed to the policy tend to become relatively stronger in the political arena as the amount of harm inflicted by the policy increases or whether recognition of the amount of harm plays a more direct role in the political process, or whether both of these factors operate, I do not know, although it would be my judgment that both of these factors exert some weight. At any rate, it may be that there is room for economists' views on public policy to play a valuable part in this process of modification and change, even though they will usually not be able to exercise a decisive influence over the choice of the policy itself. Certainly, however ill-advised policies may be, they are not in their administration devoid of sense. The demand for nonsense seems to be subject to the universal law of demand: we demand less of it when the price is higher.

A more optimistic view of the role of the economist in the formulation of public policy or, at any rate, of his future role, is presented by George Stigler in his presidential address to the American Economic Association in 1964 entitled "The Economist and the State."[14] Stigler argues that economists in the past have been willing to express views on the role of the state in economic affairs without making any serious study of how the state did in fact carry out the tasks entrusted to it or making any systematic investigation of the comparative performance of state and private enterprise. This was true both for those, like Smith and Alfred Marshall, who wanted to limit government intervention in the economic system and for those, like W. Stanley Jevons, A. C. Pigou, and a host of others, who were in favor of an expanding governmental role. Stigler's comments on our predecessors seem a little harsh—they faced difficulties which we do not encounter, they were few in number, and they were mainly engaged (particularly the better among them) in developing the analysis of a pricing system—but I do not wish particularly to quarrel with his main conclusion. I have argued that our knowledge is very limited—and we are able to read what our predecessors wrote.

Stigler ascribes the lack of influence of economists on the formulation of public policy—which he asserts and I would not wish to deny—to their ignorance. "Lacking real expertise, and lacking also evangelical ardor, the economist has had little influence upon the evolution of economic policy."[15] But that is the past. The future, according to Stigler, will be very different.

> The age of quantification is now full upon us. We are armed with a bulging arsenal of techniques of quantitative analysis, and of a power—as compared to untrained common sense—comparable to the displacement of archers by cannon. . . . The desire to measure economic phenomena is now in the ascendent. . . . It is a scientific revolution of the very first magnitude. . . . I am convinced that economics is finally at the threshold of its golden age—nay, we already have one foot through the door. The revolution in our thinking has begun to reach public policy, and soon it will make irresistible demands upon us. It will become inconceivable that the mar-

14. George J. Stigler, "The Economist and the State," *American Economic Review* (March 1965):1.
15. *Ibid.*, 12.

gin requirements on securities markets will be altered once a year without knowing whether they have even a modest effect. It will become impossible for an import-quota system to evade the calculus of gains and costs. It will become an occasion for humorous nostalgia when arguments for private and public performance of a given economic activity are conducted by reference to the phrase, external economies, or by recourse to a theorem on perfect competition. . . . I assert, not that we should make the studies I wish for, but that no-one can delay their coming. . . . That we are good theorists is not open to dispute. . . . The last half century of economics certifies the immense increase in the power, the care, and the courage of our quantitative researches. Our expanding theoretical and empirical studies will inevitably and irresistibly enter into the subject of public policy, and we shall develop a body of knowledge essential to intelligent policy formulation. And then, quite frankly, I hope that we become the ornaments of democratic society whose opinions on economic policy shall prevail.[16]

I was present when Stigler delivered his address and, as he ended with these words, it was hard to restrain a cheer. When the immediate impact of this eloquent and moving address had passed, Stigler's assertions brought to mind Pope's couplet: "Hope springs eternal in the human breast;/Man never is, but always to be, blest."

But even though we do not believe that such a glittering prospect lies ahead of us, we need not despair. If, as I am inclined to believe, economists cannot usually affect the main course of economic policy, their views may make themselves felt in small ways. An economist who, by his efforts, is able to postpone by a week a government program which wastes $100 million a year (what I would consider a modest success) has, by his action, earned his salary for the whole of his life. Indeed, if we compute the total annual salaries of all economists engaged in research on public policy issues (or questions related to this), which might amount to $20 million (or some similar figure), it is clear that this expenditure (or one much larger) would be justified if it led to a minuscule increase in the gross national product. It is not necessary to change the world to justify our salaries. But does the advice of economists on public policy issues improve the situation in those

16. *Ibid.*, 16–17.

cases in which it does have some influence? I take Stigler's main purpose to be not to raise our morale but to induce us to change our ways so that our advice will be worth following. If, as a result, we achieve my modest aim, we will at least earn our keep. If Stigler's view of the future is correct, we will confer a great benefit on mankind—and be grossly underpaid.

The advice that we have had to offer in the past that was valuable—what I have called the simple truths—was, of course, the implications of a theoretical system which, while its range was restricted, has been confirmed time after time. The assumption of the theory is that producers want to make as much money as possible and that consumers want to get as much for their money as they can. Or, put more generally, and with more applications, it is assumed that people tend, in the main, to pursue their own self-interests. It has proved a very robust theory. But, of course, without knowledge of magnitudes (though they could sometimes be inferred), there were a lot of questions that the theory could not answer. But this hardly explains why the theory has been ignored for those questions for which it could give answers.

Stigler pins his high hopes for the future on the growth in quantitative work. But this development is not without its costs. It absorbs resources which might otherwise be devoted to the development of our theory and to empirical studies of the economic system of a nonquantitative character. Aspects of the economic system which are difficult to measure tend to be neglected. It diverts attention from the economic system itself to the technical problems of measurement. I do not mean to suggest that we should avoid quantitative work. But it is well to remember that there is no such thing as a free statistic.

I would like to illustrate my view that nonquantitative work, or at least work with only the crudest form of quantification, can be of value by means of an example. About 1960 Senator Estes Kefauver was holding hearings into the drug industry and particularly into its practices in introducing new drugs. The main thrust of the hearings was to suggest that the prices paid were too high, but even more that the drugs were often of little or even dubious value. Senator Kefauver concluded that it would be desirable to regulate the introduction of new drugs. At the time this proposal was under consideration the tragic side effects of the use of thalidomide by pregnant women became known. The result was to generate so much support for drug regulation that the Kefauver proposal, which might otherwise have failed to secure congressional approval, was enacted into law in 1962. Was it wise to do this? Consider what one economist said early in 1965 and long before the effects of this new law could be known:

> I ask myself a question: Suppose I am a physician in the public health service, and somebody presents to me a new drug. I can approve it now, although we do not know its full effects, and commonly we shall not know the full effects of a new drug for five to ten years after it comes out. If I approve it, and a series of tragedies such as this thalidomide tragedy comes, what will happen to me? I shall certainly be discharged, and I will be held up to public obloquy. The public at large will demand that heads roll. The penalties on me are very heavy indeed if I approve a drug I should not have. Suppose on the other hand, that it proves to be a fine drug, and in the long run its achievements are wonderful, but we do not know this yet. If I hold up the use of the drug for five years until all the results are in, a large number of people may die because it was not available. Their survivors will not write and complain that I did not approve the drug earlier. All the penalties are on me in making the mistake of approving the drug too early and none on the mistake of approving it too late. This combination of rewards and penalties . . . seems undesirable.[17]

This simple application of the view that people (including government regulators) tend to have regard to their own self-interest leads to the conclusion that the regulation will result in considerable delay in the introduction of new drugs. Those of us who have seen the great improvements in health which have taken place in recent years as a result of the use of newly discovered drugs, particularly in the period since World War II, cannot but feel that the new regulation may have done more harm than good. In this case, it so happens that by now there has been a quantitative study of the effects of the new drug regulation, by Sam Peltzman of the University of California at Los An-

17. George J. Stigler, "The Formation of Economic Policy," in *Current Problems in Political Economy* (Ind.: DePauw University), 74–75.

geles,[18] and it indicates that apprehension about the legislation was completely justified. The number of new drugs introduced each year on average in the period 1963 to 1970 was about 40 percent of what it had been in the period 1951 to 1962, and a statistical investigation carried out by Peltzman indicates that the whole of this decline was probably due to the new legislation. But he went further. Noting that while some of the drugs excluded from the market by the legislation would have been beneficial, others would no doubt have proved to be unsafe or no better than drugs already existing. Peltzman proceeded to make a calculation of the probable benefits and costs of the new drug regulation. The result: The gains (if any) which accrued from the exclusion of ineffective or harmful drugs were far outweighed by the benefits forgone because effective drugs were not marketed. This conclusion was clearly foreshadowed by the essentially nonquantitative assessment of the probable results of the new drug regulation to which I drew your attention earlier. The economist who made this assessment was Stigler. It represents a fine example of nonquantitative reasoning.

The results obtained by Peltzman were not altogether surprising, since our normal theory would suggest that there would be a decrease (probably large) in the number of new drugs marketed, and, given the benefits which seem to be derived from newly discovered drugs, one would expect that this factor would dominate the results. But what was surprising (and our theory gives us no basis for expecting it) was that there is no strong evidence that the proportion of inefficacious drugs is substantially less in the smaller number of drugs marketed now than it was in the years before 1962. All this suggests not that the decisions of doctors and patients about the use of drugs are correct but that it is not easy to devise alternative institutions that will perform better.

This is, I believe, a common situation, although economists generally appear to have assumed otherwise. The reason for this sanguine attitude is that, while most economists do not ignore the inefficiencies of a market system, which, indeed, they are often prone to exaggerate, they tend to overlook the inefficiencies inherent in a governmental organisation. It is therefore hardly surprising that economists in the last one hundred years or so have been led to support (or acquiesce in) an ever-expanding role for government in economic affairs and have not

18. Sam Peltzman, "An Evaluation of Consumer Protection Legislation: The 1962 Drug Amendments," *Journal of Political Economy* (September–October 1973):1049.

felt a need for any serious investigation of the working of governmental organisations. What is wanted, if policy recommendations are to have a solid foundation, is to take into account both how a market actually operates and how a government organisation does in fact carry out the tasks entrusted to it.

Fortunately, the situation I have described does seem to me in the process of change. Economists (along with others) are beginning to take a more critical look at the activities of government, and the kind of study which I have suggested as desirable is now being made. Certainly there have been more serious studies made of government regulation of industry in the last fifteen years or so, particularly in the United States, than in the whole preceding period. These studies have been both quantitative and nonquantitative. I have referred to studies of the regulation of natural gas and drugs. But there have also been studies of the regulation of many diverse activities such as agriculture, aviation, banking, broadcasting, electricity supply, milk distribution, railroads and trucking, taxicabs, whiskey labeling, and zoning. I mention only studies with which I am familiar; there are doubtless many others. The main lesson to be drawn from these studies is clear: They all tend to suggest that the regulation is either ineffective or that, when it has a noticeable impact, on balance the effect is bad, so that consumers obtain a worse product or a higher-priced product or both as a result of the regulation. Indeed, this result is found so uniformly as to create a puzzle: One would expect to find, in all these studies, at least some government programs that do more good than harm.

In my paper on "The Problem of Social Cost,"[19] I argued that, in choosing between social institutions, the decision should be based on how they would work in practise. I explained that there were costs involved in making market transactions and that consequently there were reallocations of factors of production which would, of themselves, raise the value of production but would not take place when the costs of the necessary transactions exceeded the gain in the value of production that would result. Such reallocations of factors can also, of course, be brought about by government regulation. Now government regulation also has costs—and government regulators may have in mind ends other than raising the value of production. But the oppor-

19. R. H. Coase, "The Problem of Social Cost," *Journal of Law and Economics* (October 1960):1–44.

tunity is there for government regulation to improve on the market. I wrote that "direct government regulation will not necessarily give better results than leaving the problem to be solved by the market or the firm. But equally there is no reason why, on occasion, such governmental administrative regulation should not lead to an improvement in economic efficiency."[20]

My puzzle is to explain why these occasions seem to be so rare, if not nonexistent. One explanation would be that these studies happen to have involved cases in which there was a failure of government regulation and that further investigation will uncover many examples of success. But it is hard to feel much confidence in this explanation—the studies have been so numerous and their range so extensive, and some of the cases of failure are found where one might have expected success, for example, the control of monopoly, the regulation of drugs or labeling, and zoning. Nonetheless, I am inclined to think that there may be something to this explanation and that, if we looked more at government activities which affected directly the costs of carrying out market transactions, we would indeed find cases in which governmental activities improved the situation. But I would not expect the inclusion of such cases to change the main conclusion, if indeed it is to be regarded as a qualification to it.

Another explanation for this record of poor performance of government would be that this is the way of the world, that the costs of government are always greater than they would be for the market transactions that would accomplish the same result. But I regard this as implausible.

I have come to the conclusion that the most probable reason we obtain these results is that the government is attempting to do too much—that it operates on such a gigantic scale that it has reached the stage at which, for many of its activities, as economists would say, the marginal product is negative. We would expect to reach this stage if the size of an organisation were allowed to expand indefinitely. I suspect that this is exactly what has happened. If further studies confirm that this really is the situation, the condition is one which can be cured only by a reduction of government activity in the economic sphere. This will not be easy to achieve, since it runs counter to prevailing attitudes. Oddly enough, the finding that many governmental activ-

20. *Ibid.*, 18.

ities do more harm than good is likely to be received sympathetically. It is common enough to read an article or the account of a speech of which the first part consists of a denunciation of the inefficiency and corruption to be found in the administration of some government program—but this is often followed by a second part which draws our attention to some pressing social problem coupled with the proposal that the government set up a new program or agency or expand an old one to deal with this problem. To ignore the government's poor performance of its present duties when deciding on whether it should or should not take on new duties is obviously wrong (old duties were once, in the main, new duties). But the sanguine view of what the government will accomplish induced by this way of thinking tends to lead to an ever-expanding role for the government in economic affairs (and has done so). If I am right that the attempt to carry out these new activities leads to the government performing worse than before in those that it is already undertaking, the continued expansion of the government's role will inevitably lead us to a situation in which most government activities result in more harm than good. My surmise is that we have reached this stage.

This makes an economist's task in one respect easy and in another difficult. It becomes easy because at the present time the advice that has to be given is that all government activities should be curtailed. Our task is made more difficult because our experience with the present overexpanded governmental machine may not give us much indication of what tasks the government should undertake when the sphere of government has been reduced to a more appropriate size. But perhaps I exaggerate the difficulty. The move to a smaller government is hardly likely to be swift—and we will gradually be able to accumulate the information needed to discover what functions should be left to the government.

But all this assumes that the investigations of economists will, as Stigler claims, in the end have a decisive influence on public policy. Whether the economist will be more successful in limiting the role of government than he has been in policies directly concerned with the operation of the markets and the pricing system remains to be seen. But as I have indicated, even a modest success is not to be despised.

FIVE

The Market for Goods and the Market for Ideas

The normal treatment of governmental regulation of markets makes a sharp distinction between the ordinary market for goods and services and the activities covered by the First Amendment—speech, writing, and the exercise of religious beliefs—which I call, for brevity, "the market for ideas." The phrase "the market for ideas" does not describe very exactly the boundaries of the area to which the First Amendment has been applied. Indeed, these boundaries do not seem to have been very clearly drawn. But there can be little doubt that the market for ideas, the expression of opinion in speech and writing and similar activities, is at the center of the activities protected by the First Amendment, and it is with these activities that discussion of the First Amendment has been largely concerned.

The arguments that I will be considering long antedate the passage of the First Amendment (which obviously incorporated views already held), and there is some danger for economists, although not necessarily for American lawyers, in confining our discussion to the First Amendment rather than considering the general problem of which it is a part. The danger is that our discussion will tend to concentrate on American court opinions, and particularly those of the Supreme Court, and that, as a result, we will be led to adopt the approach to the regulation of markets found congenial by the courts rather than one developed by economists, a procedure which already has gone a long way to ruin public utility economics and has done much harm to economic discussion of monopoly problems generally. This approach is confining in another way, since, by concentrating on issues within

Presented at a session on "The Economics of the First Amendment" at the annual meeting of the American Economic Association in December 1973. Originally published in the *American Economic Review* (May 1974). © 1974 American Economic Associated. Reprinted with permission.

the context of the American Constitution, it is made more difficult to draw on the experience and thought of the rest of the world.

What is the general view that I will be examining? It is that, in the market for goods, government regulation is desirable whereas in the market for ideas, government regulation is undesirable and should be strictly limited. In the market for goods, the government is commonly regarded as competent to regulate and properly motivated. Consumers lack the ability to make the appropriate choices. Producers often exercise monopolistic power and, in any case, without some form of government intervention, would not act in a way which promotes the public interest. In the market for ideas, the position is very different. The government, if it attempted to regulate, would be inefficient and its motives would, in general, be bad, so that, even if it were successful in achieving what it wanted to accomplish, the results would be undesirable. Consumers, on the other hand, if left free, exercise a fine discrimination in choosing between the alternative views placed before them, while producers, whether economically powerful or weak, who are found to be so unscrupulous in their behaviour in other markets, can be trusted to act in the public interest, whether they publish or work for the *New York Times,* the *Chicago Tribune* or the Columbia Broadcasting System. Politicians, whose actions sometimes pain us, are in their utterances beyond reproach. It is an odd feature of this attitude that commercial advertising, which is often merely an expression of opinion and might, therefore, be thought to be protected by the First Amendment, is considered to be part of the market for goods. The result is that government action is regarded as desirable to regulate (or even suppress) the expression of an opinion in an advertisement which, if expressed in a book or article, would be completely beyond the reach of government regulation.

This ambivalence toward the role of government in the market for goods and the market for ideas has not usually been attacked except by those on the extreme right or left, that is, by fascists or communists. The Western world, by and large, accepts the distinction and the policy recommendations that go with it. The peculiarity of the situation has not, however, gone unnoticed, and I would like to draw your attention to a powerful article by Aaron Director. Director quotes a very strong statement by Justice William O. Douglas in a Supreme Court opinion, a statement which is no doubt intended as an interpretation of the First Amendment but which obviously embodies a point of view not dependent on constitutional considerations. Justice Douglas said: "Free speech, free press, free exercise of religion are placed separate and apart; they are above and beyond the police power; they are not subject to regulation in the manner of factories, slums, apartment houses, production of oil and the like."[1] Director remarks of the attachment to free speech that it is "the only area where *laissez-faire* is still respectable."[2]

Why should this be so? In part, this may be due to the fact that belief in a free market in ideas does not have the same roots as belief in the value of free trade in goods. To quote Director again: "The free market as a desirable method of organizing the intellectual life of the community was urged long before it was advocated as a desirable method of organizing its economic life. The advantage of free exchange of ideas was recognized before that of the voluntary exchange of goods and services in competitive markets."[3] In recent years, particularly, I think in America (that is, North America), this view of the peculiar status of the market for ideas has been nourished by a commitment to democracy as exemplified in the political institutions of the United States, for whose efficient working a market of ideas not subject to government regulation is considered essential. This opens a large subject on which I will avoid comment. Suffice it to say that, in practise, the results actually achieved by this particular political system suggest that there is a good deal of "market failure."

Because of the view that a free market in ideas is necessary to the maintenance of democratic institutions and, I believe, for other reasons also, intellectuals have shown a tendency to exalt the market for ideas and to depreciate the market for goods. Such an attitude seems to me unjustified. As Director said: "The bulk of mankind will for the forseeable future have to devote a considerable fraction of their active lives to economic activity. For these people, freedom of choice as owners of resources in choosing within available and continually changing opportunities, areas of employment, investment, and consumption is fully as important as freedom of discussion and participation in government."[4] I have no doubt that this is right. For most

---

1. *Beauharnis v. Illinois,* 343 U.S. 250, 286 (1952).
2. Aaron Director, "The Parity of the Economic Market Place," *Journal of Law and Economics* (October 1964):5.
3. *Ibid.,* 3.
4. *Ibid.,* 6.

people in most countries (and perhaps in all countries), the provision of food, clothing, and shelter is a good deal more important than the provision of the "right ideas," even if it is assumed that we know what they are.

But leave aside the question of the relative importance of the two markets; the difference in view about the role of government in these two markets is really quite extraordinary and demands an explanation. It is not enough merely to say that the government should be excluded from a sphere of activity because the activity is vital to the functioning of our society. Even in markets which are mainly of concern to the lower orders, it would not seem desirable to reduce the efficiency with which they work. The paradox is that government intervention which is so harmful in the one sphere becomes beneficial in the other. The paradox is made even more striking when we note that at the present time it is usually those who press most strongly for an extension of government regulation in other markets who are most anxious for a vigorous enforcement of the First Amendment prohibitions on government regulation in the market for ideas.

What is the explanation for the paradox? Director's gentle nature does not allow him to do more than hint at it:

> A superficial explanation for the preference for free speech among intellectuals runs in terms of vertical interests. Everyone tends to magnify the importance of his own occupation and to minimize that of his neighbor. Intellectuals are engaged in the pursuit of truth, while others are merely engaged in earning a livelihood. One follows a profession, usually a learned one, while the other follows a trade or a business.[5]

I would put the point more bluntly. The market for ideas is the market in which the intellectual conducts his trade. The explanation of the paradox is self-interest and self-esteem. Self-esteem leads the intellectuals to magnify the importance of their own market. That others should be regulated seems natural, particularly as many of the intellectuals see themselves as doing the regulating. But self-interest combines with self-esteem to ensure that, while others are regulated, regulation should not apply to them. And so it is possible to live with these contradictory views about the role of government in these two

5. *Ibid.*, 6.

markets. It is the conclusion that matters. It may not be a nice explanation, but I can think of no other for this strange situation.

That this is the main explanation for the dominance of the view that the market for ideas is sacrosanct is certainly supported if we examine the actions of the press. The press is, of course, the most stalwart defender of the doctrine of freedom of the press, an act of public service to the performance of which it has been led, as it were, by an invisible hand. If we examine the actions and views of the press, they are consistent in only one respect: they are always consistent with the self-interest of the press.

Consider the argument of the press that it should not be forced to reveal the sources of its published material. This is termed a defense of the public's right to know—which is interpreted to mean that the public has no right to know the source of material published by the press. To desire to know the source of a story is not idle curiosity. It is difficult to know how much credence to give to information or to check on its accuracy if one is ignorant of the source. The academic tradition, in which one discloses to the greatest extent possible the sources on which one relies and thus exposes them to the scrutiny of one's colleagues, seems to me to be sound and an essential element in the search for truth. Of course, the counterargument of the press is not without validity. It is argued that some people would not express their opinions honestly if it became known that they really held these opinions. But this argument applies equally to all expressions of views, whether in government, business or private life, where confidentiality is necessary for frankness. However, this consideration has commonly not deterred the press from revealing such confidences when it was in their interest to do so. Of course, it would also impede the flow of information to reveal the sources of the material published in cases in which the transmission of the information involved a breach of trust or even the stealing of documents. To accept material in such circumstances is not consistent with the high moral standards and scrupulous observance of the law which the press expects of others. It is hard for me to believe that the main thing wrong with the Watergate affair was that it was not organised by the *New York Times*. I would not wish to argue that there are not conflicting considerations in all these cases which are difficult to evaluate. My point is that the press does not find them difficult to evaluate.

Consider another example which is in many ways more striking:

the attitude of the press to government regulation of broadcasting. Broadcasting is an important source of news and information; it comes within the purview of the First Amendment. Yet the program content of a broadcasting station is subject to government regulation. One might have thought that the press, devoted to the strict enforcement of the First Amendment, would have been constantly attacking this abridgment of the right of free speech and expression. But, in fact, they have not. In all the years which have passed since the formation of the Federal Radio Commission in 1929 (now transformed into the Federal Communications Commission), very few doubts about the policy have been expressed in the press. The press, which is so anxious to remain unshackled by government regulation, has never exerted itself to secure a similar freedom for the broadcasting industry.

Lest you think that I manifest a hostility to the American press, I would like to point out that the British press has acted in a similar fashion. In this case the contrast between actions and proclaimed beliefs is even stronger since what was established in Britain was a government-controlled monopoly of a source of news and information. It might have been thought that this affront to the doctrine of freedom of the press would have appalled the British press. It did not. They supported the broadcasting monopoly, mainly, as far as I can see, because they saw the alternative to the British Broadcasting Corporation (BBC) as commercial broadcasting and, therefore, as involving increased competition for advertising revenue. But if the press did not want competition for advertising revenue, they also did not want competition in the supply of news. And so they did their best to throttle the BBC, at least as a purveyor of news and information. When the monopoly was originally established (when it was still the British Broadcasting *Company*), the BBC was prohibited from broadcasting news and information unless obtained from certain named news agencies. No news could be broadcast before 7 P.M. and broadcasts likely to affect adversely the sale of newspapers faced other restrictions as well. Gradually, over the years, these restrictions were relaxed as a result of negotiations between the press and the BBC. But it was not until after the outbreak of World War II that the BBC broadcast a regular news bulletin before 6 P.M.[6]

6. For a discussion of the attitude of the press to the monopoly of British broadcasting, see R. H. Coase, *British Broadcasting, A Study in Monopoly* (Cambridge, Mass., 1950), 103–10, 192–93.

But, it may be argued, the fact that businessmen are mainly influenced by pecuniary considerations is no great discovery. What else would one expect from the money-grubbers of the newspaper world? Furthermore, it may be objected, because a doctrine is propagated by those who benefit from it does not mean that the doctrine is unsound. After all, have not free speech and a free press also been advocated by high-minded scholars whose beliefs are determined by what is true rather than by more sordid considerations? There has surely never been a more high-minded scholar than John Milton. As his *Areopagitica* "for the liberty of unlicensed printing" is probably the most celebrated defense of the doctrine of freedom of the press ever written, it seemed to me that it would be worthwhile to examine the nature of his argument for a free press. Milton's work has another advantage for my purpose. Written in 1644, that is, long before 1776, we can see the character of the argument before there was any general understanding of how competitive markets worked and before the emergence of modern views on democracy.

It would be idle for me to pretend that I could act as a guide to Milton's thought. I know too little of seventeenth-century England, and there is much in Milton's pamphlet the meaning of which I cannot discern. Yet, there are passages which leap across the centuries and for whose interpretation no scholarship is needed.

As one would expect, Milton asserts the primacy of the market for ideas: "Give me the liberty to know, to utter, and to argue freely according to conscience, above all liberties."[7] It is different from the market for goods and should not be treated in the same way: "Truth and understanding are not such wares as to be monopolised and traded in by tickets and statutes and standards. We must not think to make a staple commodity of all the knowledge in the land, to mark and licence it like our broadcloth and our woolpacks."[8] The licencing of printed material is an affront to learned men and to learning:

> When a man writes to the world, he summons up all his reason and deliberation to assist him; he searches, meditates, is industrious, and likely consults and confers with his judicious friends; after all which done he takes himself to be in-

7. John Milton, *Areopagitica, A Speech for the Liberty of Unlicensed Printing,* with introduction and notes by H. B. Cotterill (New York, 1959), 44.
8. *Ibid.,* 29.

formed in what he writes, as well as any that writ before him. If in this the most consummate act of his fidelity and ripeness of years, no industry, no former proof of his abilities can bring him to that state of maturity as not to be still mistrusted and suspected, unless he carry his considerate diligence, all his midnight watchings . . . to the hasty view of an unleisured licenser, perhaps much his younger, perhaps far his inferior in judgment, perhaps one who never knew the labour of bookwriting, and, if he be not repulsed or slighted, must appear in print like a puny with his guardian and his censor's hand on the back of his title to be his bail and surety, that he is no idiot or seducer, it cannot be but a dishonour and derogation to the author, to the book, to the privilege and dignity of learning.[9]

Licensing is also an affront to the common people:

Nor is it to the common people less than a reproach; for if we be so jealous over them, as that we dare not trust them with an English pamphlet, what do we but censure them for a giddy, vicious, and ungrounded people, in such a sick and weak state of faith and discretion, as to be able to take nothing down but through the pipe of a licenser.[10]

In the market for ideas, the right choices are made: "Let [truth] and falsehood grapple; who ever knew Truth put to the worse in a free and open encounter."[11] Those who undertake the job of licensing will be incompetent. A licenser should be, according to Milton, "studious, learned, and judicious." But this is not what we are likely to get: "We may easily foresee what kind of licensers we are to expect hereafter: either ignorant, imperious, and remiss, or basely pecuniary."[12] The licensers are more likely to suppress truth than falsehood: "If it come to prohibiting, there is aught more likely to be prohibited than truth itself; whose first appearance to our eyes bleared and dimmed with prejudice and custom is more unsightly and unplausible than many errors."[13] Nor does Milton fail to tell us that the licensing scheme against which he is writing came about as a result of industry pressure:

9. *Ibid.*, 27.   12. *Ibid.*, 25.
10. *Ibid.*, 30.   13. *Ibid.*, 47.
11. *Ibid.*, 45.

"And how it got the upper hand . . . there was in it the fraud of some old patentees and monopolisers in the trade of bookselling."[14]

In the formation of Milton's views, self-interest may perhaps have played a part, but there can be little doubt that his argument embodies a good deal of intellectual pride of the kind to which Director refers. The writer is a learned man, diligent and trustworthy. The licenser would be ignorant, incompetent, and basely motivated, perhaps "younger" and "inferior in judgment." The common man would always choose truth over falsehood. The picture is a little too one-sided to be wholly convincing. And if it has been convincing to the intellectual community (and apparently it often has), it is surely because people are easily persuaded that what is good for them is good for the country.

I do not believe that this distinction between the market for goods and the market for ideas is valid. There is no fundamental difference between these two markets and, in deciding on public policy with regard to them, we need to take into account the same considerations. In all markets, producers have some reasons for being honest and some for being dishonest; consumers have some information but are not fully informed or even able to digest the information they have; regulators commonly wish to do a good job but are often incompetent and subject to the influence of special interests, because, like all of us, they are human beings whose strongest motives are not the highest.

When I say that the same considerations should be taken into account, I do not mean that public policy should be the same in all markets. The special characteristics of each market lead to the same factors having different weights, and the appropriate social arrangements will vary accordingly. It may not be sensible to have the same legal arrangements governing the supply of soap, housing, automobiles, oil, and books. My argument is that we should use the same *approach* for all markets when deciding on public policy. In fact, if we do this and use for the market for ideas the same approach which has commended itself to economists for the market of goods, it is apparent that the case for government intervention in the market of ideas is much stronger than it is, in general, in the market for goods. For example, economists usually call for government intervention, which may include direct government regulation, when the market does not

14. *Ibid.*, 50.

operate properly—when, that is, there exist what are commonly referred to as neighbourhood or spillover effects, or, to use that unfortunate word, "externalities." If we try to imagine the property rights system that would be required and the transactions that would have to be carried out to assure that anyone who propagated an idea or a proposal for reform received the value of the good it produced or had to pay compensation for the harm that resulted, it is easy to see that in practise there is likely to be a good deal of "market failure." Situations of this kind usually lead economists to call for extensive government intervention.

Or consider the question of consumer ignorance which is commonly thought to be a justification for government intervention. It is hard to believe that the general public is in a better position to evaluate competing views on economic and social policy than to choose between different kinds of food. Yet there is support for regulation in the one case but not in the other. Or consider the question of preventing fraud, for which government intervention is commonly advocated. It would be difficult to deny that newspaper articles and the speeches of politicians contain a large number of false and misleading statements; indeed, sometimes they seem to consist of little else. Government action to control false and misleading advertising is considered highly desirable. Yet a proposal to set up a Federal Press Commission or a Federal Political Commission modeled on the Federal Trade Commission would be dismissed out of hand.

The strong support enjoyed by the First Amendment should not hide from us that there is, in fact, a good deal of government intervention in the market for ideas. I have mentioned broadcasting. But there is also the case of education, which, although it plays a crucial role in the market for ideas, is subject to considerable regulation. One might have thought that those who were so anxious to obstruct government regulation of books and other printed material would also find such regulation in the field of education obnoxious. But, of course, there is a difference. Government regulation of education commonly accompanies government financing and other measures (such as compulsory school attendance) which increase the demand for the services of intellectuals and, therefore, their incomes.[15] So self-interest, which, in

---

15. See E. G. West, "The Political Economy of American Public School Legislation," *Journal of Law and Economics* (October 1967):101.

general, would lead to support for a free market in ideas, suggests a different attitude in education.

Nor do I doubt that detailed study would reveal other cases in which groups of practitioners in the market for ideas have supported government regulation and the restriction of competition when it would increase their incomes, just as we find similar behaviour in the market for goods. But interest in monopolising is likely to be less in the market for ideas. A general policy of regulation, by restricting the market, would have the effect of reducing the demand for the services of intellectuals. But more important, perhaps, is that the public is commonly more interested in the struggle between truth and falsehood than it is in the truth itself. Demand for the services of the writer and speechmaker depends, to a considerable extent, on the existence of controversy, and for controversy to exist, it is necessary that truth should not stand triumphant and alone.

Whatever one may think of the motives which have led to the general acceptance of the present position, there remains the question of which policies would be, in fact, the most appropriate. This requires us to come to some conclusion about how the government will perform whatever functions are assigned to it. I do not believe that we will be able to form a judgment in which we can have any confidence unless we abandon the present ambivalence about the performance of government in the two markets and adopt a more consistent view. We have to decide whether the government is as incompetent as is generally assumed in the market for ideas, in which case we would want to decrease government intervention in the market for goods, or whether it is as efficient as it is generally assumed to be in the market for goods, in which case we would want to increase government regulation in the market for ideas. Of course, one could adopt an intermediate position—a government neither as incompetent and base as assumed in the one market nor as efficient and virtuous as assumed in the other. In this case, we ought to reduce the amount of government regulation in the market for goods and might want to increase government intervention in the market for ideas. I look forward to learning which of these alternative views will be espoused by my colleagues in the economics profession.

SIX

The Wealth of Nations

We meet today, on the ninth of March [1976], to commemorate the two hundredth anniversary of the publication of Adam Smith's *An Inquiry into the Nature and Causes of the Wealth of Nations*. We do this, I believe, not simply because of its historical importance as a landmark in the development of economics, but because it is a book that still lives and from which we continue to learn. Commentaries such as mine are only of value as a preliminary to reading the *Wealth of Nations* itself or, if this has already been done, to rereading it.

The *Wealth of Nations* is a masterpiece. With its interrelated themes, its careful observations on economic life, and its powerful ideas—clearly expressed and beautifully illustrated—it cannot fail to work its magic. But the very richness of the book means that each of us will see it in a somewhat different way. It is not like a multiplication table or a modern textbook with a few simple messages which, once absorbed, makes a rereading unnecessary. The *Wealth of Nations* has many ideas from which to choose and many problems to ponder. Though the time may come when we will have nothing more to learn from the *Wealth of Nations* or, more accurately, when what we would learn would be irrelevant to our problems, that time has not yet been reached nor will it, in my view, be reached for a long time to come.

Adam Smith was born in 1723. He went to the University of Glasgow when he was fourteen years old, according to W. R. Scott somewhat older than was usual at the time. In 1740, when he was seventeen years old, he graduated with a master of arts degree. He was

Delivered originally as a public lecture at the University of California at Los Angeles under the auspices of the Department of Economics, UCLA, and the Foundation for Research in Economics and Education. Published by the Foundation for private circulation and later reprinted in *Economic Inquiry* (July 1977). Reprinted here with permission.

then elected to what we would call a postgraduate fellowship at Oxford. There, neglected by his teachers who, as he observes in the *Wealth of Nations,* received their pay whether they taught or not, he studied on his own for six years. He then returned to Scotland and, in the period between 1748 and 1751, gave public lectures in Edinburgh on literature, rhetoric, and jurisprudence. It seems clear that the lectures on jurisprudence included an early version of some of the leading ideas which were to appear in the *Wealth of Nations.* In 1751 he was appointed professor at the University of Glasgow, at first of logic, but shortly afterwards of moral philosophy.

In 1759 Smith published, in *The Theory of Moral Sentiments,* the substance of a major part of his lectures. But he also gave lectures on jurisprudence, in them he presented his views on economics under the heading "Police." As Edwin Cannan points out, this may appear strange to us but only because Adam Smith believed that the economic system should be controlled through the operations of the market, a view which, largely because of his work, many of us share. Had Smith been, in Cannan's words, "an old-fashioned believer in state control of trade and industry," as were many of his contemporaries and most of his predecessors, this would, of course, have seemed the most natural heading in the world under which to discuss the determination of prices.[1] The surprise felt by those listening to his lectures at Glasgow would not have been at the heading, but at his conclusion.

Adam Smith resigned his professorship in 1764 to become tutor to the young Duke of Buccleuch and passed the next two and a half years with him, mainly in France. This position brought with it a pension of £300 a year for life and, after his return to Britain in 1766, Smith spent most of his time in Kirkcaldy, his birthplace, where he devoted himself to study and the writing of the *Wealth of Nations.*

From this account of Adam Smith's life it is possible to discern the special circumstances which, his genius apart, made the *Wealth of Nations* so extraordinarily influential. First, many of his main ideas were conceived very early in his life, very probably in his days at Oxford. He thought about these ideas, enriching his analysis by reading and observation, for about thirty years. He spent long periods, first in Oxford and later in Kirkcaldy, working out his position by himself, with

1. Adam Smith, *An Inquiry into the Nature and Causes of the Wealth of Nations,* editor's introduction (Modern Library, 1937), xxix–xxx.

little or no contact with others interested in economic questions. Smith called himself a "solitary philosopher," and though he also seems to have been a "clubable" man, there can be no doubt that he enjoyed his own company and could work well on his own without requiring any stimulus from others. In a letter to his friend David Hume, written from Kirkcaldy, he says: "My business here is study. . . . My amusements are long solitary walks by the seaside. You may judge how I spend my time. I feel myself, however, extremely happy, comfortable, and contented. I never was perhaps more so in all my life."[2]

Adam Smith's independence of mind and his liking for solitude which gave that independence free reign must have helped greatly in writing a book which was to launch a new subject. It is perhaps no accident that Adam Smith and Isaac Newton were both posthumous children. Historians of economic thought tell us, I am sure correctly, of the works of others, such as Francis Hutcheson and Bernard Mandeville, that influenced Smith. But he absorbed their ideas and made them serve purposes of his own.

The popular success of the *Wealth of Nations*, however, depended on another factor: its readability. Adam Smith, as is clear from the subjects dealt with in the Edinburgh lectures and later at Glasgow, was interested in the art of writing (James Boswell was one of his pupils). Joseph Schumpeter acknowledges Smith's skill in rather grudging terms: "He disliked whatever went beyond plain common sense. He never moved above the heads of even the dullest readers. He led them on gently, encouraging them by trivialities and homely observations, making them feel comfortable all along."[3] What Schumpeter means is that the *Wealth of Nations* can be read with pleasure. It is clear, amusing, and persuasive. Adam Smith's style is, of course, very different from that of most modern economists, who are either incapable of writing simple English or have decided that they have more to gain by concealment.

That Adam Smith worked alone and wrote the *Wealth of Nations* over half a lifetime was in part responsible for the qualities which made it so influential. But it also brought with it some disadvantages. It has often been remarked that the *Wealth of Nations* is not particularly well constructed, with sections awkwardly placed. Indeed, Smith

2. E. G. West, *Adam Smith, the Man and His Works* (1969), 153.
3. Joseph A. Schumpeter, *History of Economic Analysis* (1954), 185.

himself labels some very long sections "Digressions." The explanation normally given is that because he wrote the *Wealth of Nations* over a very long period, completing sections one at a time, he found it too onerous a task to make the substantial revisions in earlier sections which a finer construction would have called for. I accept this explanation. It seems clear that Smith found writing extremely painful. This seems to have been true even for the physical act of writing, and he usually composed by dictating to an amanuensis.

The *Wealth of Nations* also contains some obscurities and inconsistencies which might have been removed had Adam Smith not been so solitary but had consulted more with others, although it has to be confessed that not many of his contemporaries were capable of a close analysis of his work. There is, however, another reason why Adam Smith did not give that added attention which might have removed some of the inconsistencies: He did not know that he was Adam Smith. Had he known that we would be discussing his work two hundred years after it was published, he would undoubtedly have been even more careful about his writing. But I think we may be glad that he could not have foreseen this great interest in his work, for the most probable result would have been an unwillingness to publish the *Wealth of Nations* at all. When Adam Smith was dying he asked that his surviving manuscripts be burnt which, to the despair of all lovers of his work, was in fact done. A man so anxious that work not properly finished be withheld from the public would have been greatly concerned about the kind of scrutiny which the *Wealth of Nations* has come to receive. Another remark he made as he awaited death was to regret that he had done so little: "I meant to have done more."[4] All of which suggests that he never knew what he had achieved—that his concentrated study had produced the most important book on economics ever written, a work of genius.

What Adam Smith did was to give economics its shape. The subjects he dealt with, the approach he used, even the order in which the various topics were treated can be found repeated in economics courses as they are given today. From one point of view, the last two hundred years of economics have been little more than a vast "mopping up operation" in which economists have filled in the gaps, corrected the errors, and refined the analysis of the *Wealth of Nations*.

4. John Rae, *Life of Adam Smith* (1895), 434.

Adam Smith succeeded in creating a system of analysis—our system of analysis—by a series of masterstrokes. Some are very familiar to us. Others, it seems to me, are not, even yet, fully appreciated. Smith's starting point is well known. He abandoned the idea held by many mercantilists that wealth consists of gold or money. To Smith, the wealth of a nation was what people get for their money, that is, what is produced, either directly, or indirectly by exchange with other nations. This is the viewpoint he expresses in the opening words of the *Wealth of Nations:*

> The annual labour of every nation is the fund which originally supplies it with all the necessaries and conveniences of life which it annually consumes, and which consist always either in the immediate produce of that labour, or in what is purchased with that produce from other nations. According therefore, as this produce, or what is purchased with it, bears a greater or smaller proportion to the number of those who are to consume it, the nation will be better or worse supplied with all the necessaries and conveniences for which it has occasion.[5]

We can see immediately that what Adam Smith is concerned with is the flow of real goods and services over a period of time and its relation to the numbers of those who are to consume these goods and services. The emphasis is on real income, not money income: "The labourer is rich or poor, is well or ill rewarded, in proportion to the real, not to the nominal price of his labour" (p. 51).

This is Adam Smith's starting point. The welfare of a nation depends on its production. But the amount that is produced depends on the division of labour: "The greatest improvement in the productive powers of labour, and the greater part of the skill, dexterity, and judgment with which it is anywhere directed or applied, seem to have been the effect of the division of labour" (p. 13). To produce even the most

---

5. Adam Smith, *An Inquiry Into the Nature and Causes of the Wealth of Nations,* vol. 1 of *The Glasgow edition of the Works and Correspondence of Adam Smith,* R. H. Campbell and A. S. Skinner, eds. (1976), 10. Note that hereinafter, all text quotations are from the *Wealth of Nations* unless otherwise indicated; page numbers referenced in the text refer to the Glasgow edition.

ordinary commodities requires the cooperation of a vast number of people:

> Observe the accommodation of the most common artificer or day-labourer in a civilized and thriving country, and you will perceive that the number of people of whose industry a part, though but a small part, has been employed in procuring him this accommodation, exceeds all computation. The woollen coat, for example, which covers the day-labourer, as coarse and rough as it may appear, is the produce of the joint labour of a great multitude of workmen. The shepherd, the sorter of the wool, the wool-comber or carder, the dyer, the scribbler, the spinner, the weaver, the fuller, the dresser, and many others, must all join their different arts. (p. 22)

And so Adam Smith continues, adding more and more detail, until at the end he is able to conclude: "If we examine, I say, all these things, and consider what a variety of labour is employed about each of them, we shall be sensible that without the assistance and co-operation of many thousands, the very meanest person in a civilized country could not be provided, even according to, what we very falsely imagine, the easy and simple manner in which he is commonly accommodated" (p. 23).

Schumpeter remarks that "nobody either before or after A[dam] Smith, ever thought of putting such a burden upon division of labour."[6] But Adam Smith was right to insist on the importance of the division of labour, and we do wrong to slight it, for it turns economics into a study of man in society and poses an extremely difficult question: How is the cooperation of these vast numbers of people in countries all over the world, which is necessary for even a modest standard of living, to be brought about? Adam Smith's answer is that it is done by means of trade or exchange, the use of the market fueled by self-interest:

> Man has almost constant occasion for the help of his brethren, and it is in vain for him to expect it from their benevolence only. He will be more likely to prevail if he can interest their self-love in his favour, and shew them that it is for their

6. Schumpeter, *History of Economic Analysis*, 187.

own advantage to do for him what he requires of them. Whoever offers to another a bargain of any kind, proposes to do this. Give me that which I want, and you shall have this which you want, is the meaning of every such offer; and it is in this manner that we obtain from one another the far greater part of those good offices which we stand in need of. It is not from the benevolence of the butcher, the brewer, or the baker, that we expect our dinner, but from their regard to their own interest. We address ourselves, not to their humanity but to their self-love, and never talk to them of our own necessities but of their advantages. (p. 26–27)

This is a familiar quotation which you and I have read on innumerable occasions in one textbook or another. It seems to assert that man is wholly dominated by self-interest and not at all by feelings of benevolence. Furthermore, it seems to imply that benevolence, or love, could not form the basis on which an economic organisation could function. Neither of these inferences would be correct. Man's behaviour, as the author of *The Theory of Moral Sentiments* knew, is influenced by feelings of benevolence; the division of labour within a family, even an extended family, may be sustained by love and affection. Adam Smith is, I believe, making a more subtle and more important point than we normally assume. Benevolence or love is personal; it is strongest within a family, but it may also exist between associates and friends. However, the more remote the connection the less strongly, in general, we are influenced by feelings of love or benevolence. This is indeed Adam Smith says in *The Theory of Moral Sentiments*.

It is very strange but I do not recall anyone who, when citing this famous passage—and it has been repeated on innumerable occasions—also includes what Adam Smith says just two sentences before. "In civilized society [man] stands at all times in need of the co-operation and assistance of great multitudes, while his whole life is scarce sufficient to gain the friendship of a few persons" (p. 26). This, as I see it, completely alters one's perception of Smith's argument. To rely on benevolence to bring about an adequate division of labour is an impossibility. We need the co-operation of multitudes, many of whom we do not even know and for whom we can therefore feel no benevolence nor can they feel such for us. Indeed, if we did know them, their lives and circumstances would often be so different from our own that it would be hard for us to sympathise with them at all. Reliance on self-interest is not simply one way in which the required division of labour is achieved; for the division of labour needed for a civilised life, it is the only way.

We just do not have the time to learn who the people are who gain from our labours or to learn of their circumstances, and so we cannot feel benevolence towards them even if benevolence would be justified were we to be fully informed. The fact that when discussing Adam Smith's treatment of the division of labour economists have usually quoted his famous pinmaking example (where everyone is situated within a single factory) rather than the long passage from which I quoted earlier (where the participants in the division of labour are scattered all over the world) has also helped to divert attention from the extremely limited role benevolence could play in bringing about the division of labour in a modern economy.

I have remarked that the sentence about one's whole life being "scarce sufficient to gain the friendship of a few persons" is never quoted. Neither, curiously, are the sentences that follow the famous quotation:

> Nobody but a beggar chuses to depend chiefly upon the benevolence of his fellow-citizens. Even a beggar does not depend upon it entirely. . . . The greater part of his occasional wants are supplied in the same manner as those of other people, by treaty, by barter, and by purchase. With the money which one man gives him he purchases food. The old cloaths which another bestows upon him he exchanges for other old cloaths which suit him better, or for lodging, or for food, or for money, with which he can buy either food, cloaths, or lodging, as he has occasion. (p. 27)

Adam Smith's main point, as I see it, is not that benevolence or love *is not* the basis of economic life in a modern society, but that it *cannot be*. We have to rely on the market, with its motive force, self-interest. If man were so constituted that he only responded to feelings of benevolence, we would still be living in caves with lives "nasty, bruteish and short."

The efficient working of the market thus becomes the key to the maintenance of a comfortable standard of living and to its increase. What Adam Smith does first is to show that an efficient market system is one in which, because of the inconveniences of barter, we use money, in terms of which all prices are expressed. He then shows that the pricing system is a self-adjusting mechanism which leads to resources being used in a way that maximises the value of their contribution to production: "Every individual is continually exerting himself to find out the most advantageous employment for whatever capital he can command. It is his own advantage, indeed, and not that of the society, which he has in view. But the study of his own advantage naturally, or rather necessarily, leads him to prefer that employment which is most advantageous to the society" (p. 454). He is "led by an invisible hand to promote an end which was no part of his intention. Nor is it always the worse for the society that it was no part of it. By pursuing his own interest he frequently promotes that of the society more effectually than when he really intends to promote it." (p. 456).

Adam Smith's analytical system may seem primitive to us but in fact he reaches results we accept as correct today. He uses the concept of the natural price, what we would call the long-run supply price. The effectual demand is the amount demanded at that price. This is how Adam Smith describes the position of equilibrium:

> When the quantity brought to market is just sufficient to supply the effectual demand and no more, the market price naturally comes to be either exactly, or as nearly as can be judged of, the same with the natural price. The whole quantity upon hand can be disposed of for this price, and cannot be disposed of for more. The competition of the different dealers obliges them all to accept of this price, but does not oblige them to accept less. (p. 74)

He also goes through the operation, familiar to those taking introductory courses in economics, of supposing that the amount supplied is less than the amount demanded at the equilibrium price:

> When the quantity of any commodity which is brought to market falls short of the effectual demand, all those who are willing to pay the whole value of the rent, wages, and profit, which must be paid in order to bring it thither, cannot be supplied with the quantity which they want. Rather than want it altogether, some of them will be willing to give more. A competition will immediately begin among them, and the

market price will rise more or less above the natural price. (pp. 73–74)

And, of course, he examines what happens when the amount supplied is more than the amount demanded at the equilibrium price:

> When the quantity brought to market exceeds the effectual demand, it cannot be all sold to those who are willing to pay the whole value of the rent, wages, and profit, which must be paid in order to bring it thither. Some part must be sold to those who are willing to pay less, and the low price which they give for it must reduce the price of the whole. The market price will sink more or less below the natural price, according as the greatness of the excess increases more or less the competition of the sellers, or according as it happens to be more or less important to them to get immediately rid of the commodity. The same excess in the importation of perishable, will occasion a much greater competition than in that of durable commodities; in the importation of oranges, for example, than in that of old iron. (p. 74)

As an example of the way in which Adam Smith examined an actual situation, consider his discussion of the effect of a public mourning which increases the demand for black cloth:

> A public mourning raises the price of black cloth (with which the market is almost always understocked upon such occasions), and augments the profits of the merchants who possess any considerable quantity of it. It has no effect upon the wages of the weavers. The market is under-stocked with commodities, not with labour; with work done, not with work to be done. It raises the wages of journeymen taylors. The market is here under-stocked with labour. There is an effectual demand for more labour, for more work to be done than can be had. It sinks the price of coloured silks and cloths, and thereby reduces the profits of the merchants who have any considerable quantity of them upon hand. It sinks too the wages of the workmen employed in preparing such commodities, for which all demand is stopped for six months, perhaps for a twelvemonth. The market is here over-stocked both with commodities and with labour. (pp. 76–77)

There is a surefootedness about this analysis which demonstrates Adam Smith's ability to get at the heart of the matter. His tools may be primitive, but his skill in handling them is superb. He may not work with schedules, but implicit in his analysis is the view that if one did construct a demand schedule, more would be demanded at a lower price. Consider, again, Smith's discussion of the effects of price regulation:

> When the government, in order to remedy the inconvenience of a dearth, orders all the dealers to sell their corn at what it supposes a reasonable price, it either hinders them from bringing it to market, which may sometimes produce a famine even in the beginning of the season; or if they bring it thither, it enables the people, and thereby encourages them to consume it so fast, as must necessarily produce a famine before the end of the season. The unlimited, unrestrained freedom of the corn trade, as it is the only effectual preventative of the miseries of a famine, so it is the best palliative of the inconveniences of a dearth; for the inconveniences of a real scarcity cannot be remedied; they can only be palliated. (p. 527)

Could we do much better today if we were discussing government control of the price of oil and natural gas?

Adam Smith's handling of economic analysis has not, however, occasioned universal praise. The clumsiness of his treatment and its lack of finish have been strongly criticized by some economists, so strongly, indeed, as to suggest that if only these writers had been around in 1776 Adam Smith would not have been necessary. Many economists have criticized the way in which Smith discusses the distinction between "value in use" and "value in exchange":

> The things which have the greatest value in use have frequently little or no value in exchange; and on the contrary, those which have the greatest value in exchange have frequently little or no value in use. Nothing is more useful than water: but it will purchase scarce any thing. . . . A diamond, on the contrary, has scarce any value in use; but a very great quantity of other goods may frequently be had in exchange for it. (pp. 44–45)

This passage is, it is true, neither original nor particularly helpful. But Adam Smith's economics in no way suffers because he did not also give us the theory of diminishing marginal utility. Utility theory has always been an ornament rather than a working part of economic analysis.

Another passage which has offended economists is Adam Smith's statement about monopoly price:

> The price of monopoly is upon every occasion the highest which can be got. The natural price, or the price of free competition, on the contrary, is the lowest which can be taken, not upon every occasion indeed, but for any considerable time together. The one is upon every occasion the highest which can be squeezed out of the buyers, or which, it is supposed, they will consent to give: The other is the lowest which the sellers can commonly afford to take, and at the same time continue their business. (pp. 78–79)

What is found objectionable is that Smith, by speaking of the highest possible price rather than the price which maximises profits, seems not to take into consideration that at a higher price less would be demanded, or alternatively assumes that the decrease in the amount demanded takes place in a discontinuous fashion. But it is apparent from the quotations I gave earlier and is quite explicit elsewhere in the *Wealth of Nations* that Smith knew that the demand schedule was downward sloping. What does seem clear is that he was not able to formulate the determination of monopoly price in the rigorous manner of Cournot. However, Smith's view of competition was quite robust. He thought of competition, as the quotations given earlier illustrate, as rivalry, as a process, rather than as a condition defined by a high elasticity of demand, as would be true for most modern economists. I need not conceal from you my belief that ultimately the Smithian view of competition will prevail.

Adam Smith also discusses the relation between the number of competitors and the price that will emerge. He says that if the trade "is divided between two different grocers, their competition will tend to make both of them sell cheaper than if it were in the hands of one only; and if it were divided among twenty, their competition would be just so much the greater, and the chance of their combining together, in order to raise the price, just so much the less" (pp. 361–62). What

Smith believed was that a greater number of competitors leads to lower prices, both directly through the competitive process and also indirectly by making collusion less likely. It is not a very thorough treatment but I am not sure that modern economists can do much better. We should not object because Smith left us some problems to solve, although it may be a legitimate complaint that in the two hundred years since the *Wealth of Nations* was published we have made such little progress in solving them.

Adam Smith showed how the operations of the market would regulate an economy so as to maximise the value of production. To accomplish this required little assistance from government:

> Every man, as long as he does not violate the laws of justice [should be] left perfectly free to pursue his own interest his own way, and to bring both his industry and capital into competition with those of any other man. . . . The sovereign is completely discharged from a duty, in the attempting to perform which he must always be exposed to innumerable delusions, and for the proper performance of which no human wisdom or knowledge could ever be sufficient; the duty of superintending the industry of private people, and of directing it towards the employments most suitable to the interest of society. (p. 687)

Note that Smith, as his reference to the "laws of justice" shows, saw the necessity for the government establishing what we would call a system of property rights. But he did not favor government action that went much beyond this.

Adam Smith's opposition to more extensive government action did not arise simply because he thought it was unnecessary, but because he felt that government action would usually make matters worse. He thought governments lacked both the knowledge and the motivation to do a satisfactory job in regulating an economic system. He says: "Great nations are never impoverished by private, though they sometimes are by public prodigality and misconduct" (p. 342). Again:

> It is the highest impertinence and presumption . . . in kings and ministers, to pretend to watch over the economy of private people, and to restrain their expence. . . . They are

themselves always, and without any exception, the greatest spendthrifts in the society. Let them look well after their own expence, and they may safely trust private people with theirs. If their own extravagance does not ruin the state, that of their subjects never will. (p. 346)

Adam Smith explains that government regulations will normally be much influenced by those who stand to benefit from them, with the result that they are not necessarily advantageous to society:

The interest of the dealers . . . in any particular branch of trade or manufactures, is always in some respects different from, and even opposite to, that of the public. To widen the market and to narrow the competition, is always the interest of the dealers. To widen the market may frequently be agreeable enough to the interest of the public; but to narrow the competition must always be against it, and can serve only to enable the dealers, by raising their profits above what they naturally would be, to levy, for their own benefit, an absurd tax upon the rest of their fellow-citizens. The proposal of any new law or regulation of commerce which comes from this order, ought always to be listened to with great precaution, and ought never to be adopted till after having been long and carefully examined, not only with the most scrupulous, but with the most suspicious attention. It comes from an order of men, whose interest is never exactly the same with that of the public, who have generally an interest to deceive and even to oppress the public, and who accordingly have, upon many occasions, both deceived and oppressed it. (p. 267)

According to Adam Smith, the government has only three duties. The first is to protect society from "the violence and invasion of other independent societies" (p. 689). As he says, "defence . . . is much more important than opulence" (pp. 464–65). The second duty is to establish a system of justice, by which he means a legal system which defines everyone's rights. Economists are prone to think of Smith as simply advocating the use of a pricing system, but throughout the *Wealth of Nations* one finds him discussing the appropriate institutional framework for the working of a pricing system. Whether one agrees or disagrees with his views on apprenticeship laws, land tenure, joint-stock companies, the administration of justice, or the educational system, what distinguishes Adam Smith's approach from much of what has come since is that he obviously thinks this is a proper and important part of the work of an economist. It is, I believe, only recently that economists in any number have come to realise that the choice of an institutional framework is a subject which deserves to be studied systematically.

The final duty Adam Smith gives to the government is the establishment of certain public works and public institutions. What he mainly has in mind are roads, bridges, canals, and suchlike. It seems to me that the list of public works that Smith thought should be undertaken by government, although quite limited, was as extensive as it was because he did not foresee the potentialities of the modern corporation and a modern capital market, a position understandable in light of the history up to his day of joint-stock companies, of which he had a very unfavorable opinion. But there is nothing ordinary even about his treatment of a subject such as this. In his discussion of how these public works should be financed and administered, Smith argued that they should be financed by payments from consumers rather than by grants from the public revenue:

> It does not seem necessary that the expence of those public works should be defrayed from the public revenue. . . . The greater part of such public works may easily be so managed, as to afford a particular revenue sufficient for defraying their own expence, without bringing any burden upon the general revenue of the society.
>
> A highway, a bridge, a navigable canal, for example, may in most cases be both made and maintained by a small toll upon the carriages which make use of them: a harbour, by a moderate port-duty upon the tunnage of the shipping which load and unload in it. . . . When high roads, bridges, canals, &c. are in this manner made and supported by the commerce which is carried on by means of them, they can be made only where that commerce requires them and consequently where it is proper to make them. . . . A magnificent high road cannot be made through a desart country where there is little or no commerce, or merely because it happens to lead to the country villa of the intendant of the province, or to that of some great lord to whom the intendant finds it convenient to make his court. A great bridge cannot be thrown over a river at a place where nobody passes, or merely to embellish the

view from the windows of a neighbouring palace: things which sometimes happen, in countries where works of this kind are carried on by any other revenue than that which they themselves are capable of affording. (pp. 724–25)

It is clear that Adam Smith, had he been presented with a proposal for marginal cost pricing, would have understood the advantages but would not have neglected the effect such a policy would have on what would be supplied.

In making this survey of the *Wealth of Nations* I have concentrated on what I see as Adam Smith's main contributions to economics: the division of labour, the working of the market, and the role of government in the economic system. I am acutely aware that this does not do justice to Smith's great work. It would require, however, many lectures and many lecturers to do that. In the *Wealth of Nations* a number of subjects are dealt with that are doubtless as important as some of those I have mentioned. It is enough to note his discussion of economic development, of public finance, of education, of religious establishments, and, above all, his discussion of colonies—and particularly the American colonies. On all these subjects, and still others, Adam Smith has much to say that is profound, and his ideas appear striking and even, paradoxically, novel to someone reading him today.

I will illustrate this by considering the one subject which, on such an occasion as this, I can hardly avoid: Adam Smith's view of the American Revolution. In the *Wealth of Nations* America becomes, in effect, the minor theme accompanying the major theme, the working of a pricing system. As Fay says: "America was never far from Adam Smith's thought. Indeed, in the end it was almost an obsession."[7] On America, Smith's views were liberal. He saw the future greatness of America: it was likely to become "one of the greatest and most formidable [empires] that ever was in the world" (p. 623). He had little faith in the conduct of British policy. In a letter written from Kirkcaldy in June 1776, a month before the Declaration of Independence was adopted, he wrote that "the American campaign has begun awkwardly. I hope, I cannot say that I expect, it will end better. England tho' in the present times it breeds men of great professional abilities in all different ways, great Lawyers, great watchmakers, and great

7. C. R. Fay, *Adam Smith and the Scotland of His Day*, (1956), 98.

clockmakers etc. etc., seems to breed neither Statesmen nor Generals."[8]

Adam Smith did not underestimate the fighting quality of the American military forces. In discussing defence expenditures, he argued that although normally a militia would be inferior to a standing army, yet after a few years in the field it would become its equal. He added: "Should the war in America drag out through another campaign, the American militia may become in every respect a match for that [British] standing army, of which the valour appeared . . . not inferior to the hardiest veterans of France and Spain" (p. 701). It was no doubt in part with this in mind that Smith said elsewhere in the *Wealth of Nations:* "They are very weak who flatter themselves that . . . our colonies will be easily conquered by force alone" (p. 623). In a memorandum written in 1778, Smith gave as the probable outcome of the American conflict, out of four possibilities, that one which actually materialised.[9] And towards the end of the war, he wrote a letter of introduction to Lord Shelburne, who was to become Prime Minister, on behalf of Richard Oswald, who became the chief British peace negotiator with the Americans. Oswald signed the preliminary articles of peace in 1782 on Britain's behalf. He then lost his job, being attacked as one who supported "the Cause of America" rather than that of Britain, a view which may not have been too far from the truth. For example, Oswald not only forwarded Benjamin Franklin's proposal that Britain cede Canada to the United States, but seems to have favoured it.[10]

However, while all this is no doubt indicative of Adam Smith's attitude, he was by no means a cheering supporter of the American cause. In the *Wealth of Nations* he describes the motives of the leaders of the American Revolution in the following terms:

> Men desire to have some share in the management of public affairs chiefly on account of the importance which it gives them. . . . The leading men of America, like those of all other countries, desire to preserve their own importance.

8. Quoted in W. R. Scott, *Adam Smith, An Oration,* (1938), 23.

9. Reproduced in Fay, *Adam Smith and Scotland,* 110–14.

10. See Richard Oswald, *Memorandum on the Folly of Invading Virginia,* ed., with an essay on Richard Oswald, by W. Stilt Robinson, Jr. (1953), 38–43.

They feel, or imagine, that if their assemblies, which they are fond of calling parliaments, and of considering as equal in authority to the parliament of Great Britain, should be so far degraded as to become the humble ministers and executive officers of that parliament, the greater part of their importance would be at an end. They have rejected, therefore, the proposal of being taxed by parliamentary requisition, and like other ambitious and high-spirited men, have rather chosen to draw the sword in defence of their own importance. (p. 622)

To Adam Smith, what the American leaders wanted was not liberty nor democracy but position. He therefore devised a plan which would give it to them. He proposed to give the colonies representation in the British parliament in proportion to their contributions to the public revenues. If this were done,

a new method of acquiring importance, a new and more dazzling object of ambition would be presented to the leading men of each colony. Instead of piddling for the little prizes which are to be found in what may be called the paltry raffle of colony faction; they might then hope, from the presumption which men naturally have in their own ability and good fortune, to draw some of the great prizes which sometimes come from the wheel of the great state lottery of British politics. (pp. 622–23)

That is to say, an ambitious American could hope to become Prime Minister and, in effect, the ruler of the British Empire. Adam Smith also argued that Americans could ultimately expect that the capital of the British Empire would cross the ocean.

Such has hitherto been the rapid progress of that of [America] in wealth, population and improvement, that in the course of little more than a century, perhaps, the produce of America might exceed that of British taxation. The seat of the empire would then naturally remove itself to that part of the empire which contributed most to the general defence and support of the whole. (pp. 625–26)

George Stigler quotes Adam Smith's account of the motives of the American leaders with approval as a discussion of "political behavior in perfectly cold-blooded rational terms," and considers Smith's plan to be shrewd. He contrasts this discussion with other passages in the *Wealth of Nations* in which men are apparently "hot-blooded" or even "irrational" in their political behaviour, passages which are inconsistent with the view that political behaviour is "cold-blooded" and "rational" and are therefore wrong.[11] But the behaviour of Americans in the Revolution demonstrates to me that men can be both cold-blooded and hot-blooded. I do not myself find it difficult to understand why George Washington and Thomas Jefferson supported the American Revolution—Adam Smith adequately explains a large part of their motives. But why did they secure the support of the masses who suffered and died? Self-interest successfully pursued seems an inadequate explanation of their actions. Revolution is a risky business for all who take part in it, with the prizes going to the successful revolutionary leaders if the revolutionaries win.

Adam Smith does give an explanation of why the American leaders had followers, but this is to be found not in the *Wealth of Nations* but in *The Theory of Moral Sentiments,* in his discussion of the distinction of ranks. "The great mob of mankind are the admirers and worshippers, and, what may seem more extraordinary, most frequently the disinterested admirers and worshippers, of wealth and greatness."[12] This deference to the powerful, on which the distinction of ranks is based, is, Adam Smith explains, a human propensity necessary for the maintenance of order. But we can see that it is also, on occasion, capable of producing disorder.

Was it better for the ordinary American to have secured independence from British rule? It certainly got rid of those absurd restrictions on trade imposed for the benefit of British merchants and manufacturers which Adam Smith denounced. But the American government, through its tariff policy, was to reintroduce similar absurdities for the benefit of American merchants and manufacturers. And were taxes lower with independence than they would have been without it? As the

11. George J. Stigler, "Smith's Travels on the Ship of State," *History of Political Economy* 3 (Fall 1971):265, 270–72, 273.

12. Adam Smith, *The Theory of Moral Sentiments* (Glasgow edition, 1976), 62.

main expenditure in America by Britain was for defence, to Adam Smith the taxation question became simply, Who was the low-cost supplier of defence and, if it was the British government, would the colonies pay for it? If they would not, there was no reason for Britain to retain its control. "If any of the provinces of the British empire cannot be made to contribute towards the support of the whole empire, it is surely time that Britain should free herself from the expence of defending those provinces in time of war, and of supporting any part of their civil or military establishments in time of peace, and endeavour to accommodate her future views and designs to the real mediocrity of her circumstances" (p. 947). These are the last words of the *Wealth of Nations*.

There is indeed some reason to suppose that Adam Smith may have had a hand in Charles Townshend's taxation schemes which helped to precipitate the American Revolution.[13] Adam Smith regarded the taxes as a method of paying for the services which the mother country provided the colonies. The colonists, or rather their leaders, turned an economic problem into a political one. But had Smith's whole plan been agreed to, there would have been no American Revolution. A child's essay on 1776 which I heard read on the radio in Chicago contained the following sentence: "If it had not been for 1776, England would now rule America." But had Adam Smith's plan been followed, there would have been no 1776, America would now be ruling England, and we would today be celebrating Adam Smith not simply as the author of the *Wealth of Nations* but hailing him as a founding father.

The *Wealth of Nations* is a work that one contemplates with awe. In keenness of analysis and in its range it surpasses any other book on economics. Its preeminence is, however, disturbing. What have we been doing in the last two hundred years? Our analysis has certainly become more sophisticated, but we display no greater insight into the working of the economic system and, in some ways, our approach is inferior to that of Adam Smith. And when we come to views on public policy, we find propositions ignored which Adam Smith demonstrates with such force as almost to make them "self-evident." I really do not know why this is so, but perhaps part of the answer is that we do not read the *Wealth of Nations*.

13. Fay, *Adam Smith and Scotland*, 115–16.

SEVEN

Adam Smith's View
of Man

Adam Smith was a great economist, perhaps the greatest there has ever been. Today I am going to discuss his views on the nature of man. My reason for doing this is not that I think that Smith possessed an understanding of man's nature superior to that of his contemporaries. I would judge that his attitudes were quite widely shared in the eighteenth-century, at any rate, in Scotland, but no doubt elsewhere in eighteenth century Europe. Adam Smith was not the father of psychology. But I believe his views on human nature are important to us because to know them is to deepen our understanding of his economics. It is sometimes said that Smith assumes that human beings are motivated solely by self-interest. Self-interest is certainly, in Smith's view, a powerful motive in human behaviour, but it is by no means the only motive. I think it is important to recognise this since the inclusion of other motives in his analysis does not weaken but rather strengthens his argument for the use of the market and the limitation of governmental action in economic affairs.

Adam Smith does not set down in one place his views on the nature of man. They have to be inferred from remarks in *The Theory of Moral Sentiments* and the *Wealth of Nations*. Smith deals more extensively with human psychology in *The Theory of Moral Sentiments,* the ostensible purpose of which was to uncover the bases for what may be termed our feelings and acts of benevolence. "How selfish soever man may be supposed, there are evidently some principles in his nature,

Delivered as a public lecture at the University of Chicago Law School as part of the lecture series "1776: The Revolution in Social Thought." The lectures discussed this extraordinary year which saw the publication of a number of works that changed our way of thinking, as well as events that were to introduce the modern world. These lectures were printed in the *Journal of Law and Economics* (October 1976). This paper is © 1976 by R. H. Coase.

which interest him in the fortune of others, and render their happiness necessary to him though he derives nothing from it, except the pleasure of seeing it. . . . The greatest ruffian, the most hardened violator of the laws of society, is not altogether without it."[1]

Adam Smith makes sympathy the basis for our concern for others. We form our idea of how others feel by considering how we would feel in like circumstances. The realisation that something makes our fellows miserable makes us miserable, and when something makes them happy, we are happy. This comes about because, by an act of imagination, we put ourselves in their place and, in effect, in our own minds become those other persons. Our feelings may not have the same intensity as theirs, but they are of the same kind.

The propensity to sympathise is strengthened because mutual sympathy is itself a pleasure: "Nothing pleases us more than to observe in other men a fellow-feeling with all the emotions of our own breast" (p. 13). Because mutual sympathy is itself pleasurable, it "enlivens joy and alleviates grief. It enlivens joy by presenting another source of satisfaction; and it alleviates grief by insinuating into the heart almost the only agreeable sensation which it is at that time capable of receiving" (p. 14). One consequence is noted by Adam Smith: "Love is an agreeable, resentment a disagreeable passion: and accordingly we are not half as anxious that our friends should adopt our friendships, as that they should enter into our resentments. . . . The agreeable passions of love and joy can satisfy and support the heart without any auxiliary pleasure. The bitter and painful emotions of grief and resentment more strongly require the healing consolation of sympathy" (p. 15).

If the existence of sympathy makes us care about others, the practice of putting ourselves in the place of others, of imagining how they feel, also has as a consequence that we imagine how they feel about us. This includes not only those directly affected by our actions but those third parties who observe how we behave towards others. By this means we are led to see ourselves as others see us. This reinforces our tendency, when deciding on a course of action, to take into account the effects it will have on others.

The way in which Adam Smith develops this argument affords a

1. Adam Smith, *The Theory of Moral Sentiments* (Glasgow edition, 1976), 9. Note that hereinafter, all text quotations are from *The Theory of Moral Sentiments* unless otherwise indicated.

very good example of his general approach. He says: "The loss or gain of a very small interest of our own appears to be of vastly more importance, excites a much more passionate joy or sorrow, a much more ardent desire or aversion, than the greatest concern of another with whom we have no particular connection" (p. 135). He then considers a hypothetical example:

> Let us suppose that the great empire of China, with all its myriads of inhabitants, was suddenly swallowed up by an earthquake, and let us consider how a man of humanity in Europe, who had no sort of connection with that part of the world, would be affected upon receiving intelligence of this dreadful calamity. He would, I imagine, first of all express very strongly his sorrow for the misfortune of that unhappy people, he would make many melancholy reflections upon the precariousness of human life, and the vanity of all the labours of man, which could thus be annihilated in a moment. He would, too, perhaps, if he was a man of speculation, enter into many reasonings concerning the effects which this disaster might produce upon the commerce of Europe, and the trade and business of the world in general. And when all this fine philosophy was over, when all these humane sentiments had been once fairly expressed, he would pursue his business or his pleasure, take his repose or his diversion, with the same ease and tranquillity as if no such accident had happened. The most frivolous disaster which could befall himself would occasion a more real disturbance. If he was to lose his little finger to morrow, he would not sleep to-night; but, provided he never saw them, he will snore with the most profound security over the ruin of a hundred millions of his brethren, and the destruction of that immense multitude seems plainly an object less interesting to him than this paltry misfortune of his own. (pp. 136–37)

Note that Adam Smith is maintaining that people do behave in the way so vividly described in the example—and if we recall how few of us lost our appetites on hearing of the tremendous loss of life in recent years in Bangladesh or Chad or Guatemala, and in other places, we need not doubt the accuracy of Adam Smith's account. The quotation clearly can be used, rightly in my view, as an illustration of the strength of self-interest in determining human behaviour. What does at first sight appear strange is that this quotation is to be found in a chapter entitled "Of the Influence and Authority of Conscience," since Smith's description of the response of a man of humanity to this appalling disaster in China seems designed to demonstrate the absence of conscience.

But this is to ignore the subtlety of Adam Smith's mind. Given that people would respond to this disaster in the way he describes, he now asks the question: Suppose that it were possible to prevent the loss of those hundred million lives by sacrificing his little finger, would a man of humanity be unwilling to make the sacrifice? He gives this answer:

> Human nature startles with horror at the thought, and the world, in its greatest depravity and corruption, never produced such a villain as could be capable of entertaining it. But what makes this difference? when our passive feelings are almost always so sordid and so selfish, how comes it that our active principles should often be so generous and so noble? When we are always so much more deeply affected by whatever concerns ourselves than by whatever concerns other men; what is it which prompts the generous upon all occasions, and the mean upon many, to sacrifice their own interests to the greater interests of others? It is not the soft power of humanity, it is not that feeble spark of benevolence which Nature has lighted up in the human heart, that is thus capable of counteracting the strongest impulses of self-love . . . . It is a stronger love, a more powerful affection, which generally takes place upon such occasions; the love of what is honourable and noble, of the grandeur, and dignity, and superiority of our own characters.(p. 137)

A. L. Macfie thinks that the ending of this eloquent passage strikes a false note.[2] But I do not think so. It is the last sentence which states (no doubt a little too ornately for our modern taste) the essence of Adam Smith's position. It is not the love of mankind which makes the "man of humanity" willing to make this sacrifice, but that he sees himself through the eyes of an impartial spectator. As we would say today, if he were to act differently, had chosen to retain his little finger

2. A. L. Macfie, *The Individual in Society: Papers on Adam Smith* (1967), 96.

by letting a hundred million die, he would not have been able to live with himself. We have to appear worthy in our own eyes. It is not love for the Chinese (for whom he might have no feeling at all), but love for the dignity and superiority of his own character which, if he had to face such a choice, would lead the man of humanity to sacrifice his little finger.

Of course, Adam Smith presents us with an extreme case. But it enables him to make his point in a setting which brooks no objection. It is easy to see that if the man of humanity had been faced with the loss not of his little finger but of his arms and legs, and had the number of Chinese who would have been saved by his sacrifice been one hundred rather than one hundred million, he might, indeed probably would, have decided differently. But this does not affect Adam Smith's point. He knew, of course, that the extent to which we follow any course of action depends on its cost. The demand for food, clothing, and shelter similarly depends on their price, but no one doubts their importance when we are discussing the working of the economic system.

The force of conscience in influencing our actions is, of course, weakened by the fact, which Adam Smith notes, that while some men are generous, others are mean and less responsive to the promptings of the impartial spectator. But more important in reducing the influence of the impartial spectator is a factor which Smith discusses at length. We tend, because it is agreeable, to think more highly of ourselves than is really warranted. Says Smith: "We are all naturally disposed to overrate the excellencies of our own characters" (p. 133). Of our tendency to indulge in self-deceit, he says:

> The opinion which we entertain of our own character depends entirely on our judgment concerning our past conduct. It is so disagreeable to think ill of ourselves, that we often purposely turn away our view from those circumstances which might render that judgment unfavourable. He is a bold surgeon, they say, whose hand does not tremble when he performs an operation upon his own person; and he is often equally bold who does not hesitate to pull off the mysterious veil of self-delusion which covers from his view the deformities of his own conduct. . . . This self-deceit, the fatal weakness of mankind, is the source of half the disorders of human life. If we saw ourselves in the light in which others

see us, or in which they would see us if they knew all, a refor-
mation would generally be unavoidable. We could not otherwise endure the sight. (p. 158)

However, says Adam Smith, "Nature . . . has not . . . abandoned us
entirely to the delusions of self-love. Our continual observations upon
the conduct of others insensibly leads us to form to ourselves certain
general rules concerning what is fit and proper either to be done or to
be avoided" (p. 159). These general rules of conduct are of great importance. They represent the only principle "by which the bulk of
mankind are capable of directing their actions" (p. 162).

The picture which emerges from Adam Smith's discussion in *The
Theory of Moral Sentiments* is of man suffused with self-love. "We are
not ready," says Smith, "to suspect any person of being defective in
selfishness" (p. 304). Nonetheless, man does have regard for the effect
of his actions on others. This concern for others comes about because
of the existence of sympathetic responses, strengthened because mutual sympathy is pleasurable and reinforced by a complex, although
very important, influence, which Smith terms the impartial spectator
or conscience, that leads us to act in a way an outside observer would
approve of. The behaviour induced by such factors is embodied in
codes of conduct which because conformity with them brings approval and admiration, affect the behaviour of the "coarse clay of the
bulk of mankind." Presumably Smith would argue that everyone is affected by all these factors, although to different degrees.

It will be observed that Adam Smith's account of the development
of our moral sentiments is essentially self-centered. We care for others
because, by a sympathetic response, we feel as they feel, because we
enjoy the sharing of sympathy, and because we wish to appear admirable in our own eyes; and we conform to the rules of conduct accepted
in society largely because we wish to be admired by others. The impact of these factors is weakened by the fact that the forces generating
feelings of benevolence have to overcome those arising from self-
interest, more narrowly conceived, with our perception of the outcomes distorted by self-deceit.

Adam Smith makes no effort to estimate the relative importance
of the various factors leading to benevolent actions but he does indicate the circumstances in which, considered as a whole, they are likely
to exert their greatest influence. This subject Smith discusses in a

chapter entitled, "Of the Order in which Individuals are recommended by Nature to our care and attention." He says:

> Every man . . . is first and principally recommended to his own care; and every man is certainly, in every respect, fitter and abler to take care of himself than of any other person. Every man feels his own pleasures and his own pains more sensibly than those of other people. . . . After himself, the members of his own family, those who usually live in the same house with him, his parents, his children, his brothers and sisters, are naturally the objects of his warmest affections. They are naturally and usually the persons upon whose happiness or misery his conduct must have the greatest influence. He is more habituated to sympathize with them: he knows better how every thing is likely to affect them, and his sympathy with them is more precise and determinate than it can be with the greater part of other people. It approaches nearer, in short, to what he feels for himself. (p. 219)

Adam Smith goes on to consider the sympathy which exists between more remote relations within the same family:

> The children of brothers and sisters are naturally connected by the friendship which, after separating into different families, continues to take place between their parents. Their good agreement improves the enjoyment of that friendship— their discord would disturb it. As they seldom live in the same family, however, though of more importance to one another than the greater part of other people, they are of much less than brothers and sisters. As their mutual sympathy is less necessary, so it is less habitual, and, therefore, proportionally weaker. The children of cousins, being still less connected, are of still less importance to one another; and the affection gradually diminishes as the relation grows more and more remote. (p. 220)

Our feelings of natural affection, however, go beyond the family, beyond even the extended family.

> Among well-disposed people the necessity or conveniency of mutual accommodation very frequently produces a friend-

ship not unlike that which takes place among those who are born to live in the same family. Colleagues in office, partners in trade, call one another brothers, and frequently feel towards one another as if they really were so. . . . Even the trifling circumstances of living in the same neighbourhood has some effect of the same kind. (pp. 223–224)

Then there are the inhabitants of our own country and the members of the particular groups within a country to which we belong.

Every individual is naturally more attached to his own particular order or society than to any other. His own interest, his own vanity, the interest and vanity of many of his friends and companions, are commonly a good deal connected with it: he is ambitious to extend its privileges and immunities—he is zealous to defend them against the encroachments of every other order or society. (p. 230)

Adam Smith's view of benevolence seems to be that it is strongest within the family and that as we go beyond the family, to friends, neighbours, and colleagues, and then to others who are none of these, the force of benevolence becomes weaker the more remote and the more casual the connection. And when we come to foreigners or members of other sects or groups with interests which are thought to be opposed to ours, we find not simply the absence of benevolence but malevolence.

When two nations are at variance, the citizen of each pays little regard to the sentiments which foreign nations may entertain concerning his conduct. His whole ambition is to obtain the approbation of his own fellow-citizens; and as they are all animated by the same hostile passions which animate himself, he can never please them so much as by enraging and offending their enemies. The partial spectator is at hand: the impartial one at a great distance. In war and negotiation, therefore, the laws of justice are very seldom observed. Truth and fair dealing are almost totally disregarded. . . . The animosity of hostile factions, whether civil or ecclesiastical, is often still more furious than that of hostile nations, and their conduct towards one another is often still more atrocious.(pp. 154–55)[3]

The picture which Adam Smith paints of human behaviour is not edifying. Man is not without finer feelings; he is indulgent to children, tolerant of parents, kind to friends. But once this is said, it is also true that he is dominated by self-love, lives in a world of self-delusion, is conceited, envious, malicious, quarrelsome, and resentful. Smith's view is in fact a description of man much as we know him to be. This is not the aspect of *The Theory of Moral Sentiments* to which commentators normally draw our attention. The book is usually thought of as presenting, and here I quote Jacob Viner, "an unqualified doctrine of a harmonious order of nature, under divine guidance, which promotes the welfare of man through the operation of his individual propensities."[4] How this bland interpretation came to be made of what is a very unflattering account of human nature is something to which I now turn.

Adam Smith did not address himself directly to the question of whether there was a natural harmony in man's propensities. However, it can be inferred from various statements he made that Viner's generalisation is not far from the truth. Take as an example what he says about the fact that we judge people by what they do rather than by what they intend to do, although it would seem more reasonable if, in our assessment of their characters, it was the other way around.

Nature . . . when she implanted the seeds of this irregularity in the human breast, seems, as upon all other occasions, to have intended the happiness and perfection of the species. If the hurtfulness of the design, if the malevolence of the affection, were alone the causes which excited our resentment, we should feel all the furies of that passion against any person in whose breast we suspected or believed such designs or affections were harboured, though they had never broken out

3. Jacob Viner, who adopts a similar view, points out that Adam Smith's sentiments grow weaker with "social distance." See Jacob Viner, *The Role of Providence in the Social Order* (1972), 80–81.

4. Jacob Viner, "Adam Smith and Laissez Faire," in *Adam Smith 1776–1926: Lectures to Commemorate the Sesquicentennial of the Publication of "The Wealth of Nations"* (1928), 116–55.

into any actions. Sentiments, thoughts, intentions, would become the objects of punishment, and if the indignation of mankind run as high against them as against actions; if the baseness of the thought which had given birth to no action, seemed in the eyes of the world as much to call aloud for vengeance as the baseness of the action, every court of judicature would become a real inquisition. There would be no safety for the most innocent and circumspect conduct. . . . Actions, therefore, which either produce actual evil, or attempt to produce it, and thereby put us in the immediate fear of it, are by the Author of nature rendered the only proper and approved objects of human punishment and resentment. Sentiments, designs, affections, though it is from these that according to cool reason human actions derive their whole merit or demerit, are placed by the great Judge of hearts beyond the limits of every human jurisdiction, and are reserved for the cognizance of his own unerring tribunal. That necessary rule of justice, therefore, that men in this life are liable to punishment for their actions only, not for their designs and intentions, is founded upon this salutary and useful irregularity in human sentiments concerning merit or demerit, which at first sight appears so absurd and unaccountable. But every part of nature, when attentively surveyed, equally demonstrates the providential care of its Author; and we may admire the wisdom and goodness of God even in the weakness and folly of men. (pp. 105–6)

Adam Smith explains that this "irregularity of sentiment" is not without its positive utility.

Man was made for action, and to promote by the exertion of his faculties such changes in the external circumstances both of himself and others, as may seem most favourable to the happiness of all. He must not be satisfied with indolent benevolence, nor fancy himself the friend of mankind, because in his heart he wishes well to the prosperity of the world. That he may call forth the whole vigour of his soul, and strain every nerve, in order to produce those ends which it is the purpose of his being to advance, Nature has taught him, that neither himself nor mankind can be fully satisfied with his conduct, nor bestow upon it the full measure of applause, unless he has actually produced them. He is made to know, that the praise of good intentions, without the merit of good offices, will be but of little avail to excite either the loudest acclamations of the world, or even the highest degree of self-applause. (p. 106)

Adam Smith on many occasions observes that aspects of human nature which seem reprehensible to us, in fact, serve a useful social purpose. "Nature . . . even in the present depraved state of mankind, does not seem to have dealt so unkindly with us, as to have endowed us with any principle which is wholly and in every respect evil, or which, in no degree and in no direction, can be the proper object of praise and approbation" (p. 77). Consider his discussion of pride and vanity:

Our dislike to pride and vanity generally disposes us to rank the persons whom we accuse of those vices rather below than above the common level. In this judgment, however, I think we are most frequently in the wrong, and that both the proud and the vain man are often (perhaps for the most part) a good deal above it; though not near so much as either the one really thinks himself, or as the other wishes you to think him. If we compare them with their own pretensions, they may appear the just objects of contempt. But when we compare them with what the greater part of their rivals and competitors really are, they may appear quite otherwise, and very much above the common level. Where there is this real superiority, pride is frequently attended with many respectable virtues—with truth, with integrity, with a high sense of honour, with cordial and steady friendship, with the most inflexible firmness and resolution; vanity with many amiable ones—with humanity, with politeness, with a desire to oblige in all little matters, and sometimes with a real generosity in great ones—a generosity, however, which it often wishes to display in the most splendid colours that it can. (pp. 257–58)

Of more interest to those of us concerned with the working of the economic system is Adam Smith's discussion of the view, to which his teacher Francis Hutcheson subscribed, that virtue consists wholly of benevolence or love and that any admixture of a selfish motive detracts from that virtue. Hutcheson, according to Smith, argued that if an action, supposed to proceed from gratitude, should be discovered to have arisen from an expectation of some new favour, or if what was apprehended to proceed from public spirit should be found out to have taken its origin from the hope of a pecuniary award, such a discovery would entirely destroy all notion of merit or praiseworthiness in either of these actions. . . . The most virtuous of all affections . . . was that which embraced as its objects the happiness of all intelligent beings. The least virtuous . . . was that which aimed no further than at the happiness of an individual, such as a son, a brother, a friend. (pp. 302–3)

Adam Smith, as we have seen, did not deny the existence of benevolence nor that it contributed to human welfare. But he regarded this doctrine of Hutcheson's as being too extreme.

Regard to our own private happiness and interest . . . appear upon many occasions very laudable principles of action. The habits of economy, industry, discretion, attention and application of thought, are generally supposed to be cultivated from self-interested motives, and at the same time are apprehended to be very praiseworthy qualities, which deserve the esteem and approbation of every body. . . . Benevolence may, perhaps, be the sole principle of action in the Deity, and there are several not improbable arguments which tend to persuade us that it is so . . . . But whatever may be the case with the Deity, so imperfect a creature as man, the support of whose existence requires so many things external to him, must often act from many other motives. The condition of human nature were peculiarly hard if those affections which, by the very nature of our being, ought frequently to influence our conduct, could, upon no occasion, appear virtuous, or deserve esteem and commendation from any body. (pp. 304–5)

Furthermore, Smith points out, the notion of benevolence as encompassing "the general happiness of mankind" would require man to do something of which God is no doubt capable but that is beyond the powers of man: "The administration of the great system of the universe [and] the care of the universal happiness of all rational and sensible beings, is the business of God, and not of man. To man is allotted a much humbler department, but one much more suitable to the weakness of his powers, and to the narrowness of his comprehension—the care of his own happiness, of that of his family, his friends, his country" (p. 237).

It was not Adam Smith's usual practice to proclaim that there was a natural harmony in man's psychological propensities. What he normally did was to point out that particular characteristics of human beings which were in various ways disagreeable were accompanied by offsetting social benefits. Man's nature may seem unpleasant to our fastidious taste but man appears to be as well adapted to the conditions in which he has to subsist as the tapeworm is to his. The implication of the various remarks of Smith would appear to be that any change in man's nature would tend to make things worse. But Smith avoids stating this general conclusion. It is not difficult to see why he showed this caution. If he had asserted that there was such a natural harmony, how did it come about that this was so? Smith tended to think, as I suppose was usual at that time, of the universe as a machine. He speaks of "the various appearances which the great machine of the universe is perpetually exhibiting, with the secret wheels and springs which produce them" (p. 19). If there was such a natural harmony in human nature, how did it happen that human beings were designed in the way they were? According to Viner, Smith thought that this was due to divine guidance, that man exhibited these harmonious characteristics because he had been created by God. It is difficult for us to enter the mind of someone living two hundred years ago, but it seems to me that Viner very much exaggerates the extent to which Smith was committed to a belief in a personal God. As Viner himself notes, in those parts of the discussion where we would expect the word "God" to be used, it is rarely found and the word "Nature" (p. 86) is substituted or some such expression as the "all-wise Architect and Conductor" (p. 289) or "the great Director of Nature" (p. 78) or even, on occasion, the "invisible hand." (p. 184).[5]

It seems to me that one can gauge the degree of Adam Smith's belief from the remark he makes in the *Wealth of Nations* when he notes that the curiosity of mankind about the "great phenomena of nature" such as "the generation, the life, growth, and dissolution of plants and animals" has led men to "enquire into their causes." Smith observes: "Superstition first attempted to satisfy this curiosity, by re-

5. See Viner, "Smith and Laissez Faire," 121.

ferring all those wonderful appearances to the immediate agency of the gods. Philosophy afterwards endeavoured to account for them, from more familiar causes, or from such as mankind were better acquainted with than the agency of the gods."[6] This is hardly a remark which would have been made by a strong, or even a mild, deist.

The fact of the matter is that, in 1759, there was no way of explaining how such a natural harmony came about unless one believed in a personal God who created it all. Before Darwin, Mendel, and perhaps also Crick and Watson, if one observed, as Adam Smith thought he often did, a kind of harmony existing in human nature, no explanation could be given if one were unwilling to accept God the creator. My own feeling is that Smith was reluctant to adopt this particular explanation. His use of the term "Nature" and other circumlocutions was a means of evading giving an answer to the question rather than the statement of one. Since Smith could only sense that there was some alternative explanation, the right response was suspended belief, and his position seems to me to have come close to this. Today we would explain such a harmony in human nature as a result of natural selection, the particular combination of psychological characteristics being that likely to lead to survival. In fact, Smith saw very clearly in certain areas the relation between those characteristics which nature seems to have chosen and those which increase the likelihood of survival.

Consider the following passage from *The Theory of Moral Sentiments:*

> With regard to all those ends which, upon account of their peculiar importance, may be regarded . . . as the favourite ends of nature, she has constantly . . . not only endowed mankind with an appetite for the end which she proposes, but likewise with an appetite for the means by which alone this end can be brought about, for their own sakes, and independent of their tendency to produce it. Thus self-preservation, and the propagation of the species, are the great ends which nature seems to have proposed in the formation of all animals. Mankind are endowed with a desire of those ends, and an aversion to the contrary. . . . But though we are . . . endowed with a very strong desire of those ends, it has not been

6. Adam Smith, *An Inquiry into the Nature and Causes of the Wealth of Nations* (Glasgow edition, 1976), 767.

entrusted to the slow and uncertain determinations of our reason, to find out the proper means of bringing them about. Nature has directed us to the greater part of these by original and immediate instincts. Hunger, thirst, the passion which unites the two sexes, the love of pleasure, and the dread of pain, prompt us to apply those means for their own sakes, and without any consideration of their tendency to those beneficent ends which the great Director of nature intended to produce by them. (pp. 77–78)

This comes very close to a modern attitude. The "passion by which nature unites the two sexes" (p. 28), or love, was considered by Adam Smith, a lifelong bachelor, as "always, in some measure, ridiculous. . . . The passion appears to every body, but the man who feels it, entirely disproportioned to the value of the object" (p. 31). But, of course, the passion which unites the sexes serves to secure the propagation of the species and if rationality impedes this, we can count on the great Director of nature to make sure that in this area man is not rational. Similarly, we care much more for the young than the old. "Nature, for the wisest purposes, has rendered in most men, perhaps in all men, parental tenderness a much stronger affection than filial piety. The continuance and propagation of the species depend altogether upon the former, and not upon the latter" (p. 142). "In the eye of nature, it would seem, a child is a more important object than an old man, and excites a much more lively, as well as a much more universal sympathy. It ought to do so. . . . In ordinary cases an old man dies without being much regretted by any body. Scarce a child can die without rending asunder the heart of somebody" (p. 219).

In all these cases nature, as Adam Smith would say, or natural selection, as we would say, has made sure that man possesses those propensities which would secure the propagation of the species.[7] But even if Smith had been aware of the principle of natural selection, of itself this could not have given him an explanation of why there was a natural harmony in man's psychological propensities. That the instincts which regulate sexual activity and the care of the young were the result of natural selection poses no problem. These are, after all,

7. Michael T. Ghiselin, a biologist, has noted that Adam Smith "clearly grasped" that "our moral sentiments have an adaptive significance." See Michael T. Ghiselin, *The Economy of Nature and the Evolution of Sex* (1974), 257.

instincts which man shares with all other mammals, and natural selection has had a very long period to bring about this result. The social arrangements of the tiger, the wolf, or even the chimpanzee are, however, very different from those of human beings and unless there has been a long period during which natural selection could operate to shape human nature, we can have no confidence that man's psychological propensities are appropriately adjusted to the conditions of human society.

It was David Hume's view, and presumably also Adam Smith's, that human nature is revealed as being much the same in all recorded history:

> Ambition, avarice, self-love, vanity, friendship, generosity, public spirit; these passions, mixed in various degrees, and distributed through society, have been from the beginning of the world and still are the source of all the actions and enterprises which have ever been observed among mankind. Would you know the sentiments, inclinations, and course of life of the Greeks and Romans? Study well the temper and actions of the French and English. . . . Mankind are so much the same in all times and places that history informs us of nothing new or strange in this particular.[8]

Without being tied down to Bishop Usher's chronology, it would still have been difficult for Adam Smith to use natural selection as an explanation of what he thought he observed, that is, a harmony in human nature, unless recorded history was but a small part of human history. There had to be an earlier period in which human nature was not the same as it is now.

Fortunately we have learnt a great deal about the antiquity of man in recent years. We now know, what Adam Smith could not, that modern man (homo sapiens) has existed for perhaps five hundred thousand years and that homo erectus came into existence about one and a half million years ago, while creatures which may or may not be classified as men, but from which man almost certainly evolved, were in existence several million years ago.[9] We are thus able to fill in the gaps in

8. David Hume, "Human Uniformity and Predictability," in Louis Schneider, ed., *The Scottish Moralists on Human Nature and Society,* (1967), 44.

9. See Philip V. Tobias, "Implications of the New Age Estimates of the Early South African Hominids," *Nature* 246 (1973):79–83; and Charles E. Oxnard, *Unique-*

Smith's position. We have the principle of natural selection, a mechanism of inheritance and an extremely long period during which natural selection could play its part. Smith's view of a harmony in man's nature no longer requires us to postulate a divine creator and his use of the word Nature is singularly appropriate. The harmony in human psychological propensities should, however, be regarded as the existence of that combination of traits which makes for survival rather than as leading to the "perfection and happiness" of mankind. Such a position, which assigns a genetic basis for human psychology, is one for which there is, today, some support.[10]

I can find no essential difference between the views on human nature in *The Theory of Moral Sentiments* and those expressed in the *Wealth of Nations*. Of course, the subject is not treated systematically in the *Wealth of Nations* and Adam Smith's views have to be inferred from incidental remarks. But self-love is everywhere evident. We are more familiar with the effect of self-love on the actions of merchants and manufacturers, but in fact all men, whatever their occupations, are much the same. When speaking of teachers, he says: "In every profession, the exertion of the greater part of those who exercise it, is always in proportion to the necessity they are under of making that exertion."[11] Of those engaged in the "administration of government," he says that they are "generally disposed to reward both themselves and their immediate dependents rather more than enough."[12]

Self-love also shows itself in the "overweening conceit which the greater part of men have of their own abilities" and their "absurd presumption in their own good fortune,"[13] which is used by Adam Smith to explain why, among other things, people buy lottery tickets, invest in gold mines, become lawyers, engage in smuggling, join the army, or go to sea. It may seem strange that self-love sometimes results in self-harm, but the reason is that self-love leads to self-deceit and self-

ness and Diversity in Human Evolution: Morphometric Studies of Australopithecines (1975).

10. For a general survey of the problem, see Edward O. Wilson, *Sociobiology: The New Synthesis* (1975), 547–75. See also Robert L. Trivers, "The Evolution of Reciprocal Altruism," *Quarterly Review of Biology* 46 (1971):35–57; and *idem.*, "Parental Investment and Sexual Selection," in Bernard Campbell, ed., *Sexual Selection and the Descent of Man* (1972), 136.

11. Smith, *Wealth of Nations*, 759.   12. *Ibid.*, 866.
13. *Ibid.*, 124.

deceit colours our perception of the outcomes of alternative courses of action. This is all of a piece with Smith's view that man overestimates the difference between one permanent situation and another. "Avarice overrates the difference between poverty and riches: ambition, that between a private and public station: vainglory, that between obscurity and extensive reputation" (p. 149). This theme is illustrated by the discussion of ambition and in particular the case of a poor man's son "whom heaven in its anger has visited with ambition":

> He studies to distinguish himself in some laborious profession. With the most unrelenting industry he labours night and day to acquire talents superior to all his competitors. He endeavours next to bring those talents into public view, and with equal assiduity solicits every opportunity of employment. For this purpose he makes his court to all mankind; he serves those whom he hates, and is obsequious to those whom he despises. Through the whole of his life he pursues the idea of a certain artificial and elegant repose which he may never arrive at, for which he sacrifices a real tranquillity that is at all times in his power, and which, if in the extremity of old age he should at last attain to it, he will find to be in no respect preferable to that humble security and contentment which he had abandoned for it. (p. 181)

However, if the ambitious man is not made happy by the inner forces which drive him, the rest of us gain. Says Smith: "It is well that nature imposes upon us in this manner. It is this deception which rouses and keeps in continual motion the industry of mankind. It is this which first prompted them to cultivate the ground, to build houses, to found cities and commonwealths, and to invent and improve all the sciences and arts, which ennoble and embellish human life" (p. 183).

Benevolence is not absent from the *Wealth of Nations* but, as in *The Theory of Moral Sentiments,* it is put in its place. Consider Adam Smith's view that slavery could "afford the expence of slave cultivation" in the production of sugar and tobacco, but that this was not true for corn. He supports this conclusion by observing that the "late resolution of the Quakers in Pennsylvania to set at liberty all their negro slaves, may satisfy us that their number cannot be very great. Had they made any considerable part of their property, such a resolution could never have been agreed to."[14] This quotation reveals the weight which Smith assigns to benevolence. Freeing the slaves was certainly a benevolent action but hardly one likely to be undertaken if the price was personal ruin.

Arthur H. Cole, after referring to passages such as these, concludes that Adam Smith had a "pretty low opinion of mankind in general." This he finds difficult to reconcile with the picture drawn by Smith's biographers of a man who was "friendly and generous."[15] I do not regard this as a problem. Smith saw the less agreeable qualities of human beings as being productive of good. Self-interest promotes industry; resentment discourages aggressive actions by others; vanity leads to acts of kindness; and so on. Furthermore, one can hardly be upset by people's actions, even if in some respects disagreeable, if one believes that they are incapable of acting otherwise. Anyone who knows anything about cats will not spend much time deploring their unkindness to mice.

Many economists have thought that there is an inconsistency between Adam Smith's argument in *The Theory of Moral Sentiments* and in the *Wealth of Nations*.[16] Jacob Viner refers to this question in the following terms: "The Germans, who, it seems, in their methodical manner commonly read both the *Theory of Moral Sentiments* and the *Wealth of Nations*, have coined a pretty term, *Das Adam Smith Problem*, to denote the failure to understand either which results from the attempt to use the one in the interpretation of the other."[17] The inconsistency which Viner himself finds is that in *The Theory of Moral Sentiments*, Smith assumes that there exists a natural harmony, while in the *Wealth of Nations* he seems to have abandoned this belief, as is shown by the references to desirable government actions. Viner's view involves, I think, a misunderstanding of these two books. *The Theory of Moral Sentiments* is a study of human psychology. The *Wealth of Nations* is a study of the organisation of economic life. A harmony in human nature does not imply that no government action is

14. Smith, *Wealth of Nations*, 388.
15. Arthur H. Cole, "Puzzles of the 'Wealth of Nations,'" *Canadian Journal of Economics and Political Science* 24 (1958):1, 5.
16. See August Oncken, "The Consistency of Adam Smith," *Economic Journal* 7 (1897):443–50.
17. Viner, "Smith and Laissez Faire," 120.

required to achieve the appropriate institutional structure for economic activity.

Most economists, however, who have thought that there was an inconsistency between Adam Smith's position in these two books have come to this conclusion for another reason. In *The Theory of Moral Sentiments,* man's actions are influenced by benevolence. In the *Wealth of Nations,* this motive is apparently absent. This view is supported by a much-quoted passage: "It is not from the benevolence of the butcher, the brewer, or the baker, that we expect our dinner, but from their regard to their own interest. We address ourselves, not to their humanity but to their self-love, and never talk to them of our own necessities but of their advantages."[18] What is not quoted is something which Adam Smith says earlier in the same paragraph: "In civilized society [man] stands at all times in need of the co-operation and assistance of great multitudes, while his whole life is scarce sufficient to gain the friendship of a few persons."[19] This puts a completely different complexion on the matter. For that extensive division of labour required to maintain a civilized standard of living, we need to have the co-operation of great multitudes, scattered all over the world. There is no way in which this co-operation could be secured through the exercise of benevolence. Benevolence, or love, may be the dominant or, at any rate, an important factor within the family or in our relations with colleagues or friends, but as Smith indicates, it operates weakly or not at all when we deal with strangers. Benevolence is highly personal and most of those who benefit from the economic activities in which we engage are unknown to us. Even if they were, they would not necessarily in our eyes be lovable. For strangers to have to rely on our benevolence for what they received from us would mean, in most cases, that they would not be supplied: "Man has almost constant occasion for the help of his brethren, and it is in vain to expect it from their benevolence only."[20]

Looked at in this way, Adam Smith's argument for the use of the market for the organisation of economic activity is much stronger than it is usually thought to be. The market is not simply an ingenious mechanism, fueled by self-interest, for securing the co-operation of individuals in the production of goods and services. In most circum-

18. Smith, *Wealth of Nations,* 26–27.   20. *Ibid.*
19. *Ibid.,* 26.

stances it is the only way in which this could be done. Nor does government regulation or operation represent a satisfactory way out. A politician, when motivated by benevolence, will tend to favour his family, his friends, members of his party, inhabitants of his region or country (and this whether or not he is democratically elected). Such benevolence will not necessarily redound to the general good. And when politicians are motivated by self-interest unalloyed by benevolence, it is easy to see that the results may be even less satisfactory.

The great advantage of the market is that it is able to use the strength of self-interest to offset the weakness and partiality of benevolence, so that those who are unknown, unattractive, or unimportant will have their wants served. But this should not lead us to ignore the part which benevolence and moral sentiments do play in making possible a market system. Consider, for example, the care and training of the young, largely carried out within the family and sustained by parental devotion. If love were absent and the task of training the young was therefore placed on other institutions, run presumably by people following their own self-interest, it seems likely that this task, on which the successful working of human societies depends, would be worse performed. At least, that was Adam Smith's opinion: "Domestic education is the institution of nature—public education the contrivance of man. It is surely unnecessary to say which is likely to be the wisest" (p. 222). Again, the observance of moral codes must very greatly reduce the costs of doing business with others and must therefore facilitate market transactions. As Smith observes, "Society . . . cannot subsist among those who are at all times ready to hurt and injure one another" (p. 86).

Adam Smith allows for a good deal of folly in human behaviour. But this does not lead him to advocate an extensive role for government. Politicians and government officials are also men. Private individuals are constrained in their folly because they personally suffer its consequences: "Bankruptcy is perhaps the greatest and most humiliating calamity which can befall an innocent man. The greater part of men, therefore, are sufficiently careful to avoid it."[21] But, of course, men who bankrupt a city or a nation are not necessarily themselves made bankrupt. Therefore, Smith continues: "Great nations are never impoverished by private, though they sometimes are by public prodi-

21. Smith, *Wealth of Nations*, 342.

gality and misconduct."[22] As he later observes: "[Kings and ministers] are themselves always, and without any exception, the greatest spendthrifts in the society. Let them look well after their own expence, and they may safely trust private people with theirs. If their own extravagance does not ruin the state, that of their subjects never will."[23]

In the regulation of behaviour, Adam Smith put little confidence in human reason. When discussing self-preservation and the propagation of the species, Smith said, in a passage to which I have already referred, that the securing of these ends is so important that "it has not been entrusted to the slow and uncertain determinations of our reason" but to "original and immediate instincts" (pp. 77–78). Jacob Viner makes a similar point: "The important thing for the interpreter of Smith is to note how low down . . . reason enters into the picture as a factor influencing social behaviour. The sentiments [that is, the instincts] are innate in man. . . . Under normal circumstances, the sentiments make no mistake. It is reason which is fallible."[24]

It is wrong to believe, as is commonly done, that Adam Smith had as his view of man an abstraction, an "economic man," rationally pursuing his self-interest in a single-minded way. Smith would not have thought it sensible to treat man as a rational utility-maximiser. He thinks of man as he actually is: dominated, it is true, by self-love but not without some concern for others, able to reason but not necessarily in such a way as to reach the right conclusion, seeing the outcomes of his actions but through a veil of self-delusion. No doubt modern psychologists have added a great deal, some of it correct, to this eighteenth-century view of human nature. But if one is willing to accept Adam Smith's view of man as containing, if not the whole truth, at least a large part of it, realisation that his thought has a much broader foundation than is commonly assumed makes his argument for economic freedom more powerful and his conclusions more persuasive.

22. *Ibid.*
23. *Ibid.*, 346. The reasons that Adam Smith advocated limited government cannot be summarised in a single paragraph. J. Ralph Lindgren has argued persuasively that it was Smith's view that the institutional role of men in government will inevitably lead them to adopt attitudes dominated by a "love of system." See J. Ralph Lindgren, *The Social Philosophy of Adam Smith* (1973), 60–83.
24. Viner, *Role of Providence*, 78.

Economists

EIGHT

Alfred Marshall's Mother and Father

John Maynard Keynes in his famous "Memoir on Alfred Marshall" opens with an extraordinary sentence: "Alfred Marshall was born at Clapham on 26 July 1842, the son of William Marshall, a cashier in the Bank of England, by his marriage with Rebecca Oliver."[1] What makes this sentence extraordinary is that it is a masterpiece of concealment.

Let us start with Alfred Marshall's mother. Apart from the mention of her name in the first sentence, there is no other reference to her in the entire memoir, except for saying that she was the victim of her husband's despotic will. As Marshall thought that the "most valuable of all capital is that invested in human beings and of that capital the most precious part is the result of the care and influence of the mother,"[2] one might have expected that Keynes would have given her more attention. This would seem especially called for given Marshall's endorsement of Galton's view that "the mother's influence is most easily traced among theologians and men of science."[3] Alfred

Reprinted with permission of the publisher from *History of Political Economy* (Winter 1984). © 1984 by Duke University Press.

It is a pleasure to acknowledge my indebtedness to Professor D. E. Moggridge for giving me permission to see the file of correspondence on the "Memoir on Alfred Marshall" (now held in the Marshall Library, Cambridge), which has been of great value to me in writing this article. In subsequent footnotes, I will refer to the file as the Keynes Memoir file. I am also indebted to the Liberty Fund for a grant which financed the research on which this article is based.

1. J. M. Keynes, *Essays in Biography,* reprinted in *Collected Writings of John Maynard Keynes,* D. Moggridge, ed. (London: Macmillan for the Royal Economic Society, 1972), 10:161.

2. Alfred Marshall, *Principles of Economics,* C. W. Guillebaud, ed., 9th variorum ed. (London, 1961), 564.

3. Marshall, *Principles of Economics,* 207.

Marshall may be said to fall into both categories. As Keynes explains, Marshall had a "double nature." He was both pastor and scientist, leading him to attempt to be, in Edgeworth's felicitous phrase, an "Archbishop of Economics."[4] Marshall's mother was, according to his wife Mary Marshall, "a charming woman and Alfred was devoted to her. Whenever anything pleasant befell such as the Address on his eightieth birthday, he would say 'If only my mother were alive how glad she would be.'"[5] Marshall was certainly closer to his mother than to his father, and it is not without significance that his letters from America in 1875 were addressed to her and not to his father. Yet she is absent from the memoir.

The reason Keynes did not do more than mention Marshall's mother's name was that this was almost all he knew about her and even her name was not easily obtained. Mary Marshall wrote to Keynes while he was preparing the memoir to tell him that "the pedigree has been unearthed from a distant relation—I am glad to see that it gives the maiden name of Alfred's mother which I feared was lost."[6] How was it that all knowledge of Alfred Marshall's mother's family came to be lost? The explanation is contained in a letter which William, a nephew of Alfred Marshall's (presumably the son of his elder brother), sent to Claude Guillebaud (also a nephew, son of Alfred Marshall's sister, Mabel) after the memoir was published, the substance of which was sent on to Keynes by Mary Marshall: "William seems to know more about Marshall's mother than anyone and he says she came from Maidston [*sic*] and was the daughter of a chemist and that the Marshall family considered this a mesalliance and she had to cut herself off from her own family."[7] In fact, even the nephew William's information was defective. The truth was far worse than he knew. Marshall's mother was certainly born in Maidstone, in Kent, but she was a butcher's daughter not a chemist's daughter, and her mother, Rebecca Davenport (Marshall's grandmother), appears to have been the daughter of an agricultural labourer.[8] At the time of her marriage, Rebecca Oliver's

4. F. Y. Edgeworth to J. M. Keynes, 30 August 1924, Keynes Memoir file.

5. Mary P. Marshall to J. M. Keynes, 14 January 1925, Keynes Memoir file.

6. Mary P. Marshall to J. M. Keynes, 26 July 1924, Keynes Memoir file.

7. Mary P. Marshall to J. M. Keynes, 14 January 1925, Keynes Memoir file.

8. Rebecca Davenport's father, Thomas Davenport, was described as "husbandman," presumably an agricultural labourer, at the apprenticeship of his son, Thomas, to a papermaker in 1786.

father's family included other butchers, several curriers, at least one farmer, and a victualler (presumably an innkeeper). Her mother's family, the Davenports, seem to have been of a labouring class.[9] It is no wonder that Marshall's mother had to cut herself off from her own family. One consequence was that, lacking any direct knowledge, learning about "the life of the working classes" became, for Marshall, a research project.[10]

We now come to Alfred Marshall's birthplace. Keynes says that it was Clapham, and Bernard Corry in his article on Alfred Marshall in the *International Encyclopedia of the Social Sciences* (1968) embellishes this by adding after Clapham, "a leafy London suburb." In fact, Marshall was not born in the very respectable suburb, Clapham, but in Bermondsey, a much less desirable residential area, situated as it was in the midst of the tanneries, with their accompanying pungent smells, Bermondsey then being the centre of the leather industry.[11] The Marshalls had moved from Bermondsey to Sydenham, in Kent, by 1846, and sometime between 1846 and 1850, they moved to Clapham.[12] Alfred Marshall could not have been less than three nor more than seven years old when this happened. Did Marshall know that he was born in Bermondsey and not Clapham? The evidence is equivocal. In the census for 1871, Alfred Marshall gave his place of birth as Surrey, the county which, as it happens, includes both Bermondsey and Clapham. This inclines me to think that Marshall may have known that he was not born in Clapham, was willing to conceal his real place of birth, but was unwilling to tell a lie.

At the time of Alfred Marshall's birth, his father William is said

9. For this information, largely based on the census records for 1841 and 1851, I am indebted to Maurice W. M. Clarke.

10. Early in his study of economics, Alfred Marshall "set himself to get into closer contact with practical business and with the life of the working classes." Keynes, "Memoir," 181 n. 1.

11. In the famous nuisance case *Sturges v. Bridgman,* decided in 1879, the judges used Bermondsey as an example of a locality devoted to a trade or manufacture "of a noisy and unsavoury character," and they comment: "What would be a nuisance in *Belgrave Square* would not necessarily be so in *Bermondsey*" (11 Ch. D. 865 [1879] [emphasis added]. Clapham could well have been substituted for Belgrave Square. According to Alfred Marshall's birth certificate, he was born at 66 Charlotte Row, and the subdistrict of Bermondsey in which he was born was, in fact, called "The Leather Market."

12. Information is based on the birth certificates of Alfred Marshall's younger sisters Agnes (registered in 1846) and Mabel Louisa (registered in 1850).

by Keynes to have been "a cashier in the Bank of England." In fact, at that time he was a clerk at the Bank of England, earning £140 a year, a position he had held since 1830. Previously he had worked for two years as a clerk for his uncle, a stockbroker. He did not become a supernumerary cashier earning £410 a year until 1870, some twenty-eight years after the birth of Alfred Marshall, but he was a cashier when he retired in 1877, his salary being £510 a year.[13] On his marriage certificate, in 1840, Marshall's father does not admit to having an occupation, instead describing himself as "gentleman," an indication of his desire to avoid being included among the lower classes. There is no evidence that any members of the Marshall family attended the marriage. The only witnesses were Rebecca Oliver's brother and sister. How, with such pretensions, Marshall's father came to commit the social error of marrying a butcher's daughter is hard to understand. How Marshall's mother and father came to meet is easier to explain. Rebecca Oliver's brother, Edward, who had been apprenticed to a druggist in Ramsgate (perhaps the origin of the belief that Rebecca Oliver's father was a chemist) had left that position to become a clerk at the Bank of England, and it is understandable that, visiting her brother, Rebecca Oliver should meet a fellow clerk.[14] At the time of their marriage, William Marshall was twenty-seven and Rebecca Oliver had just turned twenty-three years of age.

The concealment of Marshall's mother's social origins, the error in Marshall's birthplace, and the misstatement of his father's position at the Bank of England all seem designed to enhance the family's social status. Nor do I doubt that this was the intention. But I do not wish to suggest that Keynes was responsible for the concealment. It is an almost unbelievable fact that the memoir, so beautifully constructed and dealing with so many aspects of Marshall's life and thought, was written in about two months. Marshall died on July 13, 1924, and the memoir appeared in the September 1924 issue of the *Economic Journal*.[15] It is therefore understandable that Keynes would not have checked all the material given to him. In the memoir, Keynes makes a

13. Information provided by the Bank of England.
14. Ibid.
15. The memoir was in galleys before the end of August 1924 (see F. Y. Edgeworth to Keynes, 30 August 1924). The September 1924 issue of the *Economic Journal* was somewhat delayed (see R. F. Harrod, *The Life of John Maynard Keynes* [London, 1951], 354 n. 1).

generous acknowledgement of the assistance he received from Mary Marshall. From an examination of her notes in the Keynes Memoir file, it would seem that all the information on family history (or almost all) came from Mary Marshall, and she must have derived this information from Marshall's relatives (on his father's side). It seems that she was not allowed to learn anything which might damage her husband's social position.

I now come to the concealment in the memoir for which Mary Marshall and Keynes were responsible. Claude Guillebaud wrote to Keynes after the publication of the memoir as follows:

> I am sorry my Aunt put pressure on you to omit one or two uncomplimentary references to my grandfather [Alfred Marshall's father]. He was a wicked old tyrant, who amongst other and numerous misdeeds, made my poor mother's life a misery to her for years. He refused to allow her to marry the man she fell in love with—an impecunious subaltern—and when she did marry my father the old gentleman hated him and made things as difficult as possible for him, merely because he had married my mother. He lived with us for many years until his death and one of my early and vivid recollections is that of dancing with joy and delight, together with my brothers, on hearing that he was at last dead. You could certainly have said much more than you did without erring on the side of excess.[16]

Claude Guillebaud once gave me a more detailed account of this early recollection. He told me that he and the other children were in the nursery when someone came in and solemnly announced, "Grandfather is dead." The children at first merely repeated what they had been told, and then they realised what had happened. In a spontaneous outburst of joy, they whooped and holloed and went around the nursery in Indian file, crying out all the while, "Grandfather is dead."

William Marshall was not a lovable man. Sure of himself and with no respect for the opinions of others, he must have been very disagreeable. Claude Guillebaud's father was a clergyman, and while living in his house, Marshall's father did not hesitate to interfere in

16. C. W. Guillebaud to J. M. Keynes, 27 November 1924, Keynes Memoir file. William Marshall died in 1901, in his eighty-ninth year, not in his ninety-second year, as Keynes stated in the memoir.

church affairs. For example, Claude Guillebaud told me that he set himself to censoring the hymns. One he objected to was "Onward Christian Soldiers," since the line "With the Cross of Jesus going on before" smacked of popery. Of course, Keynes's picture of William Marshall in the memoir is not attractive, but it seems to have been more attractive than Keynes wished it to be and very much more attractive than it should have been.

It is not possible to say exactly what it was that Mary Marshall induced Keynes to omit. One point in her notes in the Keynes memoir file that does not appear in the memoir is that Alfred Marshall's father's practice of keeping him up studying till 11 P.M. (which is mentioned) had an adverse effect on his schoolwork. Mary Marshall in these notes wrote: "Alfred said his father was affectionate but a bad educator. He used to make Alfred work with him for school up to 11 P.M. The result was that he worked very little at school. He said that if he had not been slack at school he could not have lived."

Another omission concerned William Marshall's treatment of his brothers and sisters while he was a boy. Marshall's paternal grandfather, a widower, also named William, died in 1828 while his children were still young.[17] They were put in charge of an uncle, and William as the oldest (he was then about sixteen years old) "was made boss over the other children and kept them in order with a slipper."[18] As we learn from a letter written by Edgeworth, Keynes in the galley proofs called this "slipper-discipline," but the subject is omitted from the published version.[19] This reference to "slipper-discipline" may well have been part of a passage explaining that Marshall's father was a strict disciplinarian. That he was is evident from a letter written by Alfred Marshall to John Neville Keynes about a governess, Miss Laxton, who was going to look after the children of the Guillebauds and of Alfred Marshall's elder brother, who was also living with Claude Guillebaud's mother and father:

> My brother is averse to very strict discipline, and so are my
> sister and her husband, the Guillebauds. But my Father has

---

17. Marshall's grandfather was married in 1810. He then went to South Africa, where Marshall's father was born in 1812, and later went to Mauritius. He finally lived in Leith, Scotland.

18. See Mary Marshall's notes in the Keynes Memoir file.

19. See F. Y. Edgeworth to J. M. Keynes, 30 August 1924, Keynes Memoir file.

very strong views on the subject; and is a little apt to push his views forward to the distress of my sister. My Father is wonderfully unselfish and kindly intentioned. But he does not know how hard his extremely severe discipline would have made life to all of us children, if it had not been for the gentleness of my Mother. Perhaps you will not mind giving Miss Laxton a hint that I think she will find my sister a wiser counsellor on all matters of discipline than my Father; but that as he is an old man and not easily to be convinced, it will be generally better to pass by his suggestions rather than actively oppose them.[20]

If we have regard to the normal standards of discipline in Victorian England, it is not easy to imagine what an "extremely severe discipline" would be or to guess what instrument of punishment took the place of the slipper in the Marshall household. Alfred Marshall said that his father was "wonderfully unselfish and kindly intentioned," but he was very anxious to escape from his father's control; and when he decided to study mathematics, "he used to rejoice greatly that his father could not understand them," as Mary Marshall said in her notes and Keynes repeated. Marshall's father strongly opposed his desire to go to Cambridge to study mathematics rather than to Oxford to study classics. According to Mary Marshall's notes, Marshall's father said "that he only withdrew his strong opposition to the Cambridge versus the Oxford career when he found that Alfred was making himself ill with the worry." This, coming from a man of extraordinary insensitivity to the feelings of others, does not ring true. More probably, Marshall's father withdrew his opposition only when it became clear that he could not stop Alfred from going to Cambridge. As Mary Marshall said in her notes, "in spite of the opposition of his family and in spite of want of funds," Alfred Marshall was "determined to go to Cambridge. He borrowed money from his uncle Charles and went to Cambridge to struggle with poverty and hardship in order to do the highest work of which he thought himself capable." Uncle Charles, who had felt the sting of the slipper, disliked Marshall's father,[21] and it must have given him great pleasure to know that in helping his nephew to go to Cambridge, he was also thwarting the wishes of his brother.

20. Alfred Marshall to John Neville Keynes, 4 August 1891, Keynes 1 (105) in the Marshall Library, Cambridge.
21. See Mary Marshall's notes in the Keynes Memoir file.

Retiring from the Bank of England in 1877, William Marshall became an author. According to Keynes, his works included a tract, *Man's Rights and Woman's Duties*. It is not among the seven works of William Marshall listed in the British Library catalogue; and although this is not conclusive, it must be regarded as doubtful whether he did write a tract with such a title.[22] However, the references to women in his writings show that if in fact he did do so, he would have found it a congenial task. The writings of which we have record have three goals: to lead man to a Christian life, to expose the menace of popery, and to restore the English language to what it was in the ninth century: "What a language is the English of King Alfred's time."[23] We need not wonder why Alfred Marshall was so named.

William Marshall's first book was a religious poem, *Lochlere* (1877), about a man who, after many vicissitudes, "gives himself up to God" and enters upon a "Christian life." However, he also tried to forward another of his aims by introducing Old English words into the poetry. Not surprisingly the reviewers poked fun at him for so doing, and their criticism led him to write his next book, *The Past, Present and Future of England's Language* (1878). He agreed that he may have overdone the use of Old English in *Lochlere,* but complained that his views had not been taken seriously:

Have the reviewers welcomed the literary object of the poem? . . . Have they said, The case which the author of "Lochlere" has brought before us is a case fit for trial in the supreme court of popular literary criticism? . . . Our grammar is a confusion of grammatical systems, our dictionary a confusion of languages; whilst the study of our learned men is given to the languages of aliens, of the dead, and even of the uncivilised, or else to questions of science, the most advanced of which take such forms as these, whether we may not derive our ancestry from tadpoles rather than from God; or as these, whether we should not give back the clouded daylight of the old Christianity of the Apostles in exchange for the starry darkness of the new Christianity of the Papal Fa-

22. In the last two books which he published, William Marshall refers to himself as the author of a tract entitled *Mary or Madonna?* which is not in the British Library list. Photocopies of all the works of William Marshall in the British Library catalogue are available in the Regenstein Library, University of Chicago.

23. William Marshall, *Lochlere* (1877), vii.

thers; or as these, whether we ought not to give the electoral franchise to women, and thus allow them, as being the more numerous sex, to utterly emasculate our councils, and to make the England of the Plantagenets and Tudors, of the Cavaliers and Ironsides, a female Power; nay, further, as these, whether the social advantage of English women's disdaining to be raised by the homage or to rule by the love of men, and preferring to clamber up their bearded disgust to the tallness of virility, will not be as great as will be the great political advantage of English women's trampling on the subjection ordered them by God and nature, and rushing frantically forward to outsqueal the bass of legislative debate, and to shriek through the wrenched speaking-trumpet of executive command.[24]

After which he proceeds to demonstrate, at length, the merits of "the pure English of King Alfred's days."

He followed this with *The Dangers and Defences of English Protestantism* (1879). One quotation will give the flavour of this work:

There are but two earthly standing grounds of Christianity; one is the firm rock of restful Puritanism—worship of God in only spirit and truth; the other is the flowery but marshy meadow of stayless Popery—God's worship by means of outward show, and through symbols. . . . Protestants cannot be too much on their guard against that religious aestheticism, or sensuousness, which causes those, whose love of pleasure flourishes so dangerously beside their love of God, to set up in their Churches works of art, under the specious pretence of giving to God their best things. These lovers of pleasure necessarily worship art whilst they are worshipping Him. . . . Is it not God's great object in the Gospel . . . to assert man's utter sinfulness, his utter vileness and uncleanness; and is it becoming in man to appear there before God glorifying himself in his own works, and reckoning the glorification as an honour paid to God?[25]

24. William Marshall, *The Past, Present and Future of England's Language* (1878), 14–15.

25. William Marshall, *The Dangers and Defences of English Protestantism* (1879), 22–23.

A poem, *Rinalpho's Dream* (1887) was also devoted to combatting the seductions of the Roman Church. As poetry it is without merit,[26] as are three more books of poetry published late in life, two editions of *Aarbert* (1898, revised 1899) and *Herbert* (1901). These were essentially reworkings of *Lochlere,* with the amount of Anglo-Saxon reduced so as not to stand in the way of the religious message.

In the whole of William Marshall's writings I have only noticed two references of an autobiographical character. It is perhaps not altogether surprising that both refer to instruments of punishment used in his youth. In preferring the old word *swipe* to the modern word *scourge,* he says: "The very sound of a wielded cane is given in this word. It is a word which I have not heard, I think, since my childhood, and is now thankfully remembered by me in connection with my faithful schoolmaster."[27] And after advocating that the word *tawer* should be substituted for *tanner,* he adds, "Boys in Scotland in my schooldays used to be chastised by leathern thongs called 'taws.' "[28]

Keynes obviously had little familiarity with William Marshall's writings. He says, repeating Mary Marshall, that William Marshall was a man of "great resolution and perception."[29] This is wrong. He was a man of great resolution and no perception. Alfred Marshall, the scientist, owed nothing to this bigoted man. Marshall's father was completely convinced of the correctness of his own narrow views, had little regard for the feelings and wishes of others, and thought it right to control the actions of those in his power by "an extremely severe discipline." He was, as Alfred Marshall said, "a bad educator." It is to be expected that the strict control exercised by such a father over his children would affect their attitude in later life. And no doubt Alfred Marshall's extreme sensitiveness to criticism (he suffered, Claude Guillebaud told me, the agonies of hell when he discovered that he had made a mistake), his evasiveness when there was a hint of disagree-

26. I need only give as a sample one of the better verses taken from *Rinalpho's Dream* (1887), p. 37:
Women silly and gay were then zealous to play
At Church their little parts,
In curtseying, crossing, confessing and all
Other ornamental arts.
27. Marshall, *England's Language,* 73. As his father lived in Leith, Scotland, William Marshall was probably educated at Leith Grammar School.
28. *Ibid.,* 84.
29. Keynes, *Essays in Biography,* 162.

ment, his dislike of controversy, and other traits were, to a large extent, the result of his upbringing. But it should also not be forgotten that, even when young, his mind ranged free, and notwithstanding strong parental pressure, he formed and acted on his own views; and, when it came to choosing his career, Alfred Marshall ignored his father and followed his star.

NINE

Alfred Marshall's Family and Ancestry

I have described the first sentence of Keynes's memoir[1] as a "masterpiece of concealment" (see chap. 8 in this volume). Alfred Marshall's birthplace is there given as Clapham, "a leafy London suburb," as Bernard Corry explained,[2] whereas he was actually born in Bermondsey in the midst of the tanneries. Alfred's mother gets the bare mention of her name. The reason for this became obvious when I learnt that she was a butcher's daughter. His father William at the time of Alfred's birth is said to have been a cashier at the Bank of England whereas he was a clerk. In fact, he never held any important position in the bank. It is true that he was made a "cashier" in 1867 (some twenty-five years after Alfred's birth) but the conferring of this title in the Bank of England, we are told, was usually a reward for "long and

Reprinted with permission of the publisher from Rita McWilliams Tullberg, ed., *Alfred Marshall in Retrospect* (Aldershols: Edward Elgar Publishing Limited, 1990).

The information on which the paper is based has been gathered over a long period from a great variety of sources with the aid of many research assistants. The correspondence and notes relating to this research will be deposited in the Regenstein Library of the University of Chicago. I hope they will be of assistance to those who wish to do further research on Alfred Marshall's family and ancestry. Such research is clearly needed. There are gaps in the story I tell and some of my inferences are based on very scanty evidence. The notes of Mary Marshall, to which reference is made in this paper, will be found in the file of correspondence of John Maynard Keynes related to his "Memoir on Marshall," now held in the Marshall Library, Cambridge ("Keynes memoir file"). I am indebted to the Liberty Fund for a grant which financed much of the research on which this paper is based.

1. J. M. Keynes, *Essays in Biography,* reprinted in *Collected Writings of John Maynard Keynes,* D. Moggridge, ed. (London: Macmillan for the Royal Economic Society, 1972), 10:161.

2. Bernard Corry, "Marshall, Alfred," in D. A. Sills, ed., *International Encyclopedia of the Social sciences* (New York: Macmillan and the Free Press, 1968), 10:25.

faithful service."[3] At William Marshall's marriage, he described himself as a "gentleman." By doing so, he elevated his social status and concealed his real position. Alfred Marshall's family lived on the edge of gentility and the truth had to be suppressed if this was necessary to maintain respectability. The result has been to enhance Alfred's social position but to diminish his achievement.

The second sentence in the memoir tells us that the "Marshalls were a clerical family of the West" and we can almost hear the clink of teacups on vicarage lawns. As always in the memoir, or nearly always, there is some truth in this. Keynes tells us that Alfred's great-great-grandfather, William Marshall, was the "half legendary herculean parson of Devonshire" and that his great-grandfather, John Marshall, a clergyman who married Mary Hawtrey, was the headmaster of Exeter Grammar School. This is correct. But Keynes adds, after the reference to this "clerical family of the West," "sprung from William Marshall, incumbent of Saltash, Cornwall at the end of the seventeenth century." As the "parson of Devonshire" was born in 1676 in Cornwall and his father does not appear to have been a clergyman, it would seem that the "incumbent of Saltash" from whom the Marshalls sprang was either an invention or, which I regard as more probable, that the "parson of Devonshire" became divided in the minds of Alfred's family into two people, which has the effect of making the clerical line appear longer. The genealogical information used by Keynes in writing the memoir was compiled by Ainslie, a daughter of Uncle Henry, a brother of Alfred's father,[4] and it is not surprising that she only knew what the family wished her to believe. It is true that John Marshall had other relatives (Marshalls) who were clergymen, but the fact is that the two mentioned are the only clergymen in the direct line to Alfred Marshall. As we all have eight great-grandparents and sixteen great-great-grandparents, it is hazardous to discuss genetic influences unless all lines of descent have been studied and hazardous even then until their DNA has been inspected. Nonetheless, it is not to be expected that the author who writes with such enthusiasm on "The

3. The statement about William Marshall's position at the Bank of England and the meaning of the title "cashier" is based on a letter (uncovered in the Marshall Library by Rita McWilliams Tullberg) which was written to J. M. Keynes by Mr. Nairne of the Bank of England.

4. This I learnt from a letter from Mary Marshall to "Cousin Ainslie," in the possession of Professor George J. Stigler of the University of Chicago.

Great Villiers Connection" would neglect the influence of heredity. However, as we shall see, if one indulges in such conjectures, there are stronger candidates than the Marshalls or the Hawtreys (all that are mentioned by Keynes) as the source of the genes which helped to produce the author of the *Principles of Economics*.

Let us turn to Alfred's immediate family. After the reference to John Marshall, Alfred's great-grandfather, the next paragraph of the memoir starts: "His father . . ." This is puzzling since it is apparent that Keynes has skipped a generation. In fact there is no reference at all to Alfred's grandparents in the memoir. In the case of Alfred's grandparents on his mother's side, this is understandable since any reference to them would have taken us into the labouring classes. But why was William Marshall, Alfred's grandfather on his father's side, not mentioned? His history, I think, explains why. All that Mary Marshall says in the notes that she gave to Keynes is that he was a paymaster in the navy and it is certainly true that on his gravestone in Leith in Scotland (where he died) he is described as "formerly paymaster R. N."[5] It must be unusual for a graveyard inscription to contain an untruth but the fact is that Alfred's grandfather never was a paymaster in the navy.

I will recount Alfred's grandfather's history so far as I have been able to discover it. His father, John Marshall, the headmaster of Exeter Grammar School, had three sons, two of whom became clergymen. Alfred's grandfather was the odd man out. Why he was considered (or considered himself) unsuitable for a clerical position, I do not know. My hypothesis is that he lacked the brain power needed for this particular occupation. He was born in 1780, but I have found no mention of him until the announcement (in the *Gentleman's Magazine*) of his marriage in 1810, when he was just under thirty years old. He is there described as "assistant paymaster-general at the Cape of Good Hope."

This position, to which he had obviously just been appointed, was that of assistant paymaster-general to the Cape garrison in South Africa, the permanent occupation of the Cape by the British having started in 1806. William Marshall and his bride set sail on 24 June 1810 and reached Cape Town on 1 October 1810. He held this position for several years, during which time four children were born, two of whom died as infants. One that survived was William, the father of

5. I have to thank Mr. Donald Rutherford of the University of Edinburgh for providing me with information on William Marshall's activities in Leith.

Alfred Marshall. Judging from the house in which he lived and other indications, it would seem that Alfred's grandfather was in the upper stratum of British society at the Cape.[6] However, sometime after March 1816, he gave up this position and went to Mauritius. Mauritius had been a French colony (called "Ile de France") but was captured by the British in 1810. At the end of the war in 1814, it became a British possession by the Treaty of Paris.

In Mauritius he first took a position in the commissary of police.[7] He then made an ill-fated move by purchasing, at a public auction in December 1817, the farm of the *batelage* or exclusive privilege of shipping and landing goods in the harbour of Saint Louis, for two years. Within a few months, William Marshall discovered that he had made a serious blunder. In a memorial addressed to the Acting Governor, dated April 1818, he explained that he could not pay the second installment of the sum he had bid and he asked for relief. His explanation for this debacle was that he had paid too high a price for the farm, approximately twice the sum for which it had been sold in previous years. He gave two reasons why he had done this. First, he had been "led to suppose by public report . . . that the Port would be kept open until the 1st March, 1820," whereas it was shut on 1 April 1818. Second, the bidding at the auction advanced in small sums which he had thought "the result of a fair competition" from which he had concluded "that if any other person could afford to give so much, [he] could do likewise." Economists will recognise this as a variant of the efficient-market hypothesis. However, he claimed that the bids above 17,500 Mauritius dollars (he paid 23,000 dollars) were not made by others who wanted to purchase the farm but by the government auctioneer and the price paid was not therefore "the result of a fair competition." In addition, some of his boats and implements were destroyed by a hurricane in March 1818. As a result, his expenses during the first year amounted to 60,000 dollars, while his receipts were 40,000 dollars.[8] The Mauritius dollar (a money of account) was worth about 4

6. See P. Philip, *British Residents at the Cape, 1795–1819* (Cape Town: David Philip Ltd, 1981), 267. Information was also provided by Professor Peter Wickins of the University of Cape Town.

7. Information provided by M. Ly-Tio-Fane of the Sugar Industry Research Institute, Mauritius.

8. William Marshall, "The Memorial of William Marshall of Port Louis," 6 April 1818, Colonial Correspondence—Mauritius CO 167/145, Public Records Office

shillings. His initial payment, plus first-year losses, therefore amounted to about £6,000 (a large sum of money in those days)[9] and this together with his living expenses apparently largely exhausted his capital.

It seems that the Acting Governor refused to forward his memorial to the Secretary of State for the Colonial Department unless he based his claim for relief solely on the losses from the hurricane. The next Acting Governor did, however, forward William Marshall's memorial with the comment that it was "reasonable . . . to afford Mr. Marshall some relief . . . there appearing no chance whatever, of Mr. Marshall being able to fulfill his Engagement." He added that "Mr. Marshall is represented to me as a diligent, respectable man, who was anxious to obtain Employment, but who, unfortunately, was not sufficiently informed at the time, of the exact extent of the concern into which he was entering."[10] One has the impression that Alfred's grandfather was not very smart.

How this matter was resolved I do not know. But in 1823 Alfred's grandmother died and his grandfather left Mauritius with his six young children. He settled in Leith in Scotland where he became a merchant. As was perhaps to be expected, this business venture does not appear to have been a success since by 1827 his occupation is given as a clerk.[11] He died in 1828, characteristically without having made a will, was buried with a false inscription on his gravestone, and was forgotten. It is not difficult to understand why Alfred Marshall's family did not keep his memory alive.

Custody of the children was given to John Bentall, a brother of their mother, and they went to Totnes in Devon where, according to

(PRO), London; *Idem.*, "The Memorial of William Marshall of Port Louis, Island of Mauritius," 31 December 1818, Colonial Correspondence—Mauritius CO 167/45, PRO, London.

9. Alfred Marshall tells us that the average income per head in the United Kingdom was about £15 in 1820 (Marshall, *Principles of Economics,* [London and New York: Macmillan, 1890], 45–46fn; *Principles of Economics,* C. W. Guillebaud, ed., 2 vols., 9th variorium ed., [London: Macmillan for the Royal Economic Society, (1890) 1961], 2:733).

10. Major General Darling to Earl Bathurst, 18 March 1819, Colonial Correspondence—Mauritius CO 167/45, PRO, London.

11. In the Edinburgh and Leith Directory, he is described as "merchant" in 1823–24 and 1824–25, as "merchant and clerk" in 1825–26, and as "clerk" in the issues for 1826–27 and 1827–28.

Mary Marshall, another brother took charge of them. What happened to these orphans who were to constitute Alfred Marshall's immediate family? The eldest was his father, the others consisted of an aunt and four uncles. I need add nothing to what I have already said elsewhere about that extremely disagreeable man, his father. But what of the others? Of Aunt Louisa, Mary Marshall tells us that Alfred Marshall was "devotedly fond . . . She made the care of her brothers and their families her first duty in life." Alfred Marshall owed a special debt to her (and so do we) since it was his belief that the summer holidays he spent with her saved his life after being overworked by his father during the rest of the year.[12]

Let us now consider his uncles, starting with Uncle Edward. Edward enlisted in the Royal Navy in January 1829, aged twelve, as volunteer first class. A year after his enlistment, he was made midshipman. In 1833, he was promoted to mate and in 1843 to lieutenant. He was made commander in 1853 and captain in 1857. He served on many stations, at the Cape of Good Hope, in the Mediterranean, and on the east coast of Africa among others, and in ships with such colourful names as *Thunderer, Thunderbolt, Snake,* and *Devastation,* and even one with the somewhat dubious name of *Sappho.* For three years, Commander Marshall was in charge of the *Virago* on the Pacific station. It will have been noticed that his career is similar to that of Horatio Hornblower in the C. S. Forrester novels and I believe the only reason that there never was an Admiral Edward Marshall was because he died, Captain Marshall, in 1862, aged forty-five.[13]

Next consider Uncle Henry. I know nothing of his early life but at the time of his marriage in 1854, when he was thirty-three, he was a merchant in Calcutta, India. He was still a merchant in India in 1858 but had returned to England by 1859, perhaps a result of the Indian Mutiny. He died in 1880 and was described in his will as a timber merchant. Uncle Henry was a businessman.

Next there is Uncle Thornton. In his teens he was apprenticed to a pharmacist and studied medicine at Guys Hospital, London. At the end of 1843, aged twenty-one, he applied for employment in the medical department of the army and was appointed an assistant surgeon. He

12. Pigou, *Memorials,* 2.
13. W. R. O'Byrne, *A Naval Biographical Dictionary* (London: O'Byrne Bros., 1861), 728; *Gentleman's Magazine* 13 N.S. (1862):794; for service records see ADM 9/431/2588, PRO, London.

served in New Zealand and Australia and was promoted to surgeon in 1855. There is not much to tell about him since he suffered from ill health and died in 1861, aged thirty-eight.[14]

We now come to the last member of this "clerical" family, Uncle Charles, the only one that Keynes mentions in the memoir and the most interesting of Alfred Marshall's uncles. He was, said Mary Marshall, "Alfred's favourite uncle." Certainly Alfred Marshall had good reason for gratitude. By providing Alfred with a loan, Uncle Charles played an important, perhaps decisive, part in making it possible for him to go to Cambridge to study mathematics, a step that would ultimately lead to his becoming an economist. It was also a legacy from Uncle Charles, according to the memoir, which enabled Alfred to make his visit to America in 1875. When I found that there were no legacies in Uncle Charles's will, I had doubts about whether Keynes was correct. However, I discovered that there was a letter in the Oxley Library in Brisbane written by Uncle Charles's widow to her solicitor complaining that Uncle Henry (the executor of the will) was paying the legacies out of income. Apparently there were legacies not mentioned in the will, perhaps contained in a letter.

Given the important part which Uncle Charles's financial assistance played in Alfred's life, Keynes adds that

> the story of the sources of this uncle's wealth, which Alfred often told, deserves a record. . . . Having sought his fortunes in Australia and being established there at the date of the gold discoveries, a little family eccentricity disposed him to seek his benefit indirectly. So he remained a pastoralist, but, to the mirth of his neighbours, refused to employ anyone about his place who did not suffer from some physical defect, staffing himself entirely with the halt, the blind and the maimed. When the gold boom reached its height, his reward came. All the able-bodied labourers emigrated to the gold-fields and Charles Marshall was the only man in the place able to carry on.[15]

14. A. Peterkin and W. Johnston, *Commissioned Officers in the Medical Services of the British Army, 1660–1960* (London: Welcome Historical Medical Library, 1968), 1:329; *A List of the Officers of the Army and the Corps of Royal Marines, on Full, Retired, and Half-Pay, 1859–60 and 1862–63; Gentleman's Magazine* 10 N.S. (1861):588; WO 17/577, 17/586, 17/595, 17/604, 17/613, 17/630, 17/631, 17/640, 17/649, 17/658, 17/679, 17/689, 17/699, 17/709, 25/3931, PRO, London.

15. Pigou, *Memorials*, 4.

Edgeworth thought this passage should have been omitted because behaviour based on an eccentricity had no general significance.[16] I think it should have been omitted because there is not a word of truth in it. Let us try to reconstruct the real story of Uncle Charles's life and of how he acquired his wealth. Mary Marshall in her notes for Keynes says that Uncle Charles "who disliked his brother William's control at Totnes . . . ran away and became a cabin boy." In the memoir, Keynes adopts the phrase and applies it metaphorically to Alfred who, he said, ran away "to be a cabin-boy at Cambridge and climb the rigging of geometry and spy out the heavens." But it seems likely that Mary Marshall's tale was true and that Uncle Charles really did run away and became a cabin-boy. I say this because, when he was twenty, we find his occupation given as "mariner" in the census of 1841.[17]

After 1841 I have found no reliable information about his activities until 1849, when he is recorded as owner (with Robert Campbell) of the sheep station Ellangowan on the Darling Downs in Australia.[18] According to one account, he arrived in Australia in 1847.[19] How he obtained the capital to buy his interest in this sheep station I do not know, perhaps in some business venture outside Australia or as the result of an inheritance. There is a description of a meeting with him, almost certainly in 1849, in reminiscences by John Watts, who was manager of a neighbouring property:

> We had a dispute with Ellangowan, then belonging to Mr. Charles Marshall, who had purchased it from the Forbes. . . . When we got to Ellangowan, Marshall was just preparing for shearing, and had to manage the washpool himself. Here we found him, and he said: "Oh, come up to the house and have a glass of grog and we will talk it over as soon

16. See the letter from F. Y. Edgeworth to J. M. Keynes, 30 August 1924, Keynes Memoir file, Marshall Library, Cambridge.

17. He is so described in the entry for the house of Thornton Bentall, Borough and Parish of Totnes, census of 1841.

18. Commissioner for Crown Lands, *Darling Downs Record Book, 1845–52,* New South Wales State Archives (NSWSA), Sydney; Crown Lands Office (CLO)/13 Queensland. Chief Commissioner for Crown Lands, *Darling Downs Record Book,* Register of demands made for leases to pastoral runs, 1848–65, Queensland State Archives (QSA), Brisbane.

19. See "Gooragooby" Dalveen, "Echoes of the Past: A Black Criminal," *Warwick Daily News* (Queensland), 26 March 1935.

as I have finished here." So in due course we found ourselves at the house, and it was arranged that the matter should stand over until after shearing but before this could be done Mr. Marshall had sold the station to J. Gammie.[20]

From 1849 on it is possible to give a very complete account of Uncle Charles's activities on the Darling Downs. In 1850 he became a joint owner of Glengallan with Robert Campbell.[21] In the same year he was appointed a justice of the peace, an indication of his standing among the pastoralists on the Darling Downs.[22] In 1852 he became sole owner of Glengallan.[23] Glengallan was a large sheep station of about sixty thousand acres with a grazing capacity for about eighteen hundred cattle and twenty thousand sheep.[24] The Reverend H. Berkeley Jones, who published a book about his travels in Australia, says this of his visit to Glengallan in 1852: "Mr. M. possesses a very valuable station, and in the course of a few years, with small capital and untiring perseverance, has accumulated nearly a lac of rupees."[25] In 1854 Uncle Charles brought in John Deuchar as a partner. Deuchar was a stock breeder with considerable experience; before joining Uncle Charles, he had been manager of a station owned by the Aberdeen Company. With Deuchar's assistance, Glengallan prospered and its stock became famous. Deuchar was, however, a flamboyant character and he (but not Uncle Charles) went bankrupt. The partnership was dissolved

20. John Watts, "Personal Reminiscences by John Watts," n.d., John Oxley Memorial Library, Brisbane, 24.

21. Commissioner for Crown Lands, *Darling Downs Record Book, 1845–52.*

22. T. Hall, *The Early History of Warwick District and Pioneers of the Darling Downs* (Warwick, n.d.), 60; *Votes and Proceedings,* New South Wales Legislative Council, 1856–71, 1:916–26, John Oxley Memorial Library (JOML), Brisbane; Archives Office (AO)/3256, AO/3257, NSWSA, Sydney.

23. Hall, *Early History,* 45; J. G. Steele, *Conrad Martens on Queensland: The Frontier Travels of a Colonial Artist* (Brisbane: University of Queensland Press, 1978), 60–65; Rev. B. Glennie, "The Australian Diary of Rev. B. Glennie, Jan. 16th 1848– Sept. 30th 1860," JOML, Brisbane, 15. In Steele will be found a number of reproductions of pencil sketches made by Martens of Glengallen in 1853. Some paintings of Glengallen by Martens were commissioned by Uncles Charles and Uncle Henry.

24. *Votes and Proceedings,* N.S.W. Legislative Council, 1854, v. 2, and 1859–60, vol. 3; Commissioner for Crown Lands, *Darling Downs Record Book, 1848–49;* Darling Downs Pastoral District, *N.S.W. Government Gazette,* 1848, 945–46.

25. Rev. H. Berkeley Jones, *Adventures in Australia in 1852 and 1853* (London: Richard Bentley, 1853), 164.

in 1869.[26] In 1873, Uncle Charles brought in W. B. Slade as partner. Slade also proved to be an excellent stock breeder but Uncle Charles died in 1874 and his interest in Glengallen passed to his widow. Marshall and Slade became Knighton and Slade when she remarried. There is no reason to doubt that Uncle Charles made a fortune. He married Charlotte Augusta Dring Drake in 1857, a daughter of General William H. Drake who, in 1871 became Sir William. At the time of his marriage, Uncle Charles was thirty-six; Charlotte was twenty.

How did this man who had run away to become a cabin-boy come to acquire his wealth? Alfred Marshall gives the answer. He had a sheep station on which he employed the halt, the blind, and the maimed (a "little family eccentricity," according to the memoir, although there is no evidence that any of Alfred's other relatives possessed it). At any rate, when gold was discovered in Australia, the workers on other stations left for the goldfields and Uncle Charles was the only man who was able to continue sheep farming, at least on the Darling Downs. It is an inherently improbable tale. Those working on a sheep station as shepherds or in other capacities were, in general, engaged in tasks which the halt, the blind, and the maimed could not perform. It is difficult to imagine what useful work a blind man riding his seeing-eye horse could do on a one-hundred-square-mile sheep station. But it is not necessary to insist on this. There are many reasons for thinking that this tale is a fabrication.

We should note first of all that by 1850, Uncle Charles was already a man of some substance, whereas the first payable gold discovery in Australia was not made until 1851. Second, the historical accounts of the sheep stations on the Darling Downs indicate that they all continued operating after gold was discovered. The number of sheep in New South Wales, Victoria, and Tasmania actually increased during the period of the gold boom and there is every reason to suppose that this was true on the Darling Downs (which was at this time in New South Wales).[27] Waterson says that in this period "the area exuded prosperity—1856 to 1866 was the golden age."[28] No doubt numbers

26. Hall, *Early History*, 36–38, 45–47; D. B. Waterson, *Squatter, Selector, and Storekeeper: A History of the Darling Downs, 1859–1893* (Sydney: Sydney University Press, 1968), 283; Glennie, "Diary," 17; CLO/8, CLO/13, QSA, Brisbane.

27. A. Barnard, *The Australian Wool Market, 1840–1900* (Melbourne: Melbourne University Press, 1958), 217.

28. Waterson, *Squatter*, 13.

of workers did go to the goldfields although, curiously enough, in the case of Glengallen, the only mention I have found of such a movement involves Uncle Charles himself. Nemeniah Bartley visited the Turon goldfields in 1851 and there met "Marshall, a son of the chief cashier of the Bank of England and his West Indian friend, Davson." "Son" is obviously a mistake for brother and the description of Alfred Marshall's father as "chief cashier of the Bank of England" is another example of that "little family eccentricity" of exaggerating their social position. Bartley adds: "Fearfully and wonderfully was the 'damper' compounded by Marshall and Davson; wedges of putty were digestible in comparison therewith";[29] from which we can infer that Uncle Charles was no weakling.

More important perhaps in undermining Alfred Marshall's tale is that it is inconsistent with all we know about the employment practices of this tough ex-seaman. He was a no-nonsense employer. In 1849, while he was still at Ellangowan, he accused George Munday at the Court of Petty Sessions of absconding from his service. Munday denied that he was Uncle Charles's servant and the case was dismissed. At the same time Samuel Bishop was brought before the court to answer Uncle Charles's complaint of "neglect of duty and insolence." It was held that the charge was not proven.[30] We get a more complete view of Uncle Charles's attitude from the correspondence with his new partner, W. B. Slade, written in 1873 and 1874 while on a trip to England, and now in the Oxley Library in Brisbane.

Uncle Charles emerges as a fair-minded man but one who, in his employment practices, was above all concerned with what he would gain from following one course of action or another. Just before he died he remarked that the number of hands employed seemed large for the quantity of stock kept and he hoped that there would be a considerable reduction.[31] In dealing with individuals he was sympathetic but businesslike. Here is an example:

> I often wonder whether you will be able to find work for old
> Pugh after he has finished the wool shed. I like the old fellow

29. N. Bartley, *Opals and Agates; or, Scenes under the Southern Cross and the Magelhans* (Brisbane: Gardina Gotch, 1892), 52.
30. *Moreton Bay Courier,* 29 December 1849.
31. C. H. Marshall to W. B. Slade, 26 June 1874, Glengallen Estate, *Private Papers,* JOML, Brisbane.

very much and shall be sorry that he has left our employ. He is
mostly thoroughly trustworthy and can be depended upon in
an emergency. . . . Though of course if you have no work for
him you cannot help him.[32]

Most of the comments on employees in the letters relate to the
South Sea Islanders he had taken on and whose term of employment
was nearing its end. He wanted them properly treated:

> While in Brisbane I saw the Immigration Agent Mr. Gray,
> and it was arranged that on your sending down the South Sea
> Islanders on expiration of their respective terms, you should
> remit their 3 years' wages and he would see that they were
> properly cared for and not cheated by shopkeepers.[33]

In another letter he says that he had "promised the boys that if they
behaved well I would send them each a Medal."[34] He has eight medals
struck with their names engraved on them. He takes pains to see that
this is well done, thinks about getting them reproduced in a newspaper
"to show that the boys are not treated quite as slaves"[35] but apparently
decided not to do so because it would look like "ostentation."[36] He
comments: "They will be delighted to get their medals for good conduct, and I feel they deserve them."[37] As the South Sea Islanders had
been so useful, he hopes that some would return but if they did not,
that replacements would be obtained. If Slade intended to do this, Uncle Charles gave some words of advice, " go down directly . . . the
ship arrives and select them yourself. If you trust an agent to pick them
you will get a very inferior lot."[38] This suggestion seemed designed to
avoid employing "the halt, the blind, and the maimed."
    It is easy to see from this correspondence why Uncle Charles was
able to build up a fortune. In his letters he is concerned with every
detail of the business, shows great shrewdness, and his aim is always
to increase the profits of the firm. Thus he notes that "documents of
importance, and especially Bills at sight" should be sent "by the
shorter route via Brindisi. The week's interest on £1,000 is 0/8 at 8 per

32. *Ibid.*, 4 September 1873.   36. *Ibid.*, 27 October 1873.
33. *Ibid.*, 18 April 1873.   37. *Ibid.*, 29 October 1873.
34. *Ibid.*, 28 August 1873.   38. *Ibid.*, 11 July 1873.
35. *Ibid.*, 3 October 1873

cent and of course bears no proportion to the difference in rate of postage."[39] One quotation gives an excellent illustration of his thinking:

> I hope you will not be obliged to let the number of sheep go down too low from sales. The clip forms so important a source of our profits that we must not let it fall off if possible. I begin to think it is a mistake culling sheep only on account of coarse wool. During the last two years I have observed that coarse sheep have paid much better than fine ones. The C wool fetches very nearly, and often quite as much as that marked A (principally on account of its greater length of staple) and the difference in weight of the fleeces . . . is fully in favour of C quality. The carcase is also of course larger and so more valuable. Of course it would not do to dispense with the stud flocks on account of the sale of rams, but I feel quite sure that for the general flocks the coarser long wool quality of sheep will pay best . . . and of course our great object in sheep farming is to keep the stock that *pays best.*[40]

Uncle Charles was a good businessman but he would have made a good economist. In May 1874 he reports that the Hogarth Meat Preserving Company, in which he has an interest, had been losing money and that instructions had been sent to Australia to stop working: "At present prices of stock, and tin [*sic*] meat in England, it is impossible to carry on meat preserving without loss." He believes that other meat-preserving establishments in Australia will also stop working. He concludes: "The effect of this will not be to make meat rise in England, for South America will supply the market but stock must fall [in Australia]." He adds that he is telling Slade this "in order that you may act cautiously in buying."[41]

Alfred Marshall, discussing joint supply, has this to say in the *Principles:*

> the price of mutton in the wool-producing districts of Australia was at one time very low. The wool was exported; the meat had to be consumed at home; and as there was no great demand for it, the price of the wool had to defray almost the

39. *Ibid.*, 24 September 1873.
40. *Ibid.*, 15 April 1874 (emphasis in original).
41. *Ibid.*, 13 May 1874.

whole of the joint expenses of production of the wool and the meat. Afterwards the low price of meat gave a stimulus to the industries of preserving meat for exportation and now its price in Australia is higher.[42]

My feeling is that Uncle Charles would have done as well and perhaps better.

It seems clear that Uncle Charles built up his fortune over a long period as a result of hard work, intelligence, perseverance, and attention to detail. Apart from his pastoral activities (which must have given him the bulk of his income), he had other business interests in Australia, of which the meat-preserving company already mentioned is one example. He dealt in land, had rental property in the neighbouring town of Warwick, and had investments in Australian mining companies. These companies do not seem to have been a profitable investment for him and he comments: "My tin [speculation] has proved the truth of what I have held as a golden maxim namely 'never to invest in anything that you do not understand and have no part in its control.'"[43]

Claude Guillebaud has remarked on Alfred Marshall's uncanny ability to detect error in any statement about economic facts. Why then did he accept and repeat a story so improbable on its face and, as we now know, at variance with Uncle Charles's actual behaviour? I think I may know the answer. Even before the discovery of gold there had been a severe shortage of labour on the Darling Downs and the owners of sheep stations there petitioned for the resumption of transportation which had been stopped in 1840.[44] Transportation was in fact resumed in 1849, and in 1850 it became possible for those running sheep stations on the Darling Downs to secure convict labour. Uncle Charles did not hesitate. In 1850 he is listed for seven "exiles," in 1851 for one more, and 1852 for another three, including one taken on by Robert Campbell in 1850. In addition, four passports for the employment of "ticket-of-leave" men were issued to him in 1851 and two more in 1852. He was probably also able to use the "ticket of leave" men as-

42. Marshall, *Principles of Economics*, 9th ed., 1:389.
43. Marshall to Slade, 15 April 1874.
44. *Moreton Bay Courier*, 25 January 1851; *Sydney Morning Herald*, 3 February 1851.

signed earlier to Robert Campbell.[45] A "ticket-of-leave" was a document issued to a convict allowing him to work for wages in the private sector, thus preparing himself for economic self-sufficiency after the expiration of his sentence. It was a status that a convict would normally not wish to imperil by, for example, leaving his district without a police pass.

So in the years immediately following the gold discovery of 1851, when the drain on local labour would have been most intense, a substantial portion of the labour force employed by Uncle Charles at Glengallan consisted of convict labour. This, I believe, is what the tale of "the halt, the blind, and the maimed" was intended to conceal. In reality, Uncle Charles did not employ the halt but the haltered. It becomes easy to understand why Uncle Charles's workers did not go to the goldfields. Did Alfred Marshall know that what he was saying was a falsification? It is not possible to be certain but I would regard it as very likely. The family would not wish it to be known that Uncle Charles made the fortune from which Alfred (and other family members) benefited in part through the employment of convict labour.

What I find curious about this concealment through falsehood in the case of Alfred Marshall's family is that, to me, the truth is not discreditable. Two of his uncles were successful businessmen—one very successful—and another uncle had a distinguished career in the navy. The fourth died at too early an age to assess his achievement but we have no reason to suppose that it would not have been highly creditable. The story of these orphans who were Alfred Marshall's uncles is one in which he could take pride, even though there was not a clergyman among them. I should add something about Alfred Marshall's brothers and sisters. His elder brother, Charles William Marshall, became manager of the Bengal Silk Company in India. His sister, Agnes, went to live with Alfred's elder brother in India.[46] His younger brother Walter died while a student at Cambridge. His sister Mabel fell in love with a young army officer but her tyrant father would not allow her to marry him. She ultimately married the Reverend E. D. Guillebaud. Our feelings of indignation at the high-handed action of Alfred Marshall's father may be somewhat assuaged by the thought

45. Commissioner for Crown Lands, *Darling Downs Record Book, 1845–52*, Register of Exiles and Register of Ticket-of-Leave Holders.
46. I am indebted for this information to Rita McWilliams Tullberg.

that this gave us Claude Guillebaud and the variorum edition of the *Principles*.

One aspect of this story should be noted. As all of Alfred Marshall's uncles spent most of their time abroad, he would have had little contact with them, certainly while he was young. Apart from his summer holidays with Aunt Louisa, he would have had no relief from the oppressive control of his father. That he managed to survive his father's harsh regime with the fire of his genius still alight must have been due to some inner strength, to something within him. I now turn to a possible source of that something.

Keynes's discussion of Alfred Marshall's ancestry is slight and is largely confined to the clerical connections of his great-grandfather, John Marshall, and the family of Mary Hawtrey. The neglect of the ancestry of Alfred Marshall's mother is easy to explain. But the failure to mention his grandfather, William Marshall, had the unfortunate result that no attention was paid to his wife, Alfred Marshall's grandmother. Her name was Louisa Bentall.

That Alfred Marshall's family benefited in a material way from the Bentall connection is clear. John Bentall, a stockbroker, the brother of Louisa, was made guardian of her children after the death of their father in Leith, and they went to live in Totnes with another brother, presumably Thornton Bentall, a banker. Alfred Marshall's father worked as a clerk for John Bentall before joining the Bank of England. The Bentalls no doubt aided Alfred's father and uncles in ways unknown to us. But Alfred Marshall may have benefited from the Bentall connection in a much more important way. It seems possible that he inherited through Louisa Bentall those traits of character and intellect which enabled him to withstand his father and to play a major role in building modern economics.

The Bentalls were distinguished over the centuries by the possession of considerable business ability. Robert Burnel, Lord Chancellor of Edward I, in the thirteenth century, was a member of the family. He was "a self-made man who . . . built up a widespread complex of landed property by purchase, exchange, the conversion of loans, and other ways in the course of a prosperous career."[47] It reminds one of Uncle Charles. One of his purchases was an estate in Benthall, Shropshire, and the family (or some of them) seems to have taken the

47. A. R. Wagner, *English Genealogy* (Oxford: Clarendon Press, 1960), 223–24.

name of Benthall which, in the course of time, became Bentall. Louisa Bentall's father (Alfred's great-grandfather) was a banker. In modern times the department store Bentall's of Kingston near London and Bentall and Co., the agricultural machinery company, were founded by members of the family.[48] A more recent example is Sir Paul Benthall who had a successful career in India and was later chairman of the Amalgamated Metal Corporation and a director of Chartered Bank, the Royal Insurance Company, and other financial concerns in England. A member of the family bought the old family home, Benthall Hall, in Shropshire, in 1934, and in 1958 it was given to the National Trust.[49] But Louisa Bentall had more to contribute. Her grandfather was John Bentall, wine cooper and merchant of Colchester in Essex and his wife was Elizabeth Thornton.

Elizabeth Thornton's family was even more distinguished in business and public affairs than the Bentalls. They were merchants, bankers, members of parliament, and some of them were among the most prominent members of the Clapham Sect. Economists will immediately recognise that this means that Alfred Marshall was related to Henry Thornton, author of *The Paper Credit of Great Britain,* of whom Friedrich Hayek has said that "in the field of money the main achievement of the classical period" was due to him.[50] Both Alfred Marshall and Henry Thornton were descendants of Robert Thornton, Rector of Birkin, Yorkshire, in the seventeenth century. Robert Thornton was Alfred Marshall's great-great-great-grandfather and Henry Thornton's great-great-grandfather. Ralph Hawtrey had a similar distant relationship with Alfred Marshall. Keynes, in the memoir as originally published, said of this relationship with Ralph Hawtrey, "there is not much in the true theory of money which does not flow from that single stem." How much stronger a statement could have been made had Keynes known that Alfred Marshall was also related to Henry Thornton. I should add that this comment was omitted when the mem-

48. C. Herbert, *A Merchant Adventurer: Being a Biography of Leonard Hugh Bentall, Kingston-on-Thames* (London: Waterflow, 1936); P. K. Kemp, *The Bentall Story, Commemorating 150 Years Service to Agriculture, 1805–1955* (privately printed, Maldon, 1955).

49. National Trust, *Benthall Hall, Shropshire* (Plaistow: Curwen Press for the National Trust, 1976).

50. H. Thornton, *An Enquiry into the Nature and Effects of the Paper Credit of Great Britain,* F. A. Hayek, ed. (London: G. Allen and Unwin, [1802] 1939), 36.

oir was reprinted in 1933 in *Essays in Biography*, perhaps because Keynes had found that neither Alfred Marshall nor Ralph Hawtrey were related to the author of *The Treatise on Money* (published in 1930). That Alfred Marshall and Henry Thornton were related has another consequence. E. M. Forster was the great-grandson of Henry Thornton and so Alfred Marshall was also distantly related to him— and thus to a member of those "trustees of civilization," the Bloomsbury Group.[51] Had Keynes known about this relationship, I feel sure that he would have added a page or perhaps two to the memoir, although what he would have made of it I cannot imagine. That Keynes would have found the true facts of Marshall's ancestry intensely interesting is not open to doubt. He may have been fascinated by "The Great Villiers Connection" but, as he tells us in the preface to *Essays in Biography*, what he really took pride in was "the solidarity and historical continuity of the High Intelligentsia of England."[52]

The exclusion of the Bentalls and the Thorntons from their family history in Alfred Marshall's generation is extremely hard to explain. His father, his aunt and his uncles owed a great debt to the Bentalls for looking after them as children and in helping them to get started, while they should have been aware of the Thornton connection since one of Alfred's uncles was named "Thornton." Unlike their close relationship with the Bentalls, Alfred Marshall's immediate family did not seem to have had a great deal to do with the Hawtreys and the clerical Marshalls apart from Aunt Louisa in Devon, who was in touch with them.[53] The only explanation I can give for this neglect of the Bentalls and Thorntons is that it was the result of the erasure of Alfred Marshall's grandfather from family memory. I know nothing about his early life, but my guess is that he started his career with capital derived from his father and his wife and that this was dissipated in ill-

51. According to R. F. Harrod, this was how Keynes thought of the Bloomsbury Group (Harrod, *The Life of John Maynard Keynes* [New York: Harcourt and Brace; London: Macmillan, 1951], 194).

52. J. M. Keynes, *Essays in Biography*, reprinted in *Collected Writings of John Maynard Keynes*, D. Moggridge, ed. (London: Macmillan for the Royal Economic Society, [1933] 1972), 10:xix.

53. F. M. Hawtrey, *The History of the Hawtrey Family*, in 2 vols. (London: G. Allen, 1903), 1:107. The only other connection of Alfred's immediate family with the Hawtreys I have found is that when Thornton Marshall applied for admission to Guy's Hospital he was recommended by the Reverend Dr. Hawtrey of Eton.

considered business ventures with the result that he ended up as a clerk in Leith. Failures would not be talked about in the Marshall family and as a consequence all knowledge of his wife, her family, and illustrious relations would be lost.

The effect of all these errors and omissions in Keynes's references to Alfred Marshall's family has been to give a very misleading picture of the circumstances in which Alfred Marshall was brought up. For example, Skidelsky said recently in his biography of Keynes that "Marshall was yet another product of the well-connected clerical families which colonised English intellectual life."[54] Alfred Marshall was not a member of a cultivated, comfortable and well-connected clerical family, with his father's occupation an exception, as Skidelsky seems to suppose. Alfred's home life was such as would have left most people unfit for serious scientific work. Keynes reports in the memoir that E. C. Dermer, a schoolfellow of Alfred's, said that Alfred Marshall as a schoolboy was "small and pale, badly dressed, looked over-worked . . . cared little for games, was fond of propounding chess problems, and did not readily make friends." I do not doubt the accuracy of this description. Alfred Marshall, in a letter, refers to his father's "extremely severe discipline,"[55] and what this implied in Victorian England I shudder to imagine. No doubt his father's "extremely severe discipline" left permanent scars. Nonetheless, while still a boy, Alfred Marshall rejected the fake scholarship and unscientific attitude of his father, stood his ground, and made up his mind to go to Cambridge to study mathematics. When he reached Cambridge, "the great mother of strong men," it must have seemed like heaven. The memoir tells us nothing about Alfred's undergraduate years except that, when completed, he proposed to study molecular physics. My feeling is that the ideas to which he was exposed when he arrived in Cambridge must have played a very important part in forming his views on the proper conduct of scientific work. If this is so, a detailed study of his life as an undergraduate would help us to understand better many of his basic positions. Be that as it may, what is striking to me about the story I have told is the ability of Alfred Marshall to overcome

54. R. Skidelsky, *John Maynard Keynes: Hopes Betrayed, 1883–1920* (New York: Viking Penguin, 1986; London: Macmillan, 1983), 40.

55. R. H. Coase, "Alfred Marshall's Mother and Father," *History of Political Economy* 16 (1984):523–24. [See chap. 8 in this volume.]

very unfavourable family circumstances and to emerge, not unscathed, for some aspects of his character are not admirable, but with the power of his intellect intact and with that devotion to scholarship which can serve as a model to us all and which, in his case, was to produce the *Principles of Economics*.

Addendum: Did Marshall know where he was born?

There is no question about where Alfred Marshall was born. Civil registration of births in England started in 1837 and Marshall was born in 1842. So anyone can get a copy of his birth certificate. This shows that he was born at 66 Charlotte Row, Bermondsey. Keynes, however, in his Memoir on Alfred Marshall says that he was born in Clapham, roughly the equivalent of saying that he was born in Westchester whereas he was really born in the South Bronx.

Did Marshall know that he was not born in Clapham but in Bermondsey? Someone born in the South Bronx who wished to preserve the idea that he was born in Westchester but was unwilling to tell a lie would, I believe, say that he was born in New York. So when I found that in the census for 1871 Marshall gave his place of birth as Surrey, the county in which both Bermondsey and Clapham were situated, I was inclined to think that "Marshall may have known he was not born in Clapham, was willing to conceal his real place of birth, but was unwilling to tell a lie" (see page 121 above).

However, after chapter 8 was first published, I obtained the entry for Alfred Marshall in the census for 1881, and found that it contained some surprising information. In that census, Alfred Marshall was said to have been born neither in Bermondsey nor in Clapham and not even in Surrey. His birthplace is there given as Sydenham (Kent). Sydenham in Kent was the place where Marshall's parents lived in between Bermondsey and Clapham. It is difficult to know what to make of this. Indeed, the census-taker later crossed out Kent and substituted Devon, which suggests some confusion on the part of his informant over where Marshall was born. Marshall in 1881 was married and Principal of University College, Bristol, and it seems likely that the informant was either his wife, Mary Marshall, or her brother-in-law, who was staying with them at the time. Whoever it was, Marshall had certainly given her (or him) a false idea of where he was born.

We now come to the census of 1891. Alfred Marshall was by then living in Cambridge where he was Professor of Political Economy.

In that census, Marshall's birthplace is given as Croydon, Surrey. Croydon is situated about ten miles south of London Bridge, is some miles south of Bermondsey, Sydenham and Clapham, and is a place in which, so far as I know, Alfred Marshall never lived. Apart from their servant, Sarah, no one was living with the Marshalls at the time of the 1891 census. I therefore assume that Mary Marshall was the informant of the census-taker, an assumption strengthened by the fact that her occupation is stated to be "Lecturer University," a detail that Alfred would have been unlikely to give. How Mary Marshall came to believe that Alfred was born in Croydon is a mystery. What is evident is that Alfred concealed from her his real place of birth.

Did Alfred Marshall know where he was born? My own opinion is that he did and that the changing place of birth in the 1881 and 1891 censuses was due to his vagueness in giving information about it to his wife. But the entries in the censuses for 1901, 1911, and 1921 are still to come and they can be expected to throw more light (or perhaps more darkness) on this question.

TEN

The Appointment of Pigou as Marshall's Successor

In the course of an extremely interesting article on the part played by British economists in the Tariff Reform Campaign of 1903, A. W. Coats suggested that "there is reason to believe that the events of 1903 may have directly influenced the choice of A. C. Pigou as successor to Alfred Marshall at Cambridge, a decision that ensured the preeminence of economic theory at the leading academic centre of British economics."[1] And later, he put the same point in the form of a hypothetical question: "Is it, then, too much to suggest that but for the tariff reform debate of 1903, the election of 1908 might have gone differently?"[2] H. S. Foxwell, who was a candidate for Marshall's chair, seems to have believed that this may have been the case.[3] It is, however, my belief that, in the events which led to the selection of Pigou instead of Foxwell in 1908, the roles played by each man in the tariff controversy were relatively unimportant. The decision to appoint

Reprinted from the *Journal of Law and Economics* 15 (October 1972):473–85. © 1972 by The University of Chicago.

I would like to acknowledge and to express my thanks for the assistance I received in the research leading to this article from Mr. Piero Sraffa and the staff of the Marshall Library in Cambridge, to Mr. James Claydon of the Cambridge University Library, and to Mr. K. Carpenter of the Kress Library of Business & Economics in the Harvard Graduate School of Business Administration. I am grateful to Mr. Paul Sturges of the Institute for Historical Research in London for drawing my attention to the diaries of J. N. Keynes, now in the Cambridge University Library. I am indebted to Professors George J. Stigler and Aaron Director for comments on an earlier draft of this article.

1. A. W. Coats, "Political Economy and the Tariff Reform Campaign of 1903," *Journal of Law and Economics* 11 (1968):181, 225.

2. *Ibid.*, 228.

3. See Audrey Foxwell, who was no doubt expressing her father's opinion, in *Herbert Somerton Foxwell: A Portrait* (Harvard Graduate School of Business Administration, Kress Library of Business & Economics, 1939), 9.

Pigou would, I believe, have been the same had the tariff controversy of 1903 never occurred. The purpose of this article is to explain why I hold this view.

Alfred Marshall was not one of the electors for the professorship in political economy, but it is obvious that his opinion about who should be appointed as his successor would carry great weight. In fact, Marshall apparently did everything in his power to ensure that Pigou was selected. I would not wish to suggest that the electors, left to themselves, would not have selected Pigou—they might well have done this—but Marshall's active support for Pigou must have told heavily in his favour.

Marshall was, of course, deeply concerned about the future of economics, and particularly Cambridge economics, and, given his temperament, it is unthinkable that he would not exert himself to the full to secure the election of the candidate who, in his view, would do most for Cambridge economics. If we study the relations of Marshall with Pigou and Foxwell, it seems to me that the events before 1903 and in the years after form part of a continuous story with no trace of any change brought about by the tariff controversy. Marshall's preference for Pigou is clearly foreshadowed before 1903. If the events of that year had any effect on Marshall, it could only have been to strengthen an opinion already formed.

Foxwell was, of course, an old colleague of Marshall's at Cambridge (he had in fact been one of the electors when Marshall was appointed to the chair of political economy in 1884). Pigou did not enter the picture until about 1899. On December 11, 1899, John Neville Keynes records in his diary that he and his wife (Florence) "dined with the Marshalls meeting Carter of Oxford, the Ryles and Pigou of King's." Pigou was then a student and it seems probable that one of Marshall's aims in arranging the meeting was to draw J. N. Keynes's attention to Pigou. In this Marshall was no doubt successful but in other respects the meeting was less happy. J. N. Keynes adds in his diary (a very typical reference on his part to Marshall): "Marshall is the most exasperating talker I know. He will agree with nothing you say & argues & dogmatises so as to drive one wild. He is a pro-Boer & kept making innuendoes, but without success, to draw us into argument on the subject. Florence said she agreed with absolutely nothing he said all through the evening."

Marshall had for some time felt the need for a young lecturer who would give an introductory course on economics. In a letter to J. N. Keynes written early in 1899, after referring to other problems, he said: "After these the most urgent need for the Board—& may become the most urgent of all—is, in my opinion, the need for a young lecturer on economics, who has time and strength to do drill work for men of medium ability. I cannot do that without neglecting other work that is more important; and it is not done. If such a man could be had, I should cease to give a general course, and give more specialized advanced courses."[4] Three months after the disastrous dinner, Marshall revealed his intentions with regard to Pigou. He said in a letter to J. N. Keynes:

> When the Moral Science Board was discussing its needs at the last meeting, I was under the impression that a movement for raising the Fellowships of Professors under the new statutes at St. Johns to £200 had fallen through. So I urged the Board to represent that another lecturer in addition to Foxwell was needed. But to my surprise I heard yesterday from the Bursar that he had paid £200 into my account. So I am at once reviving old schemes for action, on my own hook, wh[ich] I had set aside.[5]

What Marshall had in mind was that, instead of asking the university to pay for another lecturer, he would pay the salary of the lecturer himself (as, in fact, Marshall did for several lecturers over a number of years). The lecturer he had in mind was Pigou:

> I am now inclined to think that the ideal man is at hand:— Pigou. But he would hardly be ripe for lecturing in 1900–1: and I have not said anything to him about it yet. I have some thoughts of asking Bowley to give a course of about ten lectures on statistics and statistical method, with special reference to his own subject—U.K. wages. His work in that seems to grow in excellence and in general favour. But as the loose cash has been jingling in my pocket for less than 24 hours, I am not ready to "say something and stick to it."

4. Letter from Alfred Marshall to J. N. Keynes, 2 February 1899, on file in the Marshall Library, Cambridge, as Keynes 1 (letter no. 115). Letters in the Marshall Library are hereinafter cited by file name and letter number.
5. Letter from Alfred Marshall to J. N. Keynes, 4 March 1900, Keynes 1 (116).

The letter ends with another reference to Pigou: "I had Pigou in my mind at last Board meeting: but I had not then seen much of his papers. I have seen a good deal since then; & I think he is thoroughly satisfactory."

Foxwell did not approve of Marshall's intention to ask Pigou to give introductory lectures and does not seem to have welcomed the proposal that Bowley should lecture. At any rate, it was difficult to make arrangements which were satisfactory to Foxwell. J. N. Keynes apparently wrote to Marshall, relaying an objection from Foxwell to the proposed hour at which Bowley was to lecture since Foxwell was himself lecturing at that hour. Marshall replied, asking that his letter should be passed on to Foxwell:

> The choice of hours for Bowley's lectures was very difficult, and was long and often discussed before a final decision was taken. Twelve o'clock seems best for lectures designed, as Bowley's are, to catch some men who are not reading economics for any Tripos. On the whole it is best for Historical men, who will form his largest single contingent in all probability, and unless my untrustworthy memory has played me another trick, Foxwell agreed that Bowley should clash with his 12 o'clock than with his 11 o'clock lectures. . . . So though I much regret the clashing, I do not see how to change except for the worse. Taking account of everything, I see no reason for thinking that the conclusion originally reached with so much pains, could ever have been improved on; & change now would be an evil in itself.[6]

Marshall's letter (and also one from Bowley) were sent to Foxwell. He replied to J. N. Keynes: "Many thanks for the trouble you have taken. I did not expect much success with Marshall; his arrangements are always the best possible & the result of infinite calculation!" But later in the letter Foxwell indicates his fear that Bowley's lectures might draw off the better students from his own course and he also refers to Pigou's new course:

> It is perfectly true that I should prefer Bowley to lecture at 12 rather than at 11 on those days. But it is not the case that I only get beginners at my general lectures: & I much prefer a

6. Letter from Alfred Marshall to J. N. Keynes, 6 October 1900, Keynes 1 (121).

salting of the better class of men: but I almost fancy that Marshall does not like them to come to me: for we have had a good many differences on these matters: culminating in his having engaged Pigou to deliver an elementary course: a man, of all I have known, least qualified to deal with a general class, as he is such a prig![7]

It will not come as a surprise to learn that making the arrangements for Pigou's lectures proved to be even more troublesome than it was for Bowley's. J. N. Keynes records in his diary for May 20, 1901: "Marshall is putting on Pigou as a Lecturer in Political Economy and the relations between him & Foxwell are very strained. I am having rather lengthy letters from Marshall on the subject." The character of this correspondence can, I think, be gathered from an extract from a letter sent by Marshall to J. N. Keynes, two days after this diary entry:

My own view is that there is some, though not great, harm in Pigou's lectures clashing with Ward's; & there is no real harm at all in their clashing with Foxwell's course. But if I propose

7. Letter from H. S. Foxwell to J. N. Keynes, 6 October 1900, Keynes 1 (40). Foxwell's unfavourable view of Pigou never seems to have changed. In a letter to W. R. Scott, 24 November 1926 (in Kress Library of Business & Economics), Foxwell said, with reference to Pigou's election to the British Academy: "As to Pigou, I promised to vote for him, much against my principles, for he is the last Economist I wish to see in any position where he could influence economic study. He has ruined it at Cambridge where complaints are incessant and you have probably seen the letter of Benn in the Times. Let someone nominate him who believes in him: it is bad enough for me to swallow the necessity of a vote agst [against] my deepest convictions."

The "letter" (actually article) of Sir Ernest Benn had appeared in the *Times* (London), 17 November 1926, 15–16, under the heading, "The Teaching of Economics, Examples from Cambridge, Issues Ignored." He complained of a lack of concern with the factors determining production and claimed that teaching concentrated on "distribution, division, taxation, or confiscation." He said that universities were "led by the nose by the Socialists." This led to an angry letter from Pigou denying political bias (*Times* [London], 19 November 1926, 15): "In the University of Cambridge, when a man is appointed to teach, enquiry is not made into his political opinions. . . . It is his duty to discover and teach what is true. . . . Where there is a difference of opinion among competent authorities it is his duty to let students know that this is so, and to put the issues fairly before them. These things are our duty at once to our University and to the spirit of science. For an outsider, ignorant of our practice and an amateur in our subject to charge us with violating it is an impertinence." So far as Pigou's colleagues were concerned, the charge was "untrue."

it, I shall be told again that I am "making an attack on him."
Time does not diminish my feeling of soreness. It seems to
me the story of the wolf & the lamb. Foxwell refused for 15
years to set papers, though he knew his not doing so was regarded by me as a great oppression. Then when at last I had
got arrangements wh[ich] would (i) free me from a disagreeable position (ii) enable the better sort of beginners to have
a systematic general course from which people who want
quick & really advanced teaching wld [would] be excluded &
(iii) enable a proper advanced course to be given; wh[ich] has
never been done yet—then he instantly cuts in before Pigou
& duplicates in anticipation a part of the course wh[ich] he
knows the Mo[ral] Sc[ience] Board accepted with [and?]
heartily approved a year ago, & wh[ich] Pigou has been preparing himself to give. Of course, they will not duplicate one
another. Pigou could not duplicate him & he has never done
what I hope Pigou will ultimately do. Pigou and I care for the
men: & I think I may truly say for the men only. Foxwell does
not seem able to understand this sort of aim, & hunts for some
other.[8]

In the light of these events in 1900 and 1901, it is hardly possible
to date Marshall's breach with Foxwell from 1903 (the date of the tariff
controversy). The fact is that Marshall's conception of economics and
his views on economic teaching were very different from those of Foxwell, as he explained in a letter to Foxwell in 1906. Marshall had previously suggested that Foxwell should lecture on economic history
and that D. H. Macgregor should take over some of Foxwell's economics lectures.[9] To this Foxwell apparently replied at length, defending his methods and declining to give the economic history lectures.
Marshall replied, in part, as follows:

I have always known you to be a most excellent expositor. I
have heard you speak many times; and have thought your
method, your style, your lucidity and your geniality most attractive to your hearers, and most effective on behalf of the

8. Letter from Alfred Marshall to J. N. Keynes, 22 May 1901, Keynes 1 (124).
9. Letter from Alfred Marshall to H. S. Foxwell, 7 February 1906, Marshall 3
(48).

cause you were advocating. And everything I have heard from others, whether young or old about you has been in the same direction. . . . Of course our ideals in economics are different. I have noticed that when a book or a pamphlet pleased you greatly you describe it as "scholarly" whereas I am never roused to great enthusiasm about anything wh[ich] does not seem to me thoroughly "scientific." . . . I think it is very important that there should be considerable diversities of temperament among the teachers of any subject, and especially of one of which the past and the present are so meagre, and the future is so uncertain as economics. . . . It seems to me that our differences in temper causes you to lay greater stress upon accuracy as regards facts, & me to insist more on their wrestling with difficult analysis and reasoning. . . . That you lay what seems to me insufficient stress on what, from my own particular point of view, is at once the most arduous, the least attractive and the most essential duty of the lecturer, is the *only* objection wh[ich], as far as I am aware, I have ever raised to your lectures. I regard your lectures as a most important part of our scheme; and I should regard your being displaced by young men as a great calamity. . . . I do not wish to urge you to undertake anything for wh[ich] you were not inclined. And I trust that we may agree finally on some plan that provides fuller introduction in economics for Freshmen, and enable you to do only what you wish and that in your own way, wh[ich] I quite recognize as being excellent of its kind.[10]

Marshall did not share Foxwell's antipathy to theory[11] or his enthusiasm for the historical approach in economics. And Foxwell's specialty, the history of economic thought, was to Marshall a subject of

10. Letter from Alfred Marshall to H. S. Foxwell, 12 February 1906, Marshall 3 (49).

11. Foxwell's comment on Allyn Young (who had been responsible for arranging the purchase of his second main book collection by Harvard University, now in Kress Library of Business and Economics) made after Young's death in a letter to W. R. Scott, 5 March 1929 (in Kress Library of Business & Economics), affords an example of his point of view: "I have seldom met anyone with whom I was in more general agreement. He perhaps attached more importance to pure theory than I should: but it was clear that his interest in it was steadily diminishing."

secondary importance.[12] Pigou, with his analytical approach to economic problems, his evident ability and high potential, was bound to appeal to Marshall. Given Marshall's views, and the seriousness with which he held them, it is inconceivable that he could have preferred Foxwell to Pigou as his successor.

The election of Marshall's successor took place in 1908. The electors were A. J. Balfour (who took no part in the proceedings), Lord Courtney, F. Y. Edgeworth, J. N. Keynes, J. S. Nicholson, R. H. Inglis Palgrave, V. H. Stanton, and W. R. Sorley. It is possible to form some notion of the events surrounding the election from the entries in the diary of J. N. Keynes:

> April 30, 1908. Interview with Marshall on the subject of the Election to the Political Economy Professorship. He speaks in the highest terms of Pigou and is clearly most anxious that he should be elected. He very distinctly does not want Foxwell to be elected. I very much wish that I were not an Elector.

> May 24, 1908. (Sunday). Next Saturday's election is hanging over me.

> May 27, 1908. Another interview with Marshall about the Political Economy Professorship.

> May 28, 1908. Palgrave has come to stay with us until Saturday.

> May 29, 1908. Today Nicholson has arrived to stay until Monday. Dinner Party—Palgrave, Nicholson, Dr. & Mrs. Tanner, Miss Jones, Dr. & Mrs. Bond, Florence, Margaret

12. See letter from Alfred Marshall to J. N. Keynes, 15 December 1908, Keynes 1 (137), in which he refers to Keynes having perhaps "a higher opinion of the importance of Foxwell's specialty to Cambridge" than he does. Earlier in 1902, Marshall had argued against making the paper on the history of economic theory compulsory in the Economic Tripos. "As to the position of the paper on history of economic theory, it is not necessary to argue now. The time for that will come when the details of a scheme are being elaborated. In Germany even academic students have almost abandoned the study of the history of economic theory: wh[ich] I think goes to the opposite extreme. But, knowing the tone of your mind, I feel sure that if you had been through what I have been through during the last twenty years, you would not wish to make it compulsory." Letter to J. N. Keynes, 6 February 1902, Keynes 1 (126).

and myself. Edgeworth (who is staying with Marshall) arrived at 9:30 to discuss tomorrow's election. We gathered that he had been sent by Marshall. Nicholson is intensely annoyed at what he thinks Marshall's unfairness to Foxwell.

May 30, 1908. V.C. [Vice Chancellor] 12–1.45 Political Economy Professorship Election. V.C., Lord Courtney, Palgrave, Edgeworth, Nicholson, Stanton, Sorley, and myself. Balfour did not come. The candidates were Ashley, Cannan, Pigou, Foxwell. Pigou was elected. I am extremely sorry for Foxwell. The whole thing has worried me very much. We dined with the Marshalls. Nicholson tells me that Marshall did not speak to him the whole evening.

May 31, 1908. Palgrave left yesterday. Nicholson will stay till tomorrow. We have enjoyed having them both & Margaret is full of admiration for Palgrave. I think Palgrave thoroughly enjoyed his visit, and even enjoyed the election, which I certainly did not. . . . Nicholson went in to see Foxwell. N is very severe on Marshall's manoeuvring, & I certainly do not think that Marshall has come out of the whole thing well.

June 1, 1908. Foxwell has expressed his intention of no longer lecturing in Cambridge. At the request of Dickinson & Pigou I went in to see him & to try and persuade him to reconsider the question. But I knew of course that he would not. It was one of the most painful interviews I have ever had. He had felt so confident of being elected that he had even begun to write his introductory lecture. He was quite cordial to me personally, but he was very excited, & at one time I thought he wd [would] break down. I felt and still feel exceedingly grieved on his account. He is very bitter against Marshall, and at this I do not wonder.

June 2, 1908. Foxwell told me yesterday that Marshall wrote him a very fulsome letter. Foxwell seems to have written rather frankly in reply.

June 14, 1908. I am a little tired. Perhaps I have not yet recovered from the Political Economy Professorship Election & all that it has brought in its train. It has been like a black cloud throwing its shadow over the whole of the term.

Marshall's "fulsome" letter was preserved by Foxwell:

> My dear Foxwell
>
> Pigou is in my opinion likely to be recognized ere long as a man of quite extraordinary genius: and I hoped that he wd [would] be elected to the Professorship. But I have just written a letter to the Master of Peterhouse expressing my gratitude to the Economics Board in general, & to him in particular, for his kindly treatment of me, & for their recent most generous resolution. And I should like to add a word of special gratitude to you, the oldest of my colleagues. We differ in opinion a good deal, and in temperament perhaps even more: so that some things, for which I cared much, seemed of little importance to you. But so far as these differences permitted, you have cordially, heartily, and generously supported and furthered my poor endeavours: sometimes even your genial friendship has perhaps induced you to go a little further in the direction in which I was working, than your own unbiassed judgment would have prompted. For all this I shall ever feel myself your debtor: I shall ever look back on our association with pleasant & grateful memories.
>
> I am sure that the University as a whole cherishes feelings of high regard for your whole hearted & very poorly remunerated services to it. I have not heard very much about it: the proceedings of the election between 12 and 2 yesterday have been kept absolutely secret; but I have heard no one, not even among the most enthusiastic supporters of Pigou's claims, who is not deeply pained by the thought that it has not been possible to crown your long and trusty work by a high reward.
>
> Please do not answer this just now: for you must be feeling sore. But I wish you to know that though I think the Electors, acting as trustees, did their duty, I share with all of them to whom I have spoken a deep sorrow on your account and an affectionate gratitude towards you.
>
> Yours in sympathy,
Alfred Marshall[13]

After the election, Henry Higgs, a pupil and friend of Foxwell, and at that time holding a position in the Treasury, suggested that money

13. Letter from Alfred Marshall to H. S. Foxwell, 31 May 1908, Marshall 3 (56).

should be raised to provide a professorship for Foxwell. Marshall's attitude to this proposal may be gathered from the following letter which he sent to J. N. Keynes:

Dear Keynes,
    There has been much more correspondence with Higgs. Its chief items on my side are
(1) a letter on the 9th resuming that part of my earlier letters which is entirely free from personal references, with an intimation that he may show it to any one
(2) a letter in continuation of that, written two days later to the effect that after consideration I have decided to urge him to enter into direct communication with you, on the grounds that:—"Keynes has perhaps a higher opinion of the importance of Foxwell's specialty to Cambridge than I have: he has not committed himself, as I have for the last forty years, to the opinion that Professors ought as a rule to resign at the age of sixty: partly for that reason he does not rate as highly as I do the evils which might arise from the precedent that would be set by founding a temporary Professorship on the understanding that Foxwell should be elected to it". I add other reasons connected with your personal qualities and your access to the Council by means informal as well as formal.
(3) Some letters marked "private" in which I have explained —in answer to his continual urging as to the importance of Foxwell's experience and judgment—that in my view the specialty of Cambridge teaching is to develop faculty, and to leave judgment to be formed later: and that a lecturer, who imposes his own judgment on youth, is not acting up to the best Cambridge tradition.
    [I did *not* add that as Foxwell's judgments while always confident, are apt to turn in opposite directions at six months notice, I have a fear of his judgments. On Finance in particular, one of the subjects proposed for him, I think his judgment is extraordinarily bad. He seems never to see more than one side of any complex question.]
    In Higgs' last letter but one he half asked my opinion as to the danger of there being "two Kings in Brentford". I replied that—though I had not mentioned the matter to Pigou—I felt sure there wd [would] be no trouble on that side: but that recent events had made me a little anxious on the other side. And I lifted the veil which covers those events

so far as to say "Foxwell wrote to me in June declaiming against electors, who had set aside the claims of friendship. I shuddered. I did not answer: but that was the forerunner of trouble."

Holding the opinions which you do, I think you would be right to provide(?) Higgs' scheme, provided it is so worked as not to undercut the expected appeal of the Cambridge Association on behalf of the Economic school. But at most I can be "benevolently" neutral. And if, as is possible, the question is raised whether a second Professorship—should there be one—should go to Clapham or Foxwell, I *must* speak for Clapham. I know you have not come much in his way, & do not have my eager admiration for him. But you must have heard rumours of his success as a lecturer. And I, who have seen a good deal of him, would always go to him as counsellor of the first weight in any difficult matter of judgment. I think his achieved work is of a very high order, full of individuality and strength. Even if Foxwell were still in his prime, I should hesitate to put him on the same intellectual level with Clapham.

I now leave the matter in your hands. For the sake of auld lang syne, I will stretch my academic conscience as far as it will go. But it has a stiff neck. It may be well that you should have learnt at an early stage how far my benevolent neutrality towards Higgs' proposal is likely to reach. I am clear that I cannot *actively* support it in its present form.

Yours very sincerely,
Alfred Marshall[14]

14. Letter from Alfred Marshall to J. N. Keynes, 13 December 1908, Keynes 1 (137). How much Foxwell knew about these efforts or of Marshall's views, particularly his preference for Clapham, I do not know. Foxwell later attempted to get Higgs elected to the British Academy and was disappointed that he did not succeed and particularly that Clapham was preferred to Higgs, as is shown in the following extracts from letters to W. R. Scott (in Kress Library of Business & Economics): "I am surprised to hear of the apathy about Higgs. There is no living economist more brilliant, & none to whom *English economics is more profoundly indebted*" (Foxwell to Scott, 18 November 1927); "[Higgs] is really a born scholar, with a touch of genius added. That such a common-place & in some respects objectionable person as Clapham should have been preferred to him is the greatest blow I have received since Marshall got me rejected at Cambridge & harder to understand. It seems to me that those who really devote themselves to public service, & do the real work, get laughed at for their pains, & only earn the familiarity that breeds contempt" (Foxwell to Scott, 10 June 1928).

Whether because of the lack of any active support from Marshall or for some other reason, the professorship for Foxwell was not established. So far I have concentrated on Marshall's views and actions. But, as I have indicated, it seems quite possible that Pigou would have been selected had Marshall not engaged in any "manoeuvring." A modern appointments committee would not have had any doubt, assuming that the choice was one between Foxwell and Pigou.[15] Pigou's writings (excluding writings in nonprofessional journals and book reviews) up to and including 1908 consisted of the following articles, all in the *Economic Journal:* "A Parallel Between Economic and Political Theory" (1902); "A Point of Theory Connected with the Corn Tax" (1902); "Some Remarks on Utility" (1903); "Pure Theory and the Fiscal Controversy" (1904); "Monopoly and Consumer's Surplus" (1904); "Professor Dietzel on Dumping and Retaliation" (1905); "The Unity of Political and Economic Science" (1906); "The Incidence of Import Duties" (1907); "Social Improvement in the Light of Modern Biology" (1907); and "Equilibrium under Bilateral Monopoly" (1908). In addition, during this period the following books by Pigou had been published: *Robert Browning as a Religious Teacher* (1901); *The Riddle of the Tariff* (1903); *Principles and Methods of Industrial Peace* (1905); *Protective and Preferential Import Duties* (1906); and *The Problem of Theism, and other essays* (1908). During this same period, Foxwell's published work consisted of an introduction of just over a page to the printing of a letter from Malthus to Ricardo in the *Economic Journal* (1907) and an article on "The Goldsmiths' Company's Library of Economic Literature" in Palgrave's *Dictionary of Political Economy* (1908).

J. N. Keynes does not tell us how the various electors voted. He is indeed silent about his own preference and although it seems probable

15. I have discussed the selection procedure in terms of a choice between Foxwell and Pigou, which was, I believe, the actual situation. However, a modern appointments committee would have found Edwin Cannan a strong candidate. His publications, among others, were *Elementary Political Economy* (1888, plus two editions in 1897 and 1903); *The History of the Theories of Production and Distribution in English Political Economy from 1776 to 1848* (1893, plus a second edition in 1903); *The History of Local Rates* (1896); his edition of Adam Smith's *Wealth of Nations* (1904) as well as numerous articles in the *Economic Journal* and elsewhere. But Cannan was not a Cambridge man and his interests in economics and his approach (not to mention his connection with the London School of Economics) would not have commended him to Marshall, and I do not think he received serious consideration as Marshall's successor.

that he supported Foxwell's candidature, it is by no means certain that he did not, in the end, vote for Pigou. Pigou was a close friend of his son, Maynard Keynes,[16] he was a visitor at his home, and although there is only one comment in the diary indicating an opinion about Pigou (on March 25, 1905), it is laudatory: "Yesterday and today I have been putting together questions in political economy for the Economics Tripos. Pigou has sent me his questions and I think them excellent."[17]

Unless J. S. Nicholson's attitude simply represented annoyance at Marshall's efforts to influence the electors, it would seem that he supported Foxwell's candidature.[18] But, as against Nicholson, F. Y. Edgeworth obviously supported Pigou.[19] It seems to me that no selec-

16. It was at Pigou's suggestion that Marshall wrote to Maynard Keynes on April 3, 1908, about the possibility of him returning to Cambridge to lecture on economics. And one of Pigou's first acts after being appointed professor of political economy was to invite Maynard Keynes to lecture, an offer which was accepted. Pigou paid the salary of £100. Marshall's letter was cautiously worded since Pigou was then still a candidate for the professorship. Marshall said that the proposal for Maynard Keynes's appointment would be made at the Economics Board on "(probably) June 3," that is, after the election. He felt obliged to add that this was "subject to some reserve in the case of one possible election to the Professorship," that is, if Foxwell was appointed instead of Pigou. Marshall's caution led J. N. Keynes to say, in a letter dated April 23, 1908: "Is not Marshall's letter in some respects very vague? I am glad you have not committed yourself at present." See *Collected Writings of John Maynard Keynes,* Elizabeth Johnson, ed. (1971), 15:13–15.

17. This is a sharp contrast to the references to Marshall in the diaries, which are uniformly hostile. Thus, in the month before the reference to Pigou, we find an entry (February 1, 1905) noting a meeting of the Economics Board which reads: "I really have not time to be on a Board of which Marshall is a member." This antagonism to Marshall should be borne in mind when interpreting J. N. Keynes's account of the election and Marshall's part in it. But it would be wrong to assume that this antagonism extended to Pigou. Nonetheless, I am inclined to accept as correct Foxwell's account of the voting given in the letter reproduced by Coats (see A. W. Coats, "The Appointment of Pigou as Marshall's Successor: Comment," *Journal of Law and Economics* 15 [1972]:493), which indicates that J. N. Keynes did in fact support Foxwell.

18. Nicholson's attitude tends to weaken somewhat the view that Foxwell's opposition to the "Professors' Manifesto" was an important element in the decision, since Nicholson was himself a signatory of the Manifesto. For a discussion of the "Professors' Manifesto," see A. W. Coats, "The Role of Authority in the Development of British Economics," *Journal of Law and Economics* 7 (October 1964):99–103.

19. Edgeworth had a high regard for Pigou as an economist. In his review of Pigou's book, *The Riddle of the Tariff,* he said: "The power with which he wields the organon of economic theory is of the highest promise. One who had observed the early

tion committee would have failed to be swayed by the fact that the professors of political economy at both Oxford and Cambridge were agreed that Pigou should be appointed. Even if Marshall had not taken steps to make his views clear, it seems improbable that the electors would not have wished to discover what they were.

Foxwell's daughter, in a passage to which Coats refers, does not go beyond saying that Foxwell, "partly as a result [of the tariff controversy], was not chosen as a successor to Marshall."[20] In fact, Marshall had many reasons for preferring Pigou to Foxwell, and their respective roles in the tariff controversy must have been one of the least important. C. W. Guillebaud, in his obituary of Foxwell, gives what I consider to be a correct assessment of the position: "A bimetallist and protectionist, an anti-Ricardian with a profound suspicion of abstract economic analysis on classical lines, Foxwell was opposed to much for which Marshall pre-eminently stood. It was understandable therefore that when Marshall retired from the Cambridge Chair of Political Economy in 1908, he should have favoured the candidature of his own pupil, A. C. Pigou."[21]

An account of why Pigou and not Foxwell was chosen to succeed Marshall draws attention to Foxwell's weaknesses. But it should be recorded that if Foxwell was an anti-Ricardian, he was also a champion of Jevons. He had a most extensive knowledge of economic literature. His assembling of the books which formed the basis of the Goldsmiths' Library in London and the Kress Library at Harvard has

---

work of Clerk Maxwell remarked: 'it is impossible for that man to go wrong in physics.' For 'physics' substitute what Jevons called the 'mechanics' of industry and trade, and the dictum might be applied without extravagance to the author of the analysis that we have mentioned." (*Economic Journal* 14 [1904]:65, 67.) Also compare Edgeworth's discussion of some of Pigou's contributions in his "Appreciations of Mathematical Theories," *Economic Journal* 17 (1907):221–26, reprinted in F. Y. Edgeworth, *Papers Relating to Political Economy* (1925), 2:321–26. Austin Robinson has described Pigou's method in his book, *Principles and Methods of Industrial Peace*, published in 1905: "He applied to economics the method of the philosopher, clarifying the issues, dissecting them and analyzing them, trying to see how different assumptions regarding the material might modify conclusions—the analytical method applied with great precision to an essentially qualitative argument." (Article on Arthur Cecil Pigou, *International Encyclopedia of the Social Sciences* (1968), 12:91.) It is easy to see that such an approach, handled with skill, would greatly appeal to Edgeworth.

20. Audrey Foxwell, *Herbert Somerton Foxwell*, 9.
21. *The Eagle* (St. John's College, Cambridge, 1935), 49 (218):275.

put all scholars of the history of economic thought in his debt. Foxwell was not a negligible figure. And his reservations about Pigou proved, in the event, to have some substance. It seems clear to me that Pigou did not fulfil the high hopes which Marshall had of him.[22] In many respects his influence on the development of economics has been bad. He seems to have lacked any feeling for the working of economic institutions.[23] But this does not mean that I consider the electors wrong in preferring Pigou to Foxwell. The difficulty that they faced in choosing a successor to Marshall was that there was no-one comparable to Marshall that they could have chosen.

My criticism of what was, in the context of Coats's article on the tariff reform campaign, a minor point, does not affect Coats's main argument or detract from the significance of his findings. Coats's study shows that the entry of the economists into the tariff controversy did not raise the quality of the debate, brought economics into public disrepute, was divisive within the academic community, and weakened the professional *esprit de corps* of economists. I agree with him that "one of the general lessons to be drawn from this example is that such quasi-political activities pose a threat to the economics profession." Nor would I wish to disagree with his surmise that "few economists would conclude that this is too high a price to be paid for the opportunity of shaping policy," although for most economists the word "illusion" should probably be substituted for "opportunity."[24]

22. That Marshall had reservations about the character of Pigou's work is clear from his comments on *Wealth and Welfare*. See Krishna Bharadwaj, "Marshall on Pigou's *Wealth and Welfare*," *Economica* 39 (1972):32.

23. Compare Austin Robinson's comment on Pigou: "He was never, as an economist, quick to see intuitively the order of magnitude and the potential dangers of economic forces, and he was never a person to whom colleagues turned instinctively for advice in the sphere of economic policy making." (Robinson, article on Pigou, *International Encyclopedia of the Social Sciences* 12:94.) For my own criticisms of Pigou, see R. H. Coase, "The Problem of Social Cost," *Journal of Law and Economics* 3 (1960):28–42.

24. Coats, "Tariff Reform Campaign," 229.

ELEVEN

Marshall on Method

We are inclined to think of the Cambridge economists working together at Cambridge in the period before the publication of Alfred Marshall's *Principles of Economics* as a "little band of brothers" and of a work such as John Neville Keynes's *Scope and Method of Political Economy* as embodying a Cambridge point of view. In fact this picture is incorrect. They were not a "little band of brothers." They did not have a common view. John Neville Keynes's references to Marshall in his diaries are uniformly hostile. For example: "Marshall's long disquisitions are very tiresome"; "Marshall said a good many silly things"; "I really have not time to be on a Board of which Marshall is a member."[1] All of which suggests a certain lack of sympathy with Marshall, not only with his manners but with his aims. And we know from other evidence that this inference is correct.

In the Marshall Library in Cambridge, there are a number of letters from Alfred Marshall to John Neville Keynes about the draft of Keynes's *Scope and Method of Political Economy* in which Marshall expresses reservations about Keynes's treatment of the subject. Not possessing the draft on which Marshall was commenting or Keynes's side of the correspondence, it is not possible to define their differences in view as sharply as one would like. That they did differ in their views is clear, as the following comment by Marshall, made after there had

Reprinted from the *Journal of Law and Economics* 18 (April 1975):25–31. © 1975 by The University of Chicago.

This article is a revised version of a paper presented at the meeting of the Midwest Economics Association, April 6, 1973. I am grateful to the staff of the Marshall Library in Cambridge and the Cambridge University Library who, as always, did everything possible to aid me in my researches.

1. The diaries of John Neville Keynes are in the Cambridge University Library. The quotations given are from entries on 8 October 1900, 29 May 1902, and 1 February 1905.

been some considerable exchange of correspondence, shows: "I find we differ more than I thought. I have expressed my views freely: you will I fear not be convinced."[2] What we do find in this correspondence is a fresh statement of Marshall's views, although not essentially different from what we find in the *Principles,* which is hardly surprising since both the *Scope and Method* and the *Principles of Economics* first appeared in 1890 and both would have been going through the press about the same time. Of course, when interpreting Marshall, one has to realise that he commonly becomes somewhat evasive whenever there is a hint of disagreement or controversy, a trait I attribute to the strict discipline exercised by his father when he was a child. But whatever the reason, Marshall often states his views in a way which tends to minimise differences in viewpoint.

In an early letter, Marshall states his general position:

I take an extreme position as to the *methods & scope* of economics. In my new book I say of *methods* simply that economics has to use every method known to science. And as to scope, I say "Economics is a study of mans actions in the ordinary business of life it inquires how he gets his income & how he uses it."

I extend income so as to include non-exchangeable "goods"; & generally I never discuss any line of division or demarcation except to say that Nature has drawn no hard & fast lines, & that any lines Man draws are merely for the convenience of the occasion: & shld never be treated as though they were rigid.

So I am not a good judge of the views expressed by your more orderly nature. I have simply indicated where we differ. But I don't think it will do for you to pay much attention to what I say. What Nicholson says is likely to be far more helpful to you.[3]

Marshall, I should add, does not appear to have had a high opinion of J. S. Nicholson.

Later in the correspondence, Marshall develops his views as to the

2. Letter from Alfred Marshall to J. N. Keynes, on file in the Marshall Library, Cambridge, as Keynes 3 (letter no. 70). Letters in the Marshall Library are hereinafter cited by file name and letter number.
3. Letter from Alfred Marshall to J. N. Keynes, Keynes 3 (66).

relation of induction and deduction in economics and sets out his notion of how economics should be presented to students.

You make all your contrasts rather too sharply for me. You talk of the inductive & the deductive methods: whereas I contend that each involves the other, & that historians are always deducing, & that even the most deductive writers are always implicitly at least basing themselves on observed facts. And in consequence you *first* allow to the inductive method pure and simple more by far than I shd allow to it, & similarly for the deductive method, and *afterwards* take back a great deal of what you have allowed by saying that all deduction involves induction & *vice versa*. Thus in the end you come to pretty nearly the same result as I shd: but you start by saying things that seem to me not true. It is a mere question of arrangement: but I think it is a very important one practically. I think the right order is *first* to emphasize the mutual dependence of induction & deduction, & *afterwards* to show in what kinds of inquiry the economist has to spend the greater part of his time in collecting arranging & narrating facts, & in what kinds he is chiefly occupied in reasoning about them & trying to evolve general processes of analysis & general theories which shall show the Many in the One & The One in the Many.

My second point is that you continually use the word *theory* where I shd use *analysis*. This seems to me in itself to cause confusion wh is increased by the fact that later on you exclude modern facts from history; & yet you do not boldly say that they are part of theory. If they are then I agree with you that a study of theory shd come before a study of history. But I do not myself like to put the case in this way.

My own notion is [and here Marshall is I take it describing how economics should be presented to students]

i. Begin with analysis, which is an essential introduction to all study of facts whether of past or present time, with perhaps a very short historical introduction.

ii. Go on to call to mind the students knowledge of the economic conditions in wh he lives. Show the relations in wh they severally stand to one another & carry analysis further, making it more real & concrete.

iii. Build up a general theory or process of reasoning applicable to Value Money Foreign Trade etc, with special

169

reference to the conditions in wh the student lives, & pointing out how far & in what ways, it can be made to bear on other conditions.
iv. Give a general course of economic history.

* * *

vi. Consider economical conditions in relation to other aspects of social life.
vii. Treat of the economic aspects of practical questions in general & social reform in particular.[4]

I have omitted step v. Marshall says of this, which he describes as "Return to economic theory and carry it further," that this may come almost anywhere and for some classes of student, may be omitted altogether.

The fact that Marshall moves quickly from a discussion of method to the question of how we should study economics, considered in quite a concrete way, is, I think, indicative of his attitude. He had little interest in what he termed "philosophical economics." And in a sense he can be said to have held no views on method. As A. C. Pigou has said: Marshall "would have nothing to do with controversies between deductive schools, inductive schools, historical schools and so on. There was work for all, and he welcomed all. Constructive work was what he wanted."[5]

Marshall's general position was that, at any given time, in some parts of economics more induction was required and in other parts more deduction but that, in general, more inductive work calls for more deductive work and vice versa. He recognised that individual economists might be better at one or the other but did not think it was possible to be a good economist without, to some degree, engaging in both inductive and deductive work: "Every genuine student of economics sometimes uses the inductive method and sometimes the analytical, and nearly always both of them together."[6]

In a letter to H. S. Foxwell, Marshall said: "Most of the suggestions which I made on the proofs of Keynes's *Scope and Method* were aimed at bringing it more into harmony with the views of Schmoller. Some were accepted. But it still remains true that as regards method I

4. Letter from Alfred Marshall to J. N. Keynes, Keynes 3 (74).
5. A. C. Pigou, ed., *Memorials of Alfred Marshall* (1925), 88.
6. *Memorials*, 309.

regard myself midway between Keynes + Sidgwick + Cairnes and Schmoller + Ashley."[7] Although Marshall claims to occupy this middle ground, and in a sense he does, if we study what Marshall says, it seems to me that he always emphasises induction, the collection and assembly of facts, and plays down what we would term "theory," a word which, as we have seen, he did not much like when applied to economics. Indeed in one letter to Foxwell he says that in economics there is "no 'theory' to speak of."[8] This may, as John Maynard Keynes tells us, in part reflect the attitude of someone who, trained as a mathematician, had earlier thought of working in molecular physics and found economic theory rather "small beer." Marshall, according to John Maynard Keynes, "always felt a slight contempt from the intellectual or aesthetic point of view for the rather 'potty' scraps of elementary algebra, geometry, and differential calculus which make up mathematical economics."[9]

However this may be, the main reason why Marshall speaks in this way and emphasises induction is, I think, that his aim was to understand the working of the real economic system, a system whose operation we could observe in the factories, in the streets, and in the homes of ordinary people. Marshall himself, of course, was a great collector of economic facts not only from such sources as government reports but also from visits to factories and from questioning businessmen and workers. His factual knowledge was apparently formidable. His nephew, Claude Guillebaud, told me that Marshall had an unerring sense of the magnitude of economic factors and that he would immediately pounce if one made an error—so that a conversation with Marshall could be an unnerving experience.

Marshall himself had come to economics because he wanted to help in eliminating poverty and in enhancing the quality of man and man's life. The economic system which Marshall studies always had this concrete character—it was a system which, leaving the study or the library, one could observe. And for Marshall it was important that one should get it right since it was this real system that one had to explain. This leads Marshall to appraise the work of other economists

7. See J. M. Keynes's article on "Herbert Somerton Foxwell" in *Collected Writings of John Maynard Keynes*, D. Moggridge, ed. (1972), 10:271–72 n.5.
8. Letter from Alfred Marshall to H. S. Foxwell, 25 January 1897, Marshall 3 (26).
9. *Collected Writings*, Moggridge ed., 10:186.

from a very special vantage point. John Neville Keynes uses J. H. von Thunen in his *Scope and Method* as an example of an economist who uses "a highly abstract method of treating economic problems."[10] Marshall greatly admired von Thunen but did not like this way of describing him. In the correspondence to which I have referred, in what is evidently a comment on this passage, Marshall writes to Keynes: "You know von Thunen's *Metier* was that of an agricultural reformer. His abstract economics come in by the way. He was up to his eyes in facts about rye and manure and so on."[11]

Marshall did not think of economics, as is common today, as economic theory. This is what he says, writing to F. Y. Edgeworth:

> In my view "Theory" is essential. No one gets any real grip of (?on) economic problems unless he will work on it. But I conceive no more calamitous notion than that abstract, or general, or "theoretical" economics was economics "proper." It seems to me an essential but a very small part of economics proper: and by itself sometimes even—well, not a very good occupation of time. . . . General reasoning is essential, but a wide and thorough study of facts is equally essential. . . . A combination of the two sides of the work is *alone* economics *proper.* Economic theory is, in my opinion, as mischievous an imposter when it claims to be economics proper as is mere crude unanalysed history.[12]

Marshall had expressed a similar point of view in a letter to W. A. S. Hewins, Director of the London School of Economics, written in 1899, that is, nine years after the publication of the *Principles:*

> It seems strange to me to be asked my views as to the study of pure economic theory; as tho' that were a subject on wh I were fit to speak. For indeed I was never a partisan of it; and for more than a quarter of a century I have set my face away from it. As early as 1873 (I think it was the year) Walras

10. J. N. Keynes, *The Scope and Method of Political Economy,* 4th ed. (1917), 21.
11. Letter from Alfred Marshall to J. N. Keynes, Keynes 3 (67). Compare with Marshall's statement that von Thunen "was a careful experimenter and student of facts with a mind at least as fully developed on the inductive as on the deductive side. . . . I loved von Thunen above all my other masters." (Pigou, *Memorials,* 360.)
12. Pigou, *Memorials,* 437.

pressed me to write something about it; & I declined with emphasis. The fact is I am the dull mean man, who holds Economics to be an organic whole, & has as little respect for pure theory (otherwise than as a branch of mathematics or the science of numbers), as for that crude collection & interpretation of facts without the aid of high analysis which sometimes claims to be a part of economic history.[13]

It is illustrative of Marshall's attitude that, when he gave what he termed "advanced lectures," these did not deal with the kind of technical and mathematical problems with which such a course today would be likely to deal. There was such a course at Cambridge, but it was given by the scientist Arthur Berry (who also wrote on economics) and later, I believe, by Pigou. Marshall himself dealt in his "advanced lectures" with the analysis of some real but difficult economic problems. It was, I think, work of this character that Marshall had in mind when he wrote:

> The function then of analysis and deduction in economics is not to forge a few long chains of reasoning, but to forge rightly many short chains and single connecting links. This however is no trivial task. If the economist reasons rapidly and with a light heart, he is apt to make bad connections at every turn of his work. He needs to make careful use of analysis and deduction, because only by their aid can he select the right facts, group them rightly, and make them serviceable for suggestions in thought and guidance in practice.[14]

As a final illustration of Marshall's attitude to the way in which an economist should study his subject, we may take his views on the use of mathematics in economics. His general position has been described by Pigou:

> Starting out then with the firm view that economic science is chiefly valuable, neither as an intellectual gymnastic nor even as a means of winning truth for its own sake, but as a

13. Letter from Alfred Marshall to W. A. S. Hewins, 12 October 1899, University of Sheffield Library.

14. Alfred Marshall, *Principles of Economics,* C. W. Guillebaud, ed., 9th variorum ed. (1961), 1 (app. C):773.

handmaid of ethics and a servant of practice, Marshall reso-
lutely set himself to mould his work along lines conforming
to that ideal. Though a skilled mathematician, he used mathematics sparingly. He saw that excessive reliance on this instrument might lead us astray in pursuit of intellectual toys,
imaginary problems not conforming to the conditions of real
life: and further, might distort our sense of proportion by
causing us to neglect factors that could not easily be worked
up in the mathematical machine. [15]

As a young man, Marshall was a mathematician of considerable ability. He was not therefore unaware of the advantages which come from
the mathematical treatment of a problem. He said in the *Principles:*

a training in mathematics is helpful by giving command over
a marvellously terse and exact language for expressing
clearly some general relations and some short processes of
economic reasoning; which can indeed be expressed in ordinary language, but not with equal sharpness of outline. And,
what is of far greater importance, experience in handling
physical problems by mathematical methods gives a grasp,
which cannot be obtained equally well in any other way, of
the mutual interaction of economic changes. [16]

Later in life (in 1906), Marshall wrote to one of his favourite pupils, A.
L. Bowley, the statistician, about how mathematics should be used.
These are Marshall's views: "(1) Use mathematics as a shorthand language, rather than as an engine of inquiry. (2) Keep to them till you
have done. (3) Translate into English. (4) Then illustrate by examples
that are important in real life. (5) Burn the mathematics. (6) If you
can't succeed in (4), burn (3). This last I did often." Later on in the
same letter to Bowley he says: "Mathematics used in a Fellowship
thesis by a man who is not a mathematician by nature—and I have
come across a good deal of that [and these days he would have come
across even more]—seems to me an unmixed evil. And I think you
should do all you can to prevent people from using Mathematics in
cases in which the English language is as short as the Mathematical." [17]

15. Pigou, *Memorials,* 84.
16. Marshall, *Principles of Economics,* 1 (app. D):781.
17. Pigou, *Memorials,* 427.

What was it that Marshall found objectionable about the use of mathematics, at any rate, when used extensively? He thought we lacked the data to support any but relatively simple constructions. He feared that factors that could not easily be dealt with in mathematical form would be neglected. But above all, he thought that we would be tempted to engage in what he termed "mathematical diversions" or, as Pigou put it, we would be led to pursue "intellectual toys, imaginary problems not conforming to the conditions of real life." Marshall thought it would tend to divert our attention from the real world in which poverty causes degradation and to the study of which he thought we should devote our whole energies.

In these days, when the mathematical method rides triumphant in economics, one may ask whether Marshall's fears were well-founded. Have we been tempted to embark on "long chains of reasoning" without adequate supporting data? Do we neglect factors difficult to put into mathematical form? Do we concern ourselves not with the puzzles presented by the real economic world but with the puzzles presented by other economists' analysis? It is not, of course, possible to indict the whole economics profession—and much good work is done nowadays and some of this work is carried out with mathematical methods. Furthermore, I feel sure that Marshall would have agreed that this was so. But it would be hard to deny that the extensive use of mathematics has encouraged the tendencies that he thought would be its probable consequence. Marshall's thought was that the extensive use of mathematics would lead us away from what he considered to be "constructive work." I very much doubt that what has happened in recent years would have led him to change his mind.

Marshall welcomed all methods providing that they assisted in constructive work, and mathematics was not excluded from this. What is I think distinctive in his position is his belief that we should not investigate "imaginary problems not conforming to the conditions of real life." He thought that we should start with the real economic system, that it was our high calling to try to explain how it worked, and that we should be interested in techniques of analysis only to the extent that this helped us to achieve the main goal.

TWELVE

Arnold Plant

Arnold Plant was born in 1898 in Hoxton in East London, the son of a
municipal librarian. He was educated at the Strand School and, on
leaving, joined a mechanical engineering organisation controlled by
Dr. Wingfield, a German engineer and inventor, who came to England
in 1902 and became naturalised, later changing his name from Wie-
sengrund. One of the two companies controlled by Wingfield, the
Power Plant Company, did important work for the Admiralty, and an
agitation based on his "enemy alien origin" led Wingfield to dispose of
his interest in that company in 1918 while retaining control (with a
partner) of his other company, the Steam Fittings Company. Returning
from a period in the Army, Plant, who had obviously displayed considerable business ability since joining Wingfield's organisation, was
made Manager of the Steam Fittings Company in 1920 (at which time
he was only twenty-one years of age).

Plant was advised by William (later Lord) Piercy that he ought to
learn something about management before doing much more of it.
Living in Hoxton as a boy, Piercy had come to know the Plant family.
After leaving school, Piercy had worked for a timber-broker but, aided
by two full-time scholarships, became in 1910, at the age of twenty-
four, a full-time undergraduate at the London School of Economics
(LSE), specialising in economic history under Lilian Knowles. After

Originally published as "Professor Sir Arnold Plant: His Ideas and Influence" in
The Unfinished Agenda: Essays in Honor of Arthur Seldon (London: Institute of Economic Affairs, London 1986), and reprinted here with permission of the Institute. The
article has been slightly revised for this book.

I am very grateful to Mr. Roger Plant for giving me much valuable information
about his father's career and views, and for allowing me to consult his father's papers; to
Professor Z. Gurzynski for providing me with details of Arnold Plant's activities at the
University of Cape Town; and to Professor H. C. Edey for providing information on
Arnold Plant's work at the London School of Economics.

graduating in 1913 he was appointed to the staff of the LSE, but on the outbreak of the First World War was absorbed into government service and, the war over, began his distinguished career in business. This included his appointment in 1945 as the first chairman of the Industrial and Commercial Finance Corporation, a position he held until his retirement in 1964.[1]

It is hardly surprising that Piercy's advice led Plant, in 1920, to enroll at the LSE for the B.Sc. (Econ.) degree; even his decision to specialise in modern economic history, which seems strange for someone whose aim was to learn about management, seems almost certainly due to Piercy's influence. But the commerce degree (B. Com.) had been created after the First World War with the active support of Piercy and other businessmen, and while at the LSE, Plant also followed courses for the B.Com. as an external student. He was awarded the B.Com. in 1922 and the B.Sc. (Econ.) with first-class honours in 1923. Plant's demonstration that it was possible to study for these two degrees simultaneously and with distinction led to a change in university regulations which would make it impossible for this feat to be repeated. Plant enjoyed his time at the LSE but he did not adopt either the protectionist views of Lilian Knowles or the socialist views of R. H. Tawney and Harold Laski. The teacher who had most influence on him was Edwin Cannan, the professor of political economy, whose views and commonsense approach to economic analysis and economic policy were to be reflected in Plant's own work.

At this stage Plant seemed destined to return to business management. His career until then had closely paralleled that of Piercy, and had he gone back to business he would undoubtedly have achieved a similar success. But this was not to be. At the University of Cape Town, South Africa, a proposal for a degree in commerce had recently been approved, and in 1923 it was decided to create a professorship in commerce. When the position was advertised, Theodore (later Sir Theodore) Gregory told Plant that he would be a fool not to apply. Gregory was then a lecturer at the LSE working under Cannan but, like Piercy and Plant, had taken his B.Sc. (Econ.) in economic history under Lilian Knowles. There were twenty-four applicants for the chair

1. Plant (with John B. Kinross) wrote the obituary of Piercy for the *Journal of the Royal Statistical Society,* series A (general) 130 (pt. 2, 1967). He also wrote the obituary of Wingfield, the other man who played a decisive part in his early career, for the *Journal of the Institution of Electrical Engineers* 77 (July–December 1935).

but it was Plant who was selected—notwithstanding his meagre teaching experience and his youth (he was twenty-five)—no doubt because of his experience in management and the high regard for his abilities held at the LSE.

He took up his appointment in 1924 and set about carrying out his duties with great energy. Most of the teaching for the commerce degree fell on him and he lectured on an amazingly wide range of subjects, including banking and currency, insurance, factory organisation and administration, business finance, the economics of transport, public administration and marketing, as well as subjects dealing specifically with conditions in South Africa, such as South African railways. It was not until 1928 that a senior lecturer, W. H. Hutt, was appointed to assist him. During this period he must also have been collecting the material which he used in the chapter on "Economic Development" he wrote for the volume on South Africa of the *Cambridge History of the British Empire*.[2]

His academic writings while in South Africa were not extensive (hardly surprising, given the demands on his time of his other duties) and were concerned with South African banking and customs tariffs. The only one of his writings in South Africa which he decided to reprint in *Selected Economic Essays and Addresses*[3] was one dealing with the economic relations of the races, a subject which could hardly be ignored by someone seriously interested in the economic problems of South Africa. The article, "The Economics of the Native Question," was written in 1927 and published in the journal *Voorslag* (May–July 1927). It was a trenchant attack on the policy of the South African government of separation of the races. Plant argued that the policy arose from a desire to stifle competition from the native peoples and was economically injurious to South Africa. It was competition that forced individuals to co-operate in an efficient way. What the South African government ought to be doing was, by providing educational opportunities and in other ways, to bring the natives into Western society. It was wrong to justify its policy by arguing that the natives were uncivilised while withholding the means which would

2. *Cambridge History of the British Empire* (Cambridge and London: Cambridge University Press, 1936, rev. ed. 1963), 8:788–836.
3. Plant, *Selected Economic Essays and Addresses* (London: Routledge and Kegan Paul, in association with the IEA, 1974), 3–17.

enable them to become part of Western civilisation. A few quotations will give the flavour of this article:

> the refuge which some degenerate white people are prone to seek in the colour of their skin as a basis for privileged treatment is but one particular phase of the universal habit among the lazy or inefficient of seizing hold of an entirely irrelevant characteristic of their competitors and endeavouring to persuade the general public that it constitutes a sufficient ground for legislation differentiating against that particular class as a whole. . . . If the competitor is a Jew, or a married woman, or an Indian, or a native, or an unapprenticed skilled worker, or a professional man who did not pay his premium as an articled pupil, then the general public is besought to clamour for legislation which will put an end to the competition. . . . While the provision for native education remains as meagre as it is today, the number of natives who will seek social intercourse and full co-operation with civilised, well-educated people is doomed to remain small. . . . Our failure to provide for the native population the opportunities for the fullest co-operation of which they individually are capable is *economically* deplorable; and the depressing outlook of many Europeans towards native questions suggests that the *non-economic* reasons for regretting our lack of intercourse with the native peoples are no less potent.

In 1930 Plant left South Africa and returned to the LSE to fill the newly created chair of commerce ("with special reference to Business Administration"). Plant became responsible for the Industry and Trade group in the B. Com., where his teaching in seminars and lectures had a profound influence on his students. He also taught in the new postgraduate Department of Business Administration which had been started in 1930, and in 1935 became its head. From then on, running the Department of Business Administration took up much of his time and energies. Closed down during the Second World War, it was restarted when the war ended; but it never seems to have taken root at the LSE and, on Plant's retirement in 1965, it was quietly allowed to die, a decision no doubt made easier by the inauguration of the London Business School in the same year.

The character of Plant's views and his style emerge very clearly in his inaugural lecture in 1931, "Trends in Business Administration."[4] This lecture was clearly designed both to indicate what Plant thought important and to mollify those at the LSE who might be hostile to the creation of a professorship devoted to the study of business. Thus, the Webbs are referred to for their writings on business problems "from the special angle which [they] have made essentially their own" but without saying what that "special angle" was. The "pathbreaking" work by specialists in government at the LSE comparing and contrasting public and private administration is noted. Graham Wallis and Harold Laski are praised for teaching that "the unfettered expression of our individuality [is] the most precious ingredient of liberty," but in such a way as to make advocacy of a free-enterprise system seem a natural development of their views.

Plant's theme in the main section of his lecture is that the businessman does not dominate the economic system. He is "merely the organising agent of that relentless controller and employer, the community of consumers." He has to anticipate consumer wants and "the more accurately he interprets the unspoken wish, the more likely he is to remain in favour, the more able he will be to command the capital and the labour which he needs for his production, and for which he has incessantly to bargain against the other businessmen who also serve the ultimate employer." To achieve economic progress, "there is one fundamental condition: the preservation . . . of the freedom of the individual to modify his habitual conduct, whether as consumer or producer, whenever he may believe a change to be advantageous to himself."

Businessmen, of course, seek to free themselves from their relentless controller, the consumer, by the use of various defensive devices: advertising, rebates to regular customers, season tickets, coupons, the deferred rebate, trade boycotts, and so on. Direct attacks on competitors, however, are not likely to be successful. "Local price-cutting to eliminate rival traders is expensive; new rivals spring up as soon as the attempt is made to recoup the loss by raising prices." But so long as the state was not "interventionist in its attitude towards trade practices, so long as it confined itself to the protection of life and limb and to the eradication of misrepresentation and fraud, the public lost

4. Plant, "Trends in Business Administration," *Economica* 12, no. 35 (February 1932):45–62.

little from the transient victories of monopoly, and gained enormously from the strenuous struggle of competition." This is not what the state has done. Of "state intervention aimed at the conservation of natural resources—of oil, timber and the like," Plant says: "There can surely be few fields of State activity in which intervention has been more arbitrary in its manifestations and less securely based on economic principle." Particularly in the field of public utilities, state intervention has changed from intervention to *prevent* monopoly to intervention to *promote* it:

> It is still perhaps an unsettled question of economics whether the attempts both at control and at public operation do not make bad worse; whether indeed the State is not best advised to leave these undertakings to unfettered private management and apply itself rather to the question of encouraging new enterprises and stimulating competition in these fields.
>
> The continued profitability of all monopolies is conditional on the absence of alternatives and substitutes. Public control either of the prices charged or of the disposal of aggregate profits places the harassed monopolist in a straitjacket when the time comes for a struggle for existence against unhampered competition. It carries with it an almost irresistible claim to protection against free competition, and the State becomes involved on the side of monopoly in schemes to prevent the public from benefiting from the introduction of new inventions and new processes.

As is apparent from these quotations, Plant did not think of the study of business administration as being primarily concerned with how to run a business. He studied business practices in order to understand why they existed. His field of interest would be described today, I believe, as industrial organisation. His analytical system was unsophisticated but powerful. He thought of the consumer as the ultimate employer, with competition as the mechanism through which the consumer exercised his control. Monopoly he considered to be transitional and usually unimportant. The state had a legitimate role in providing law and order and preventing misrepresentation and fraud. But state intervention was commonly designed to help special interests, did not promote competition but monopoly, and imposed economic regulation which often made matters worse. These were some of the ideas that his students carried away from him. They are now more widely held in the economics profession than they were then. A continuing interest of Plant's was the subject of property and the economic freedom of ownership. He said that his interest was inspired by reading David Hume's treatment of this subject.[5] No doubt it was, but it is difficult not to see in this, as in other aspects of his work, the influence of Edwin Cannan. At any rate, it led Plant to write articles which rank as his major academic achievements in economics. In the early 1930s he wrote two articles, one on patents for inventions and another on copyright in books.[6] In them he questioned the need for establishing property rights in patents and copyright. They did not arise out of scarcity, but by setting up a monopoly they created scarcity. He pointed out that British authors had been handsomely rewarded by American publishers even though their works were not copyrighted in America. Furthermore, much invention goes on in many trades, even though the resulting improvements are not patentable. He suggested that, even though the existing law were retained, modifications could be made (such as the use of Licences of Right as a normal practice) to improve the situation. But his general stance was one of hostility. Today his discussion seems somewhat incomplete; but it has to be remembered that it was Plant who opened up the subject, and his articles raised questions which still have not been answered satisfactorily.

After World War II he returned to the subject in his Stamp Lecture in 1953, "The New Commerce in Ideas and Intellectual Property."[7]). Here Plant examined the problems created for copyright and analogous protection by recent technological changes, such as the recording of sound and broadcasting. It is an interesting lecture but it lacks the fire of his papers of the early 1930s and it adds little to the analysis in them. It seems clear that after World War II Plant did not continue his earlier research on property, and it is doubtful whether there was a manuscript on the economics of property, at the existence of which

5. Plant's references to Hume can be found in Plant, *Selected Economic Essays and Addresses* (1974), 30–31, 35–36, 169.

6. Plant, "The Economic Theory Concerning Patents for Inventions" (35–56), and "The Economic Aspects of Copyright for Books" (57–186), in *Selected Economic Essays and Addresses* (1974).

7. Plant, "The New Commerce in Ideas and Intellectual Property," in *Selected Economic Essays and Addresses* (1974), 87–116.

Arthur Seldon hints in his foreword to *Selected Economic Essays and Addresses*.[8]

Plant's ill health (he suffered from diabetes) was undoubtedly one reason for his reduced scholarly work after the Second World War. His pre-occupation with the Department of Business Administration was another. His work on government committees must also have had the same effect. Plant had served on government committees before the Second World War. He was, for example, appointed in 1938 as one of the original independent members of the Cinematograph Films Council. But after the Second World War, perhaps because his wartime service as an adviser of cabinet ministers gave him a taste for power and influence, Plant was, as Arthur Seldon indicates, almost continuously engaged on government committees. With his energies sapped by ill health, such activity, combined with his administrative duties at the LSE, was bound to divert him from scholarly work and it is understandable that his research on property was put aside.

But there was perhaps another reason that this happened. Plant was the ex-business manager who went to the university to learn more about management. He saw it as an important function of the university and it was one that was dear to his heart. His inaugural lecture at the University of Cape Town was on "University Education for Commercial Careers," and at the LSE, as we have seen, he devoted himself to the Department of Business Administration. For many years Plant was also head of the Commerce Degree Bureau of the University of London. It was no doubt a consequence of his concern with the practical application of economics that he had little interest in developing economic theory. But, as we can now see, improvements in theory were required if useful work on property rights was to proceed. The LSE was, at that time, a temple of truth dedicated to the improvement of economic theory but the economists, except to some degree Hayek, were not interested in business practices, and so Plant got no help from them. Perhaps Plant felt that in his articles of the 1930s he had gone as far as he could in the study of property rights. But for many other purposes, the theory he possessed, the theory of competition, was quite serviceable and, armed with it and a realistic view of what a government could and would do, he was able to destroy many widely held

8. Arthur Seldon, Foreword in Arnold Plant, *Selected Economic Essays and Addresses* (1974), vii.

views and to pass on to his students an approach to economic policy which would protect them from much fashionable error and would enable them to devise policies more solidly based.

Arnold Plant was a good teacher who took a deep interest in his students and he exerted himself to further their careers. The work of his students, Arthur Seldon and others, will ensure that his influence neither dies nor fades away.

THIRTEEN

Duncan Black

Duncan Black, son of Scotland, was born on May 23, 1908, in Motherwell, an industrial town situated about twelve miles from Glasgow. His father was born in the western Isle of Mull. Black's grandfather, a blacksmith, died some twelve years after his marriage, and his widow left Mull and returned with her young family to her native village, Tayvallich in Argyle. There, while in his teens, Black's father worked on a farm but later, when the family moved to Motherwell, he became a boilermaker.

If, on his father's side, Black's ancestors were Highlanders, his mother's family were Lowlanders. His mother, Margaret Brown Muir, was born in Motherwell, her father also having been a blacksmith. At the age of twelve, she was apprenticed to a milliner. A clever woman, it was a great regret to her that she had had to leave school at such an early age. Bible classes and music lessons at the church did something to make up for the loss. Shortly before her marriage, she opened a drapery and millinery shop in Motherwell, which she continued to run after her marriage, indeed, until the coming of buses, which made the large Glasgow stores accessible to Motherwell shoppers, led to a decline in business, and to the disposal of the shop in 1931. It was Alfred Marshall's opinion that the "most valuable of all capital is that invested in human beings and of that capital the most precious part is

This paper reprints the obituary memoir that I contributed to the proceedings of the British Academy after the death of Duncan Black in 1991. It is based on my own recollections of Duncan Black, on conversations that I have had with him about his life, and on biographical notes that he gave to me. It reproduces, with permission, a biography that I wrote for *Toward a Science of Politics: Essays in Honor of Duncan Black*, ed. Gordon Tullock (1981) but which I have revised and brought up to date.

the result of the care and influence of the mother."[1] He refers with approval to Galton's view that "the mother's influence is most easily traced among theologians and men of science, because an earnest mother leads her child to feel deeply about great things, and a thoughtful mother does not repress, but encourages that childish curiosity which is the raw material of scientific habits of thought."[2] It would seem that Margaret Black was such a mother. Certainly Duncan Black had no doubt that his mother had been the dominant influence in his life.

Black was educated in the Motherwell schools. Particularly important for his intellectual development was Dalziel High School, then enjoying a period of high academic achievement. A number of students from this period later joined the faculty of the University of Glasgow. The teaching at Dalziel High School encouraged a love of scholarship. Of his English teacher, Black says: "One got the feeling of all the treasures of civilization being poured into one's lap." To Black his school work was a source of great pleasure, the subjects which he most enjoyed and in which he did best being languages and literature. It would have seemed natural that these would have been the subjects which he would choose to study at the university. But when he enrolled at the university, it was to study mathematics. As an honours degree had to be taken in two cognate subjects, he decided to study mathematics and physics. The explanation he gave for what, considering his interests, seems a strange decision, is that he regarded mathematics as a means to truth, a view which he continued to hold throughout his life. But he also added another reason: vanity. Mathematics was difficult and a good degree would win approbation. In all this, one cannot but suspect that Black's Scotch Presbyterian upbringing played an important part. Most of us like approbation but we usually choose the easiest way of securing it.

Black did not enjoy mathematics as it was taught at Glasgow. The mathematical courses were designed for engineers and did not excite him. There were no new materials and nothing about the relation of mathematics to formal logic. The physics lectures were more to his taste but he had no interest in physical phenomena. Consequently he eagerly looked forward to the end of these courses. The award, in

1. Alfred Marshall, *Principles of Economics,* C. W. Guillebaud, ed., 9th variorum ed. (London, 1961), 564.

1929, of a master of arts degree (the first degree at Glasgow) with second-class honours may have secured approbation but it afforded little else. Black next turned to the social sciences, his intention then being to enter the civil service. With the help of a scholarship of £50 per annum and a similar sum earned as a demonstrator in the medical physics laboratory, he was able to enroll for an M.A. in political economy and political philosophy. His studies for this second degree proved to be much more congenial than his earlier studies in mathematics and physics. The professor of political economy, W. R. Scott, was a distinguished scholar, the author of works on Francis Hutcheson and Adam Smith and of a three-volume history of joint-stock companies. Scott's main interest was in the relationship between philosophy and economics. The questions he discussed, such as whether the theory of value in economics might benefit from the work of philosophers and whether the philosophers' views on value could benefit from the techniques of analysis employed in economics, struck a responsive chord in Black. Another teacher whose influence on his later work seems evident was A. K. White, a lecturer in politics.[3] White considered most of the literature on this subject to be of little value and Duncan Black recalled that he spent a large part of one term discussing the possibility of constructing a pure science of politics. Black also remembered that he quoted, with approval as a key notion, Mary Parker Follett's description of how an idea develops in a committee.[4] But an equally or more important influence was provided by the class in moral philosophy and particularly by C. A. Campbell's exposition and defence of the Idealistic doctrine of desire.[5]

In 1932 Black obtained his M.A. in economics and politics, with first-class honours. In the previous year he had been awarded (jointly with Alec Cairncross) the Certificate of Merit in Social Economics. In 1932 he was appointed an assistant lecturer at the School of Economics and Commerce, Dundee. In 1934, he became a lecturer in economics at the University College of North Wales, Bangor, where he stayed (with a period during the war in the civil service) until 1945. In 1945, he became a senior lecturer in economics at Queen's University,

2. *Ibid.*, 207.
3. See A. K. White, *The Character of British Democracy* (Glasgow, 1945).
4. Mary Parker Follett, *The New State: Group Organization the Solution of Popular Government* (New York, 1918), 24–25.
5. See C. A. Campbell, *Scepticism and Construction* (London, 1931), 201–11.

Belfast, but a year later, in 1946, he returned to his alma mater, the University of Glasgow, as senior lecturer in social economics. In 1952, Black became professor of economics at the University College of North Wales, Bangor, and remained there until he retired in 1968.

Of all these positions, the first, at the School of Economics and Commerce, Dundee, was the most significant in its effect on his intellectual development. The Dundee School of Economics was founded in 1931 by George Bonar, a leading member of the Dundee jute industry. James A. Bowie, from the Manchester College of Technology, was the first principal. In the planning of the School, assistance was provided by the London School of Economics (LSE), by its director, Sir William Beveridge (later Lord Beveridge), by its secretary, Mrs. J. Mair (later Lady Beveridge), and by others at LSE. It was therefore not surprising that the first lecturers to be appointed, J. K. Eastham and J. C. Gilbert, both came from LSE. In 1932, two assistant lecturers were added to the staff. One was Black. I was the other. I had been educated at LSE and had been recommended for the post by Professor Arnold Plant. Gilbert had been my tutor during my first year at LSE. Black and I, the two assistant lecturers, saw a good deal of each other and a friendship developed which has continued ever since. Eastham had studied economics not only with Lionel Robbins when he was a lecturer at LSE but also with Allyn Young, the great American economist who had been appointed to the chair in economics at LSE after the retirement of Edwin Cannan. Gilbert, who specialised in money and banking, came to Dundee eager to expound the theories of Robertson, Keynes, and Hayek.

I came to Dundee after having spent a year in the United States on a Cassel Travelling Scholarship, my head, according to Black, full of my ideas on the firm. It is certain (as I have learnt from a letter which I wrote in October 1932) that my first lecture in a course on the organisation of the business unit contained the main points which were to appear in my article on "The Nature of the Firm." A draft of that article was completed by the spring of 1934 while still at Dundee. That my article was not published until 1937 was mainly due to our belief that getting it right was more important than getting it published. The discussions between the four of us (Eastham, Gilbert, Black, and myself) were lively, thorough, and continuous. Whether at meals or elsewhere, the subject we discussed was economics, and particularly those new ideas which emerged, to a large extent in England and often at LSE, in the 1920s and 1930s. All problems in economics seemed to be on the verge of solution. And so our days passed happily by. The impact of these discussions on Black was dramatic. He came from the University of Glasgow, where economics was still treated, as it had been in the days of Adam Smith, as a branch of moral philosophy. Black came to Dundee with an interest in philosophy and politics as great, or perhaps greater, than his interest in economics. At Dundee, he was brought into contact with the analytical approach to economics which, through the influence of Allyn Young, Lionel Robbins, Friedrich Hayek, and John Hicks, was dominant at LSE. He also attended Eastham's graduate theory lectures and this gave him a grasp of recent theoretical developments in economics. But if Black increased his knowledge of economic analysis at Dundee, the problems which really absorbed him, although to my recollection he did not discuss them with us (with good reason since we probably would not have understood them), were those which had struck his imagination while listening to the lectures of Scott, White, and Campbell at Glasgow. Indeed, Black's major contributions may be regarded as the result of using the analytical approach of LSE to solve the problems which had been raised in his mind by the teaching at Glasgow. The point of view he came to hold was expressed succinctly in an article which he wrote many years later. It was his belief "that when we do eventually obtain a 'satisfactory' Political Science it will have the same distinguishing marks as Walras' *Elements* or Pareto's *Manuel*—or perhaps Marshall's *Principles,* with the admixture of the rigorously formal and the descriptive treatment—rather than those of the existing texts in Politics. And the core of the treatment . . . will consist of a set of formal or mathematical propositions."[6] To find this "set of formal or mathematical propositions" was to be his life work.

The reference in this account to C. A. Campbell as an influence leading Black to his theory of committees may have caused some puzzlement. In fact, the influence was very real and had been strengthened when, for four years in the 1930s, they were colleagues at Bangor, where Campbell held the chair in philosophy. At first sight, Campbell's discussions of the Idealist doctrine of desire would seem to have little to do with Black's thinking on the committee. But this

6. Duncan Black, "The Unity of Political and Economic Science," *Economic Journal* (September 1950):506.

was not so. Campbell, according to Black, was wrestling with the problem of the relation of an individual's choices and actions to his various desires. An individual's actions depended on the composition of his desires (some favouring and some opposing each particular action). Substitute individual voters for these desires and the analysis of the committee and of the individual become formally the same. As it happens, Black did not reach his theory of the committee through an analysis of the choices made by the individual but Campbell's way of looking at human choice undoubtedly played its part in the development of Black's thought. I would argue, and I am not sure how far Black held the same view, that the case for thinking of individual choice in the same way as we think of a committee is even stronger than these remarks may have suggested. Substitute genes for desires and it becomes easy to see that an individual's choice among alternative courses of action is in fact determined by a kind of voting system. If I am right, the theory of committees (or something analogous) can be applied directly to the analysis of individual choice and we should not therefore be surprised to find intransitivities or even cyclical movements in individual choices. Such an approach would, of course, mean the abandonment of the assumption, commonly made in economics, that man is a "rational utility maximiser" and that an individual's choices are consistent, a change in viewpoint which, for my part, I would welcome. The attempt to use the analytical approach of economics to increase our understanding of the political system may therefore have the unexpected result of leading to an improvement in economic analysis itself.

In 1934, after leaving Dundee and going to Bangor, Black began to work seriously on the analysis of a political system, using economic concepts. But although he made some progress, he did not feel that he had secured a handle on the problem and in 1935 active work was put aside. In this connection, I should refer to a statement made by Black in the preface of his book, *The Theory of Committees and Elections:* "At a very early stage I was helped to find the general lines of development by discussion with my colleague Professor Ronald H. Coase on his view of the nature of the firm."[7] This statement is over-generous. When Black first started to apply the kind of analysis used in eco-

7. Duncan Black, *The Theory of Committees and Elections* (Cambridge, 1958), *xi.*

190

nomics to the problems of the political system, he certainly used the concept of transaction costs to explain the emergence of political parties and legislative assemblies, and in this was influenced by my approach to the firm. But this part of his work has never, to my knowledge, been published. While it is literally true that my discussions with Black were a stage on the way to his theory of committees, the solutions which he ultimately found to the problems that were vexing him were along lines which owed nothing to my work on the firm. When I discussed this question with him, Black's recollection was that consideration of the firm led us to discuss Edgeworth's treatment of contracting in *Mathematical Psychics* and that it was these discussions which helped him to find his way. In this he could well be right.

The main reason why Black ceased to work actively after 1935 on the problem of the political system was not lack of progress. He had published nothing up to this point and to excuse this lack of publication by explaining that he was engaged on the construction of a pure science of politics was hardly likely to advance the professional career of a young economist. He therefore turned back to a student thesis which he had written under Scott at Glasgow on "The Incidence of Income Taxes." Work on taxation was made easier because he was lecturing at Bangor on public finance and was pleasurable because he had to study once again the Italian writers on public finance, whose work he had greatly enjoyed in his student days, and which had the added advantage of also being relevant to his real interest, the pure theory of politics. Articles were published on taxation in 1937 and 1938 and finally his book, *The Incidence of Income Taxes,* was published by Macmillan in September 1939, just after the outbreak of the war. The book served its purpose. It was favourably regarded and Black's academic position was secure. Frederic Benham concluded his review in *Economica* by stating: "Good books on the theory of public finance are rare. It is a pleasure to welcome an addition to their number." The book was reprinted in 1961.

The outbreak of the war led to Black joining the civil service but his mind never ceased to play on the problems which really interested him. It was in fact during his period in the civil service that he found the key to the problem with which he had wrestled for so long. Black gave an account of the discovery he made in February 1942, in notes which he provided me with. He said:

I was "fire-watching" in case of air raids, around midnight in the green drawing room of Warwick Castle, one of the most stately rooms in the whole of England, though now there was a strange contrast between the coats of medieval armour and the walls and the long narrow tables strewn about the room and cluttered with civil-service paraphernalia. Acting apparently at random, I took a sheet of civil-service notepaper and wrote down a diagram bearing three curves, and I saw in a shock of recognition that if I interpreted points on the horizontal axis as motions before the committee, and took the preferences of the members in relation to these motions to be represented by the three single-peaked curves, the decision by a committee using a simple-majority procedure must correspond to the median optimum. The diagram showed the relation in which the decision of the committee stood to the preferences of the members. Drawing two more diagrams left the conviction that now I would be able to say things which previously I had only felt and had been unable to communicate or even formulate properly. Not only so but the technique, hit on apparently accidentally, would allow an investigation of government to be made along systematic lines which were fairly clearly delineated. Or so, that night, the future seemed to stretch out.

He added:

After lying dormant in my mind for some years, the problem to which I had at one time given my full attention had changed its nature: it had become a problem in Mathematics. The queries that arose could be posed as mathematical problems. You arrived at a political theory by translating back from the mathematical symbols, just as in Economics and Mathematical Physics, and as had been the rule in pure science since the seventeenth century.

In October 1942, owing to the illness of a colleague, Black returned to college teaching. This enabled him to begin serious work on his theory of the committee. He soon discovered the existence of intransitivities and, after writing up parts of his theory, enlisted the help of R. A. Newing, a colleague in the mathematics department at Bangor. Newing suggested the use of a matrix notation to deal with the case of a finite number of motions and was helpful in other ways. Black was concerned about the complications which arose when the preferences of voters relating to one topic depended on the decisions made on other topics, and he and Newing collaborated in an attempt to find a way of handling this problem. Considerable progress was made but at some points the mathematics involved seemed to bulk disproportionately large in comparison with the conclusions it furnished for political theory and the work was put aside. In the meantime, Black had returned to the civil service.

After the war in Europe was over, Black was appointed a senior lecturer at Queen's University, Belfast, but the teaching and administration involved in this position left him little time for writing. All this changed when, in 1946, at the invitation of A. L. Macfie, he was appointed a senior lecturer at the University of Glasgow. He now had time for writing. The years of patient thought on the theory of committees paid off. Four articles were quickly completed and, early in 1947, two were submitted to the *Economic Journal* and two to *Economica*. But Duncan Black's troubles were not at an end. All four articles were rejected. Black also attempted to have his ideas published in book form. A draft of a book, entitled *The Pure Theory of Politics,* was completed by October 1947. The chapter headings give a good indication of its character and scope:

1. The Problem Investigated
2. Some Definitions and the Symbolic Representation of a Motion
3. The Theory of Independent Valuation
4. The Decisions of a Committee using a Simple Majority
5. Correspondence of the Theory with Reality
6. Examination of Some Methods of Electing Candidates
7. The Decisions of a Committee using a Special Majority
8. The Nature of International Agreements
9. The Elasticity of Committee Decisions with an Altering Size of Majority
10. The Elasticity of Committee Decisions with Alterations in the Members' Preference Schedules
11. The Unity of Political and Economic Science.

The book was submitted to four British publishers, all of whom rejected it.

Economics, however, is an international discipline and Black had, in the meantime, sent his articles to journals published abroad. His first success came when his article "On the Rationale of Group Decision-Making" was accepted for publication in the *Journal of Political Economy* and appeared in the issue of February 1948. Another article was printed in Italian in the issue of May–June 1948 of the *Giornale degli Economisti*. Finally, two articles were published in the July 1948 issue of *Econometrica*. Black continued to draw on the store of materials he had built up and in March 1949 an article was published in the *South African Journal of Economics,* and in May and August 1949, two more articles were published, this time in the *Canadian Journal of Economics and Political Science.*

In August 1949, Black returned to Bangor to spend some time with Newing in the hope that they might be able to finish the work which they had begun some six years before. As a result of three weeks of intensive work, they were successful and, using geometric methods of exposition, which Black hoped would make their results more accessible to economists, they completed their paper. They examined the situation in which the preferences of voters on any given topic depended on what other decisions had been made and in which therefore the order in which decisions were made played a crucial role in the outcome. They also analysed in detail the conditions under which a majority motion would exist. The title given to the paper was "The Decisions of a Committee of Three." The restriction of the analysis to a committee of three was to facilitate a geometrical treatment, the authors believing that an extension of their results to larger committees would be a routine matter.

The paper, which had been written in August 1949, was revised by correspondence and the final version was submitted to *Econometrica* in November 1949. Black then had a piece of very bad luck. *Econometrica* did not give a decision about publication for eighteen months. Whether this was due to editorial responsibility for manuscripts submitted by European authors being transferred from Professor Ragnar Frisch to the managing editor in Chicago or for some other reason, I do not know. And when the decision came in a letter from the managing editor dated May 24, 1951, it had a very peculiar character. The letter stated that he was prepared to recommend their paper for publication "if the interrelationships with Arrow's recent monograph could be brought out clearly throughout the paper." Kenneth Arrow's monograph *Social Choice and Individual Values* had been published in 1951 shortly before the managing editor's letter was written. The suggestion that Black and Newing should revise a paper written and submitted for publication in 1949 so as to relate to a book which had recently appeared in 1951 (and which they had not even seen) was obviously completely unacceptable. They withdrew the manuscript from *Econometrica* and it was published by William Hodge in 1951 as a booklet of fifty-nine pages with a new title, *Committee Decisions with Complementary Valuation*.

Black had become aware that Borda and Condorcet had written in eighteenth-century France about the theory of elections and at the end of 1948 he learnt more about them from a visit to the British Museum. Deciding to probe deeper, he went to Paris in the spring of 1949 and gathered more information about these French writers and also about Laplace, who had written on the same subject. It was natural that he would try to discover whether he had any British precursors. He soon came across the work of E. J. Nanson. But his search among English writers was to be richly rewarded when, in 1951, he discovered the contributions which Lewis Carroll had made to the theory of the committee. Lewis Carroll showed great insight and skill in handling the analysis, was aware of the existence of cyclical majorities and of the problems of complementary valuation, and had even employed the matrix notation which Black had used at the suggestion of Newing. Black's methodical scholarship also led to the discovery of documents relating to Lewis Carroll which had been hitherto unknown.

Black's theory of the committee was dispersed among articles in journals published in the United States, South Africa, and Canada. In order to make his theory accessible to more readers and to make clearer the interrelationships between its various parts, he decided to write a book which would bring together the ideas which he had expounded in these articles. In 1958, largely through the support of the philosopher R. B. Braithwaite and the economist E. A. G. Robinson, his book, *The Theory of Committees and Elections*, was published by Cambridge University Press. This book also contained a second part, which gave an account of the work of Borda, Condorcet, and Laplace in France and of Lewis Carroll in England. He also reprinted Lewis Carroll's three pamphlets dealing with the theory of the committee.

Black's views did not find a ready acceptance in Britain. We have seen that when he submitted his first four articles on the theory of committees to English journals they were rejected. His 1947 book failed to secure a publisher. This response reflected a general attitude. As I can testify from my personal knowledge, Black's work was regarded as an eccentricity, an attempt to use a mathematical treatment in spheres for which it was completely inappropriate. Nor was I more perceptive than the others. I shared the general scepticism. It was not until Black spent an evening, while I was staying with him in North Wales, taking me through the argument of the booklet which he had written with Newing, that I came to realise how powerful were the ideas that he was developing. With my lack of mathematics, I could never have obtained this understanding of Black's theory by reading his articles. This points to another reason why his colleagues in Britain failed to perceive the importance of the work on which he was engaged. Black in his writing made no concession to his readers and presented his theories in an austere form which, though it might have seemed reasonable to a physicist, reduced his chance of influencing his British colleagues. However, it was Black's devotion to the ideals of high scholarship which, though it made him disinclined to cater to the weakness of his readers, gave him that inner strength which enabled him to persevere in spite of this lack of encouragement.

But, once more, the New World was called in to redress the balance of the Old. In the United States, there has been much more interest in Black's work than has been the case in Britain. In 1962, Black was a visiting professor in the department of economics of the University of Virginia and in 1963 a visiting professor in the department of political science of the University of Rochester. After his retirement in 1968 from the chair of economics at Bangor, he visited the United States on many occasions. He was a Research Fellow in law and economics in the University of Chicago Law School in 1968–69 and in 1970–71 was a National Science Foundation Fellow in the department of economics, Virginia Polytechnic Institute. He was a visiting professor in the department of political science of the University of Chicago in 1969, 1972, 1973, and 1976, and was a visiting professor in the department of political science of Michigan State University in 1971, 1972, 1973, 1975, and 1976. These appointments were a great source of pleasure to him and this was particularly true of his visits to Michigan State University, where he came to feel completely at home. At all these institutions, he found what had lacked in Britain— colleagues who were sympathetic to what he was doing and graduate students interested in his approach and of a caliber to benefit from his teaching. In 1981 a festschrift in honour of Duncan Black, edited by Professor Gordon Tullock, entitled *Toward a Science of Politics,* was published by the Public Choice Center in Blacksburg, Virginia. In that same year 1981, Duncan Black was elected a foreign honorary fellow of the American Academy of Arts and Sciences.

While this recognition in the United States gave Black much pleasure, the lack of interest in his work in Britain somewhat embittered him. It was therefore a source of great satisfaction when, at the age of eighty-one, he was elected to the newly created category of Senior Fellow of the British Academy in 1989. Up to that time (apart from Honorary Fellows), there had been no provision for the election of fellows above the age of seventy. The new category now allows election of scholars whose work had been undervalued at seventy, which was certainly true for Duncan Black in Britain. The Academy's citation spoke of Black's "pioneering work in the field of tax incidence" and his "key position as founder of the modern theory of public choice."

After his retirement Black moved to Cambridge where, in 1977, he suffered a cruel blow through the death of his wife, Almut, who had spared no effort to be of assistance to him. Later he went to live in Paignton in Devon, where he died in January 1991. Duncan Black continued with his scholarly work until his death, devoting most of his time to reading and writing, "a mind for ever voyaging through strange seas of thought, alone." The results of this continuous scholarly activity will not be lost to us. His papers are to be archived at his alma mater, the University of Glasgow. They will be the source for at least two (and perhaps four) books to be published by Kluwer Academic Publishers. The first book will republish both *The Theory of Committees and Elections* and *Committee Decisions with Complementary Valuation.* These books will contain versions based on Duncan Black's annotations, along with some published and unpublished articles. The editor will be William Riker of the University of Rochester. The second book will contain Duncan Black's work on Lewis Carroll. It will be edited by Iain McLean of Warwick University. There may be other books based on previously unpublished manuscripts. In this way the academic world will come to learn of the range and power of Duncan Black's ideas.

I cannot end without some personal remarks about my old friend. He was a man of great simplicity, self-effacing, completely honest, conscientious, and dedicated to scholarship. To know him was to like him. Although he lived much of his life in England, he had an abiding love for Scotland. In a letter I received from him about a week before he died, he spoke of planning to visit once again Oban and the old camping grounds during the coming summer. It would have been a source of the greatest pleasure to him had he known that his papers would rest at the University of Glasgow. He had another love, cricket. As a young man, Duncan Black was a fine batsman, playing for Motherwell Cricket Club. He took a great interest in the game until his death. In his will he left his interest in his apartment in Cambridge and his house in Paignton as well as his residuary estate to the Motherwell Cricket Club.

FOURTEEN

George J. Stigler

"If I had known David Ricardo, I would be better able to understand his written words." So said George Stigler. I had met him on a number of occasions but it was not until I joined the faculty of the University of Chicago in 1964 that I came to know him at all well. As a result, I understand his writings better and I admire them more. What I have not been able to understand is how he does it. But no matter. To quote George Stigler once again: "A superior mind and its products must be the most fascinating of scholarly objects." And I have been fascinated. I wish I had the literary skills to describe George Stigler as a person: his affability, his kindness, his honesty, his jocularity, all of which overlay but do not conceal his inner seriousness. What I feel capable of doing in this essay is to describe George Stigler's work as an economist. But there is much to tell.

George Stigler was born in 1911 in Renton, a suburb of Seattle, Washington, but was obviously destined for the University of Chicago. In his autobiography he tells us of the circuitous route that brought him there. He first went to the University of Washington, taking, among others, courses in business administration such as real estate principles. Graduating in 1931, a year which did not afford him much opportunity of putting these principles into practice, he accepted a fellowship at Northwestern University, obtaining, at the end of a year, his M.B.A. After returning to Washington for another year, he

Previously printed in *Remembering the University of Chicago*, Edward Shils, ed. (Chicago: University of Chicago Press, 1991), 469–78. © 1991 by The University of Chicago. It incorporates much of what I said earlier in "George J. Stigler: An Appreciation," *Regulation* (November–December 1982), and I am grateful to the Cato Institute for permission to do this. When this paper was published in 1991, it was unimaginable that, before the year was out, George Stigler would die. But it happened. As a result, economics has suffered a terrible loss and life has become poorer for all who knew him.

made the decision which was to make possible all that he would achieve: he went to the University of Chicago to obtain his Ph.D., having been told by his teachers at the University of Washington that Chicago had good economists in Frank Knight and Jacob Viner. They were right. He learned from both of them but it was Knight, under whom he wrote his thesis, who most influenced him. Knight gave him his vision of economics and strongly reinforced what must have been innate in George Stigler, his love of scholarship.

His first academic appointment was at Iowa State University in 1936. In 1938 he went to the University of Minnesota and remained there until 1946. What then happened in 1946 does little credit to the authorities of the University of Chicago. George Stigler was offered a professorship by the economics department but it was subject to approval by the central administration. He met with the president, Ernest Colwell, and was vetoed, the ostensible reason being that he was too empirical. Colwell had been dean of the Divinity School. While it has to be admitted that theology is a subject in which prudence and faith combine to discourage the empirical testing of doctrines, Colwell's decision is nonetheless difficult to understand. It had as a result that Stigler went to Brown University for a year and then joined the strong economics department of Columbia University.

The rejection of Stigler was not all loss for the University of Chicago since it made possible the appointment of Milton Friedman to a professorship in the economics department. It seems that the university administration would not have agreed to this had Stigler's appointment gone through. As it enabled Friedman to come to Chicago, George Stigler has described his failure to be appointed in 1946 as perhaps "my greatest service to Chicago." But Stigler was not to be denied to Chicago, although "God moves in a mysterious way his wonders to perform." Charles Walgreen in 1936 withdrew his niece from the University of Chicago because he had been informed that the university taught free love and communism. I know nothing about the university's teaching on communism but presumably Mr. Walgreen would not have been mollified to learn that the true Chicago view is that there is no such thing as a free love. Eventually, however, Mr. Walgreen was convinced that he had been misinformed and he made handsome amends by endowing a chair in American Institutions. For reasons unknown to me the chair was not filled for many years. Then, in 1956, Allen Wallis, a fellow student of Stigler's at Chicago in the

1930s, a close friend and an able administrator, was made dean of the Graduate School of Business. In 1958 Wallis offered the Walgreen Chair to Stigler and he was at last welcomed into his spiritual home. Once there he became an editor of the *Journal of Political Economy,* established the famous Industrial Organization Workshop, and later, in 1977, founded the Center for the Study of Economy and the State, of which he became the director. In 1982 he was awarded the Nobel prize in economic science.

The Swedish Academy of Sciences stated that it had awarded the Nobel prize to Stigler for his "seminal studies of industrial structures, functioning of markets, and causes and effects of public regulation." This is just. But this citation, with its long account of Stigler's work, nonetheless conveys an inadequate notion of the character of his contributions to economics. His range of subject matter is wide. He is equally at home in the history of ideas, economic theory, and the study of politics. Even more remarkable is the variety of ways in which he handles a problem; he moves from the marshaling of high theory to aphorism to detailed statistical analysis, a mingling of treatments which resembles, in this respect, the "subtle and colourful" Edgeworth. It is by a magic of his own that Stigler arrives at conclusions which are both unexpected and important. Even those who have reservations about his conclusions will find that a study of his argument has enlarged their understanding of the problem being discussed and that aspects are revealed which were previously hidden. Stigler never deals with a subject which he does not illuminate. And he expresses his views in a style uniquely Stiglerian, penetrating, lively, and spiced with wit. His writings are easy to admire, a joy to read, and impossible to imitate. He is a man *sui generis.* Age shall not wither nor custom stale George Stigler's infinite variety.

In its citation, the Swedish Academy made no mention of Stigler's studies of the history of economic thought, but in them he is, I believe, seen at his best. His first book, *Production and Distribution Theories* (1941), which shows the influence of his great teacher, Frank Knight, is wholly concerned with this subject. Of course, being Stigler, his critical comments, which he rightly suspects some will consider hypercritical, on the handling of the analysis by the great economists whose work he examines, end by being a substantial contribution to economic theory in their own right. This interest in the history of economics and of the men who made it has remained with

Stigler, and articles such as "The Development of Utility Theory" or "Perfect Competition Historically Contemplated" (reprinted in his *Essays in the History of Economics* [1965]) are masterly treatments of their subjects.

Stigler also uses his extensive knowledge of the history of economics to examine more general questions, and in particular to attempt to uncover the forces which have governed the development of economic theory itself. The thesis of his essay "The Influence of Events and Policies on Economic Theory" (also reprinted in the 1965 volume) is striking. He argues that "neither popular economic problems nor heroic events influence much the development of economic theory. . . . The dominant influence on the working range of economic theorists is the set of internal values and pressures of the discipline." Similarly, in his Tanner lectures, given at Harvard in 1980, and reprinted in *The Economist as Preacher and Other Essays* (1982), he argued that "economists are not addicted to taking frequent and disputatious policy positions. . . . The typical article in a professional journal is unrelated to public policy, and often apparently unrelated to this world. Whether the amount of policy-advising activity is rising or falling I do not know, but it is not what professional economics is about."

The claim that the development of economic theory is not much influenced by current events in the economic world and that the work of the economic theorist is not much concerned with economic policy is not, at first sight, very plausible, but I am convinced that Stigler's conclusions are largely true. While Stigler's knowledge of the history of economics is mainly used, as one would expect, in his historical studies, it never fails to influence his treatment, no matter what subject is being discussed. Unlike most modern economists, his investigation of an economic problem is always enriched by his knowledge of the work of earlier economists.

Most academic economists presumably know Stigler, above all, as the author of a very successful textbook dealing with what is now called microeconomics. It first appeared in 1942 with the title *The Theory of Competitive Price,* but in later editions the title was changed to *The Theory of Price* (1946, with revised editions in 1952, 1966, 1987). Though there are many revisions, rearrangements, and substitutions from one edition to another, fundamentally the book has remained unchanged. There must, however, be many who have regretted the disappearance of some of the illustrations to be found in the 1946 edition, such as the extremely amusing account of the difficulties of getting effective collusion on prices among bakers in Illinois. It is not an easy text but it is excellent for anyone seriously interested in training to become an economist.

A textbook, however, is not the place to display innovations in economic analysis, and despite the fact that there are some very Stiglerian passages, particularly in the later editions, the Swedish Academy was no doubt right to ignore it when it set out those of Stigler's contributions to economics for which the award was given. The subjects dealt with in *The Theory of Price* are those that one expects to find in a textbook on the theory of price, and even the treatment is, in many respects, quite conventional. Of course, as in all his writing, Stigler's exposition is lively and spiced with wit, but these are not the qualities which lead to a Nobel prize.

What the Swedish Academy singled out for commendation was Stigler's work in the fields of industrial organisation and the economics of regulation. In economics the subject of industrial organization means the study of market processes and the structure of industries. However, for reasons which are not altogether clear to me, it is a field which has come to concentrate on "the monopoly problem" and, more specifically in the United States, on the problems thrown up by the administration of the antitrust laws. The result has not been a happy one for economics. By concentrating on the problem of monopoly in dealing with an economic system which is, broadly speaking, competitive, economists have had their attention misdirected and as a consequence they have left unexplained many of the salient features of our economic system or have been content with very defective explanations. The link with the administration of the antitrust laws has tended to make matters worse by importing into economics the imprecise analysis (if that is the proper word) which abounds in the opinions of the judiciary in antitrust cases.

Most of Stigler's articles on industrial organization (reprinted in *The Organization of Industry* [1968]) are concerned with monopoly and antitrust policy. However, he transcends the weakness of most discussions of these questions by an impressive use of empirical data (as in "The Economic Effects of the Antitrust Laws"), by an analysis more precise and more searching (as in "Price and Nonprice Competition" or "A Theory of Oligopoly"), and by discussing interesting and significant problems (as in "The Division of Labor Is Limited by the Extent

203

of the Market"). Nonetheless, although the analysis proceeds at a much higher level than is usual, it remains true that most of the subjects discussed are those commonly dealt with under the heading of industrial organization. But Stigler is not like the others. Like a mountain raised by a volcanic eruption, standing high and strange in the surrounding landscape, there is to be found in *The Organization of Industry* a paper of a quite different kind. It is his article on "The Economics of Information," rightly regarded as Stigler's major contribution to economic theory, and it is no surprise that it was picked out by the Swedish Academy for special commendation.

Stigler's starting point is that at any one time there exists an array of prices charged by different suppliers for the same good or service. Those wishing to discover the lowest price will engage in what Stigler calls "search." The more suppliers who are canvassed, the lower the price that a buyer can expect to pay. But as there are costs to search and the marginal gains from increased canvassing tend to diminish, there will be an optimum amount of search for each buyer. This conclusion is not invalidated by the fact that the actual dispersion of prices will be affected by the amount of search undertaken by buyers. There are, of course, ways in which search costs can be reduced—by localisation, advertising, specialized dealers, firms which collect and sell information, and so on. The analysis throws considerable light on the function of these business arrangements and on the way in which a competitive system operates. Particularly important is that it has led to a greater recognition of the role of advertising as a provider of information. But the effect of the analysis is pervasive. As the Swedish Academy said, "phenomena such as price rigidity, variations in delivery periods, queuing and unutilized resources, which are essential features of market processes, can be afforded a strict explanation within the framework of basic economic assumptions." Economists have started to probe, and can be expected to continue to probe, the implications of Stigler's analysis, and with considerable benefit to economics.

Although Stigler had written on rent controls and minimum wage legislation in the 1940s, it was not until the 1960s that he began writing the articles on the economics of regulation that were reprinted (along with many previously unpublished essays) in *The Citizen and the State* (1975). Three of these articles appeared in 1964. At the end of that year, Stigler gave the presidential address to the American Economic Association on "The Economist and the State." His message was twofold. First, economists, whether they were in favour of limiting government intervention or of expanding it, had not hesitated to express their views on what the role of the state in economic affairs should be, without making any serious attempt at discovering what the effects of government intervention had been and without making a systematic comparative study of the results achieved by private and public enterprise. Second, we now have at our disposal quantitative methods to investigate such questions. "The age of quantification is now full upon us . . . economics is at the threshold of its golden age." Stigler had himself already done extensive quantitative work, his book *Capital and Rates of Return in Manufacturing Industries* having been published in 1963. In the context of his presidential address, what Stigler was calling for was a study, using quantitative methods, of the effects of regulation.

One did not have to look far to see what he had in mind. Earlier in 1964 Stigler had published the results of a quantitative investigation into the effects of regulation on electricity rates (written with Claire Friedland). The study could not discover significant effects. Again, in the same year, in the course of reviewing a report on the regulation of the securities markets, Stigler compared the result of investing in new issues in the periods before and after the formation of the Securities and Exchange Commission. No important difference could be detected. In the years which have followed there has been a flood of similar studies investigating the effect of regulation on a wide range of economic activities. Some were directly influenced by Stigler's work. Others were no doubt independently conceived and executed. The results of these studies were uniformly depressing. Either, as in Stigler's studies, no effects of regulation could be detected or, when they could be discovered, the effects, on balance, made matters worse. With regulation, prices were higher, products were less well adapted to consumer demands, and competition was restrained.

About twenty years ago, most economists, under the influence of the writings of Pigou and others, thought of the government as standing ready to put things right whenever the results produced by the working of the market were in some respect defective. This led them to support extensive government regulation. The studies which have been made since then have shown how pernicious the results of regulation have commonly been. It has become difficult to argue with plausibility that the ills of society can be cured by government regulation, and the views of most economists have changed accordingly. Stigler has played a major part in bringing about this change of view.

Stigler has not been content merely to investigate the effects of regulation. He went on to inquire why the regulations are what they are, and this led him to analyse the workings of a political system. His approach was that of an economist, treating political behaviour as utility-maximising, political parties as firms supplying regulation, with what is supplied being what is wanted by those groups (or coalitions) which are able to outbid others in the political market. What each group will bid depends on the gain to be derived from the regulation less the costs of organising for political action. In practice the highest bidder was very likely to be the industry regulated, and it is not therefore surprising to find that the regulation, as Stigler puts it, "is designed and operated primarily for its benefit." The examination of the interrelationships between political behaviour and the economic system has been greatly helped through the creation by George Stigler in 1977 of the Center for the Study of the Economy and the State. It has resulted in the publication of many articles by talented economists who have held fellowships at the Center and has, in consequence, had a considerable impact on the views on regulation held by economists. Acceptance of Stigler's approach (and it, or some variant, has been adopted by many economists) will change the way economists look at regulation since it means, as the Swedish Academy pointed out, that "legislation is no longer an 'exogenous' force which affects the economy from the outside, but an 'endogenous' part of the economic system itself."

Just how much political behaviour can be explained in this way seems to me problematical. As I watch people who are engaged in political activities, whether through voting in a parliamentary system or by taking part in political, including revolutionary, movements, supporting with enthusiasm policies which seem likely to greatly harm or even destroy their countries and perhaps themselves, I find it difficult to believe that such behaviour is best described as rational utility-maximising. However, that does not mean that in some areas, and particularly those of most interest to an economist, Stigler's approach may not have great explanatory power. And I think it does. The Swedish Academy spoke with caution about his analysis of the causes of regulation: "It is still too early to assess its ultimate scope." But, in any case, we should not assess the worth of an economist's contributions

206

by deciding whether the profession will ultimately conclude that he is right. All theories will in time be superseded by others and all will, ultimately, come to be regarded as false (or incomplete or irrelevant). What really matters is whether the contribution moves the subject forward, makes us aware of possibilities previously neglected, and opens up new and fruitful avenues of research. Stigler's contributions clearly meet this test.

I said at the beginning of this essay on George Stigler that because I knew him I understood his writings better. For those who do not know him there is a way to offset the disadvantage of not knowing him. In 1988 George Stigler's autobiography, *Memoirs of an Unregulated Economist,* was published. In it he tells the story of his intellectual development and sets out his main positions with clarity, with honesty, and with charm. Reading it is the next best thing to a personal acquaintance.

Marshall defined a classical economist as one who "by the form or the matter of his words or deeds . . . has stated or indicated architectonic ideas in thought or sentiment, which are in some degree his own, and which, once created, can never die but are an existing yeast ceaselessly working in the Cosmos." If we use Marshall's definition, George Stigler is a classical economist.

FIFTEEN

Economics at LSE in the 1930s: A Personal View

Lionel Robbins, Friedrich Hayek, or John Hicks could give a comprehensive account of economics at the London School of Economics (LSE) in the 1930s. They were, after all, the main contributors to the development of economic analysis at LSE at that time. I was a student and later a junior member of the staff, not fully aware of what was going on. Furthermore, although my appointment at LSE was in the economics department, I had taken the B.Com degree and had worked, and continued to work, more closely with Arnold Plant than with Robbins. I can give some information about the state of economics at LSE in the 1930s but my account is inevitably very incomplete.

I was a student at LSE from 1929 to 1931, having passed the intermediate B.Com examination while still at school. I spent 1931–32 in the United States on a Cassel Travelling Scholarship, my work being supervised by Plant. The year was counted as the third year of residence at LSE (required for the award of a degree), the regulations being somewhat loosely interpreted. From 1932 to 1934, I was an assistant lecturer at the School of Economics and Commerce, Dundee, and, in 1934–35, at the University of Liverpool. I was appointed an assistant lecturer at LSE in 1935. Although I was not at LSE between 1931 and 1935, in fact my association with LSE never ceased.

In the United States, I worked under the supervision of Plant, and while there, I had a long and full correspondence with my friend and fellow student, Ronald Fowler, who had received an appointment in the commerce department, and this kept me informed of developments at LSE. While at Dundee and Liverpool, I spent my vacations at LSE,

Reprinted with permission from the *Atlantic Economic Journal* (1982):31–34. This paper was presented at the eleventh annual conference of the Atlantic Economic Association held on August 14–21, 1981, at the London School of Economics.

collaborated with Ronald Fowler in a study of the pig cycle, and knew generally what was going on. However, I did not attend the seminars which were held at LSE during the period 1931–35. From 1935 on, of course, I had direct contact with what was happening at LSE.

In the late 1920s when I began to study economics, the analytical apparatus used by students was quite crude by modern standards, although serviceable enough for discussing many economic problems. H. D. Henderson's *Supply and Demand* or Edwin Cannan's *Wealth* give a good idea of what was offered to students at that time. However, even established economists lacked the tools to tackle many problems, as was made clear by the controversies over price theory in the *Economic Journal* of the 1920s. The 1930s brought about a great improvement in the analytical tools available to economists. I can give an example. I had been taught to think of marginal cost as the cost of the marginal firm and one day in 1931 I expressed dissatisfaction with this way of looking at things to Plant. He answered that it was probably better to think in terms of the cost of the additional units of output for all firms. Acting on this hint, Fowler and I constructed marginal cost schedules and worked out the relationship to average cost schedules. Then, on looking at one of the appendices to the *Economics of Welfare* we discovered that A. C. Pigou had got there first. However, though possessing marginal cost as a concept, we lacked marginal revenue.

I remember that when Fowler told me in a letter in 1932 about the lectures which Hicks was then giving at LSE and made reference to the marginal revenue schedule, I could not understand what he was talking about and I found the 1928 Theodore Yntema article (to which he also referred) equally puzzling. Of course all this changed with the appearance in 1933 of Joan Robinson's *Economics of Imperfect Competition* and Edward Chamberlin's *Theory of Monopolistic Competition*, and we were then able to cover the blackboard with the most intricate geometry. However, this tale does illustrate the relatively underdeveloped state of economic analysis at the beginning of the 1930s.

At LSE in the 1930s, economists were very receptive to new ideas. For this, a good deal of credit must go to Hayek. Today, we tend to think of him as the author of such works as *The Road to Serfdom* and *The Constitution of Liberty*. But at that time these books had not appeared and the important part he played at LSE in the early 1930s was in encouraging rigour in our thinking and in enlarging our vision. Unassertive, Hayek nonetheless exerted considerable influence through his profound knowledge of economic theory, the example of his own high standards of scholarship, and the power of his ideas.

Hicks was also extremely influential. Robbins says that Hicks, appointed in 1928, "for the next three years played a useful, but not very conspicuous, part in the routine duties of undergraduate teaching."[1] This is a Robbinsian way of saying that Hicks was unsuccessful as an undergraduate teacher. As a student attending Hicks's lectures, I can attest that this was so. Today, one might jump to the conclusion that this was because his lectures were too advanced for his young students. But this was not so. Whether the subjects on which he lectured did not really interest him or for some other reason, Hicks failed to inspire his undergraduate audience. However, Hicks's standing at LSE soon underwent a dramatic change. In 1931, at Robbins's instigation, in part because he had some mathematical training, Hicks began to give lectures on advanced economic theory and his power as a theorist was immediately apparent. Hicks's first course of lectures on advanced theory was given jointly with R. G. D. Allen. Allen, who lectured on statistics and mathematical economics, was an accomplished mathematician who did not scorn those who were not and he played an important role in furthering the movement to theoretical rigour at LSE.

The topics dealt with by Hicks in this course were a comparison of the analysis of the Lausanne school with the methods of Alfred Marshall and an examination of the theory of marginal productivity (obviously a presentation of the ideas which were later to appear in *The Theory of Wages*). Hicks in the next few years lectured on monopoly theory, the economics of disequilibrium, the foreign exchanges, the theory of risk and insurance, the theory of value, and economic dynamics, as well as giving a general course on advanced economic theory, described as a non-mathematical treatment of the general equilibrium theories of Walras and Pareto.

Robbins says that if "Hayek must be credited with bringing Austrian and Wicksellian thought to the School, the introduction of Walras and Pareto must be chiefly attributed to Hicks."[2] The failure of LSE to

1. Lionel Robbins, *Autobiography of an Economist* (London: Macmillan, 1971), 129.
2. *Ibid.*

promote Hicks and prevent his leaving for Cambridge in 1935 was a major mistake and, according to Robbins, was due "to [Sir William] Beveridge's insensate hostility to pure theory."[3] After Hicks's departure, lectures on advanced theory were given by Robbins and Hayek, as well as by Abba Lerner and Nicky Kaldor, but a major force had been lost.

I now come to the most influential figure of all, Lionel Robbins. Edwin Cannan had resigned as professor of political economy in 1927 and Allyn Young, who had been appointed in his place, died suddenly in 1929. Robbins was appointed to fill the gap, with the active, and perhaps crucial, support of Hugh Dalton, and so became professor at LSE in 1929, the same year I came to LSE as a student. Robbins's appointment encountered opposition because of his age—he was then thirty. Hayek was slightly younger than Robbins, while Hicks was twenty-six at that time. What was accomplished at LSE in the 1930s was the product of a very young group of economists.

It is unfortunate that Robbins in his autobiography says so little about the development of his own views on economics, although the little he says is very significant. Robbins had been a student of Cannan's at LSE, but he was early attracted to the writings of continental and American economists. The footnotes in his writings of this period reveal how widely he had been reading. The appointment of Hayek and the encouragement of Hicks was a reflection of this interest in developments in economics originating outside the British Isles.

Robbins's own contribution to economics at LSE was made through his lectures. In the years following his appointment, Robbins gave many courses of lectures on economic analysis, on methodology, and on the history of economics. Robbins's description in the School Calendar of the contents and purpose of a course on comparative economic theory reveals much about his own attitude:

> This course will deal mainly with the economic theories of earlier generations, but it will attempt to exhibit these theories, not as so much antiquarian data but as the raw material out of which by a process of refinement and elimination the economic theories of today have been evolved. That is to say, its ultimate purpose will be to provide a negative preparation for modern analysis.

3. *Ibid.*

That is, in this course, Robbins examined the work of earlier economists not so much to learn from them as to understand what had to be given up or changed in order to reach the economic analysis of today. The latest was the best.

Robbins's direct influence on the views of young economists at LSE came, however, through his course, General Principles of Economic Analysis, mainly devoted to what was then called Value and Distribution and is now called price theory or microeconomics. It seems to have been Robbins's intention to publish these lectures but unfortunately this was never done. Of their contents and character, Robbins says next to nothing in his autobiography. Not being an economics student I did not attend his lectures, apart from one or two, to which I went mainly to observe the expository skills of the lecturer. I did, however, copy out the lecture notes of this course taken by Vera Smith (later Vera Lutz) and so was familiar with Robbins's treatment. Unfortunately, my notes have been lost but Duncan Black made a copy of my notes and these have survived. So we have Duncan Black's copy of my copy of Vera Smith's notes on Robbins's lectures. A photocopy will be deposited in the Regenstein Library of the University of Chicago.

These lectures were not so much a statement of Robbins's own position as an exposition, carried out with care and elegance and in a very systematic way, of the ideas (of other economists) that Robbins considered important. The description of the course in the School Calendar indicates that after an introduction dealing with the evolution of economics and the character of economic analysis, Robbins first dealt with statics, the theory of valuation and exchange, followed by the theory of production and distribution, then with comparative statics and finally with dynamics.

The structure of the course was apparently much influenced by Frank Knight's *Risk, Uncertainty, and Profit,* although Robbins discussed, of course, the work of a wider range of economists than did Knight.

It is noteworthy that the two books which Robbins recommended that we all read were Philip Wicksteed's *Commonsense of Political Economy* and Knight's *Risk, Uncertainty, and Profit,* a very unusual choice which demonstrates both Robbins's independence of mind and his fine judgment. These two books provided an excellent training for the young economists at LSE and it was, I believe, our close study of them which gave us such a firm hold on cost theory, leaving aside whether what emerged should be considered, as James Buchanan contends, as a view special to LSE.

I now turn to the contribution of Plant, about which, as one of his students, I can speak with some assurance. Plant had been a student of Cannan's, contemporary with Robbins, but did not share Robbins's delight in high theory. Plant was an applied economist and his main field of interest was what today is called industrial organisation. Those of us who were associated with him were greatly interested in economic theory and, therefore, in the new analysis then being developed at LSE which we discussed with the economics specialists and among ourselves. But our interest was in using this analysis to understand the working of the real economic system. Because of this, Plant, it seems to me, retained in his teaching Cannan's interest in institutions and his commonsense approach, whereas Robbins was largely working along lines which owed little or nothing to Cannan.

Plant was interested in the subject of property and did important work on the economics of patents and copyright.[5] So far as I was concerned, perhaps his main influence was in bringing me to see that there were many problems concerning business practices to which we had no satisfactory answer. Plant had many able students, among them Ronald Fowler, Ronald Edwards, Arthur Lewis, Arthur Seldon, and Basil Yamey, and his influence has been greater than might be apparent from his own writings or the work at LSE of his contemporaries. Nonetheless, it is the case that the main thrust of the work at LSE was the development of pure theory and did not reflect Plant's interests.

What characterized LSE in the 1930s was that, despite the holding of firm views, there was a lack of doctrinal commitment, which resulted in an openness to new ideas. The main new ideas came from America and the continent. Not that their provenance mattered. Ideas were quickly absorbed and they became the basis for further work without much regard for their source. Economists at LSE were not self-consciously Austrians or Paretians or Walrasians, and certainly not Marshallians. In the United States I have heard it said that, until the late 1930s, English economics was largely confined to a study of Marshall. This was not true at LSE. Marshall was in the calendar of saints

4. For a selection of Plant's papers, including those on patents and copyright, see Sir Arnold Plant, *Selected Economic Essays and Addresses* (London: Routledge and Kegan Paul, in association with the IEA, 1974).

but few of us prayed exclusively to him. Marshall was one among many economists studied.

As a student of Plant's, I studied *Industry and Trade* rather than the *Principles* but we did not slavishly adopt Marshall's views. In fact, we thought his views on cost confused and his analysis of business practices questionable. What was done by the economists at LSE, principally by Robbins, Hayek, and Hicks, was to play a leading role in what we can now see was an international movement which brought into being, for good or ill, the modern age in economics.

At LSE we were a community of scholars. The intellectual atmosphere was extremely agreeable. Although the effect of the teaching of Robbins, Hayek, and Plant was to make students look to private enterprise for solutions to economic problems, very different views were also held in the economics department, expressed, for example, by Abba Lerner, Brinley Thomas, and Evan Durbin (Kaldor had not, I think, shown his colors at that time). In general, differing political views did not impede economic discussion. And so, in the 1930s, with its mass unemployment, its horrors in Russia, Germany, China and elsewhere, and with worse to come, we spent our time working on, and, we thought, improving our economics.

Index

215

Controversy, 74
Corry, Bernard, 121, 130
Cost-benefit analysis, 40

Dalton, Hugh, 211
Data
  function in economic analysis, 44
  requirement for testing new theory, 24
  response to lack of, 13–14
Decentralisation, 4
Demsetz, Harold, 3, 4
Dermer, E. C., 148
Director, Aaron, 65–67, 72
Disciplines
  determining boundaries of, 35–36
  factors binding scholars in, 38–39, 41
Division of labour
  cooperation required in, 114
  importance to Adam Smith's idea of, 79–82
Douglas, William O., 65–66
Downs, Anthony, 36n3
Dundee School of Economics, 188–89
Durbin, Evan, 214

Eastham, J. K., 188
Economic method
  of Marshall, 173–74
  Marshall's ideas about, 168–71
  See also Nonquantitative method; Quantitative method
Economics
  development since Adam Smith, 4
  expansion of boundaries, 36–42
Economic system
  of Adam Smith, 4, 76
  different views of, 28–30
  neglect of some aspects of, 4–5
  relationship to legal system, 11–12
  tools for understanding, 45–46
  transaction costs to explain use of money, 9–10
  unsolved problems in, 37
  value of institutional factors, 6

Economic theory
  analysis of competition in, 22–24
  to approach social science analysis, 40–41, 45
  changes in acceptance of, 18–24
  Coase on development of, 202
  criteria for choice of, 23–24, 29
  economists' choice of, 16–18, 24–25
  Friedman's criteria for choosing an, 16–18, 23–24, 26
  function of, 16–17
  incorporation of transaction costs in, 12–13
  Keynesian system in, 19–22, 24
  at LSE, 183
  Marshall's position on, 171–73
  motives for choice of, 29–31
  role of testing predictions of, 24
  in social sciences other than economics, 36–39
  Stigler on development of, 202
  study of institutions using, 5–6
Edgeworth, F. Y., 120, 122n15, 137, 164
Edwards, Ronald, 213
Election theory
  of Duncan Black, 189–96
  of economists, 36

Fay, C. R., 90, 91n9, 94n13
Firms
  political parties as, 206
  studies of activities, 8–9
  See also "Nature of the Firm"
First Amendment, 64, 65–66, 67, 69
Follett, Mary Parker, 187
Forster, E. M., 147
Fowler, Ronald, 208–9, 213
Foxwell, Audrey, 151n3, 165
Foxwell, H. S., 151
  academic performance of, 163
  Marshall's attitude toward, 155–58, 161–62
  preferences in economic thought, 165–66

view of Pigou, 154–56
writings of, 163
Free market (in ideas), 66
Free press, 68–70
Free speech, 70
Friedland, Claire, 205
Friedman, Milton, 16–17, 47–48, 200
Friendship
Adam Smith's idea of, 101–2
opposed to cooperation, 81–82
Furubotin, Erik, 46n21

Ghiselin, Michael T., 109n7
Gibbon, Edward, 35
Gilbert, J. C., 188
Glennie, B., 138n23, 139n26
God (Smith's representation), 106–8
See also Nature
Government activity. *See* Government
regulation; Public policy
Government intervention
conditions creating demand for, 72–
73
in markets for ideas and goods, 67,
69, 73
Government regulation
as accepted policy, 30
Adam Smith's objection to, 85, 87–
88
of advertising, 65, 73
of broadcasting, 69, 73
of education, 73–74
effect of, 49–50
effects studied by Stigler, 205–6
intervention through, 205
of markets for goods, 65
of markets for ideas, 65, 73–74
opportunities for improvement
through, 61–62
quantitative methods in effect of,
59–60
Smith's analysis of price control,
50–52
studies of effect of, 61
study of design, 206
in *The Wealth of Nations*, 4, 50–52

Government role
Adam Smith's opposition to, 87–88
Adam Smith's perception of, 88–90
curtailment of, 63
expansion of, 62–63
in markets for ideas and goods, 67–
68
Gregory, Theodore, 177
Guillebaud, Claude (nephew of Alfred
Marshall), 120, 123–24, 143,
171
Guillebaud, Mabel Marshall (sister of
Alfred), 144–45

Hall, T., 138nn22, 23, 139n26
Hamermesh, Daniel S., 36n5
Harrod, R. F., 21, 122n15, 147n51
Hawtrey, F. M., 147n53
Hawtrey, Ralph, 146–47
Hayek, Friedrich von, 21
acceptance and displacement of the-
ory, 19, 21–22
diffused knowledge concept, 9
influence and contribution of LSE,
183, 189, 208–10, 214
Henderson, H. D., 209
Hicks, John R., 21, 39n10
influence and contributions of, 189,
208, 210, 214
on Keynesian theory, 19–20
Hitch, Charles J., 37n8
Holmstrom, Bengt, 5
Human behaviour
Adam Smith's idea of, 96–103
economics as study of, 41–43
role of reason in Smith's idea of,
108–10, 116
self-interest in determining, 95–98
Human nature
Adam Smith's view of, 95, 111,
113, 115–16
Hume's view of, 110
in *The Theory of Moral Sentiments*,
113
in *The Wealth of Nations*, 113–14
Hume, David, 110

Hutcheson, Francis, 77, 105–6
Hutt, W. H., 178

Impartial spectator (of Adam Smith),
  26, 98–99, 100, 102
Industrial organisation
  lack of knowledge about, 48
  obstacles in study of, 13
  Plant's interest in, 213
Information theory (of Stigler), 204
Institutions
  economics as study of, 41
  governing exchange process, 6, 9–
    13
  See also Committee theory; Firms
Invisible hand. *See* Pricing system

Jevons, W. Stanley, 9, 56
Jones, H. Berkeley, 138n25

Kahn, Richard, 21
Kaldor, Nicholas, 21, 22, 211
Keynes, John Maynard
  acceptance of theory of, 19–21
  on Alfred Marshall's uncle Charles,
    136
  memoir on Alfred Marshall, 119–20,
    122–24, 128, 130, 132, 146–48
  references to Alfred Marshall, 171
Keynes, John Neville
  Marshall on work of, 167–68
  references to Alfred Marshall, 152,
    167
Keynesian revolution, 19–22
Kitch, Edmund, 49–50
Knight, Frank
  on attributes of a good scholar, 15,
    32
  influence of, 200, 201, 212
  on price control and public policy,
    53–54
Knowles, Lilian, 176, 177
Kuhn, Thomas S., 13, 26–28, 29

Lancaster, Kelvin, 43
Laplace, Pierre Simon, 195
Laski, Harold, 177, 180

Law and economics, 12, 32
Legal system
  approach to market regulation, 64–
    65
  effect on working of economic sys-
    tem, 11
  influence of social cost argument on,
    10
  relationship to economic system,
    11–12
Lerner, Abba, 20, 21, 211, 214
Lewis, Arthur, 213
Lindgren, J. Ralph, 116n23
Linear programming, 39–40
London School of Economics (LSE)
  Cannan's influence, 177, 182
  Hayek's contribution and influence,
    183, 189, 208–10, 214
  Hicks's contribution and influence,
    189, 208, 210, 214
  Plant's contribution and influence,
    6, 7, 179–84, 213–14
  Robbins's contribution and influ-
    ence, 189, 208, 211–12, 214
Lutz, Vera. *See* Smith, Vera

Macfie, A. L., 98, 193
Macgregor, D. H., 156
McKean, Roland N., 37n8
Mandeville, Bernard, 77
Markets
  Adam Smith on man's behaviour in,
    80–87, 114–15
  control economic system of Adam
    Smith, 76
  differentiation in regulation of, 64–
    65
  as regulators, 87
  remedy for failure of, 72–73
  See also Division of labour
Marschak, J., 37n6
Marshall, Agnes (sister of Alfred), 144
Marshall, Alfred
  active support of Pigou, 152–54,
    156, 158, 165–66
  attitude toward Foxwell, 155–58,
    161–62, 165–66